RETHINKING UNIVERSITIES

Also available from Continuum

Pedagogy and the University, Monica McLean
Teaching and Learning in Higher Education, Linda Evans

Research in Higher Education series

Philosophies of Research into Higher Education, Brian Brown and Sally Baker
Dispositional Theory of Good Teaching, John Fazey
Teaching in Higher Education, John Fazey and Eben Muse

RETHINKING UNIVERSITIES
The Social Functions of Higher Education

SALLY BAKER AND BRIAN BROWN

continuum

Continuum International Publishing Group
The Tower Building, 11 York Road, London SE1 7NX
80 Maiden Lane, Suite 704, New York, NY 10038
www.continuumbooks.com

British Library Cataloguing-in-Publication Data
A catalogue record for this book is available from the British Library.

ISBN-10: HB: 0-8264-9419-6 (hardcover)
ISBN-13: HB: 978-0-8264-9419-1 (hardcover)

Library of Congress Cataloguing-in-Publication Data
Brown, B. J. (Brian J.)
    Higher learning : the philosophies of research into higher education / by B. J. Brown and Sally Baker.
        p. cm.
    ISBN-13: 978-0-8264-9417-7 (hardcover)
    ISBN-10: 0-8264-9417-X (hardcover)
    1. Education–Research–Philosophy. 2. Education, Higher. I. Baker, Sally. II. Title

    LB1028.B758 2007
    378.007'2–dc22

                                                                            2007006776

Typeset by Aarontype Limited, Easton, Bristol
Printed and bound in Great Britain by Biddles Ltd, King's Lynn, Norfolk

For Xylia. And for Alaric,
whose contribution,
as he knows, has been immeasurable

Contents

Chapter 1

Thinking About the University: Theories, Histories and Knowledge

Introduction: some fragments of context

Most people who work and study in universities will be aware that they are changing. Yet few have so far grasped the extent of this change or have attempted to put it in a coherent intellectual framework. This volume gives us new ways to understand how the university workforce in developed nations is being encouraged to change and how the social role of these institutions has shifted from places of higher learning towards agents for social change and the promotion of human welfare. The demands that are being placed on institutions and the kinds of graduates they are required to produce has changed too, with the emphasis on a new brand of vocationalism and a renewed emphasis on skills and employability. In this volume we will demonstrate how it is possible for thinking about this issue to be theoretically informed and provide a philosophically sophisticated account of what universities in developed nations are being encouraged to do and the impact this has on their staff, students and the societies of which they are a part.

Universities have often been associated with higher learning and the spirit of free inquiry but in many developed nations they are being subtly transformed to do other jobs for the state and the economy. We will explore the extent to which universities have been given new tasks later. For the moment, let us note that post-compulsory education is being encouraged to give students 'skills', to render them more 'employable' in a post-industrial economy and to support and care for a student body which often includes people whose vulnerabilities would compromise their survival in the increasingly demanding and 'flexible' labour markets of the contemporary world.

Moreover, universities and their staff are encouraged to deliver quality teaching provision which is benchmarked (sometimes against disturbingly mobile goalposts); demonstrate the international standing of their research and promote 'social inclusion', social mobility and wellbeing in the societies from which they recruit their students. To do this they are enjoined to attract and transform deprived, underprivileged and otherwise 'socially excluded' individuals. All this is taking place in a progressively more austere financial climate and against a backdrop of regulation, control and 'quality assurance', the measurement of success or failure against 'metrics', benchmarks of economic viability and a kaleidoscope of shifting objectives originating from government, the commercial sector, the mass media and public opinion.

In line with these very trends, books like this must have an identifiable 'market'. The arguments and ideas we shall expound here are formulated with various people in mind. It is intended for university staff, students, researchers and policymakers who want to understand what is happening to higher education institutions at a time when their role is increasingly in the public eye. At the same time, as Furedi (2006) notes, universities and the people in them have been relatively quiet about their role and purpose in contemporary societies. While at the time of writing there have been concerns about pay and conditions, these have been formulated as a narrowly defined labour dispute. Much of the more conspicuous and forcefully expressed thinking about the nature and purpose of post-compulsory education has come from governments, from business or derives from press reports of successes and failures. Our purpose then is to provide some intellectual tools, some stories and some kind of a framework to set universities on the road to being contributors in their own right.

External demands, internal cultures

People who work in universities might begin with the desire for a collegiate environment that prompts depth of thinking about ideas fundamental to their disciplines, yet are confronted by an environment where managerial regimes increase their demands for regulation and control (Tysome, 2006). The ramping up of demands for increased productivity and the development of a managerialist culture which is at once intrusive and chaotic have arguably led to higher education being reinvented (Trowler, 2005). Fisher (2006) contends that the relentless measurement of teaching and knowledge has led to, and has hidden, a reduction in the experience of learning. Yet this is not all: Evans (2004) characterizes the process as 'killing thinking' and Furedi (2004) laments the disappearance of intellectuals.

Higher education systems in many nations have come to be the workhorses for a variety of burdens. For example, it is often assumed that they are responsible for the health of the populace as well as the economic viability of the nation. Numbers of students have increased and the 'unit of resource' has dwindled. Complaints about the massification of higher education, 'diploma factories' and 'degree mills' have been accompanied by talk of 'dumbing down' and laments about people studying for 'Mickey Mouse degrees'.

Over three decades ago, Martin Trow identified a borderline between higher education catering for a mass clientele and being 'universal' (Trow, 1976). This borderline was then defined at around 40 per cent of the appropriate age group. As Neave (2006) remarks, many European higher education systems are now going beyond that threshold. In Britain's case, the government's ambition is to see 50 per cent attending higher education by the year 2010 (DfES, 2003), a figure that some countries have already attained. For example, France has around 52 per cent of its 18- to 20-year-olds in post-secondary education.

The casual observer might be tempted to conclude that the picture is simple. Universities and the people in them are simply staggering under the load of educating a larger and somehow 'less academic' student body as a result of widening access policies. However, the picture is a little more complicated than that. At present, it is difficult to identify exactly how complicated, or to place these complications in a systematic framework. What we shall offer instead in this opening chapter is a series of snapshots of the state of the academy in early twenty-first-century societies. These pictures will offer a sense of the context, the internal workings of the institutions and the people in them and some partial diagnoses offered by theorists and practitioners of various stripes. While these do not add up to a complete theory of the role of universities and how to survive them, they all offer important insights as to how the institutions have come to look the way they do at present and offer intimations of how this trend might be continued into the future.

What is happening in universities: fragments of a diagnosis

Clearly, universities in most countries 'are now under titanic pressure to reinvent themselves' (Considine, 2006: 255). Yet the picture presented by many commentators – that these pressures come entirely from outside the system – is perhaps too simple. The story is that the imperatives for change come from elsewhere and that the university system is being galvanized by transformations in economics, politics and educational ideologies (Considine, 2006). Changes in the world economy have thrust many institutions into a new 'ambiguous arena that looks more and more like a competitive marketplace' (Gioia and Thomas, 1996: 370).

Scholarly domains are now infused with managerial values and goals, pedagogical actions are now dominated by organizational imperatives, and the life of the student is increasingly intersected by the priorities of work, finance, and future returns. (Considine, 2006: 258)

However, universities in Considine's view are not solely in crisis as a result of pressure from outside. Their crisis exists as a result of turbulence within their very identity or sense of themselves. In Niklas Luhmann's (1990) characterization, the key to a system's viability concerns its capacity to mobilize a core value around which certain binary choices can be made. The challenge for the modern university is therefore to maintain some distinction in relation to some value or binary that it owns and that other systems do not. Once upon a time the key element of a university might have been that it was a knowledge-based binary for dividing knowledge from other things. The situation has reached a point where universities have so far imbibed these other activities and values, to such an extent that there is little left which is unique.

These developments, which as we shall see are fragments of a longer-term historical shift, do not take place in a vacuum. The situation, which has been called the 'crisis of higher education', has developed in the context of a number of other social changes in national and global contexts. During the latter half of the twentieth century, public and educational life changed in fundamental ways, reflecting different social values, new forms of global consciousness, new visions of the human community and an insistence upon social inclusion. Changes in concepts of communication, economics, space, time, transport, human development, intelligence, aptitude and the role that post-compulsory education can take in shaping and revitalizing these trends were systematically reinvented. The world inhabited by universities, their students and their workforce changed. In tandem with this, shifts also took place in the values and the systems of thought that we use in making meaning out of our lives, such that they now stand in stark contrast to the world as it was before the 1980s.

As we shall argue in this volume, a part of this change was a radical transformation of thinking by policymakers, industrialists and social reformers about knowledge transfer and learning processes. Moreover, recent events in the early twenty-first century have meant that the role of the university in the British Isles has been revised substantially in line with policy agendas designed to increase the proportion of the population undertaking higher education and which have sought to broaden the definition of what universities do in the light of a whole raft of policy objectives concerned with public health, social exclusion and public order.

Traditionally the societal role of European universities has been related to the aspirations to build the nation-state, its identity, culture and educational system. However, in recent years this has undergone revision such that as well as, or instead of, serving the social good, universities also serve the market. Since the late 1980s governments have increasingly 'replaced the idea of society by the idea of the market' (Touraine, 1995: 103).

At the same time, education is seen as vital to address the demands of this market. A dominant theme in New Labour's vision of Britain was demonstrated by a number of policy documents and announcements as they took office, epitomized by terms such as 'The Learning Age' (Department for Education and Employment, 1997) and the 'age of achievement' (Blair, 1996) in which education was seen as a means by which opportunities would be opened up for everyone in a socially inclusive society. As Estelle Morris (2002), Secretary of State for Education at the time, said at the Labour Party Conference:

> We have always wanted to tear down the barriers that hold people back. We have always said that the street that you were born into should not determine what you will achieve. We have always told people to aim high and believe that what you dream about as a child you can achieve as an adult. That gives us a responsibility. If as a party we give people hope, we must give them the means to achieve it.

The notion of hope, a seductive blend of meritocracy and egalitarianism, and an emphasis on education as a panacea for all social ills, occurred against a backdrop of increasing economic liberalism and social authoritarianism where the individual is increasingly urged to take responsibility for themselves (Clarke, 2005). Over the past two decades, the rising trend of neoliberal globalization has prompted many of these changes in social affairs. North American business, propelled by its desire for profit, has greatly accelerated its imposition of a distinctive business culture, including new patterns of social relationships and political ideologies. These have been felt most acutely in the so-called Third World regions. In moving economic activities, especially extractive and manufacturing industry, out of Europe and North America, corporations have shielded themselves from the cost associated with minimum wage laws, taxes and environmental regulations (Giroux and Giroux, 2003; Giroux, 2004; McLaren, 2005). The ascendancy of market ideologies over democratic imperatives has left more people across the globe in the throes of poverty, pollution and hopelessness. In essence, corporate culture is gaining increasing control over every aspect of life. As McLaren (2005: 27) notes 'capital is in command of the world order as never before'. Downes (2001: 63) puzzles that so many authors talk about 'late capitalism', for as he sees it, capitalism has only just been 'let off the leash'.

Higher education is no exception to this trend and, as we shall see later, this aspect of life in the academy is one with which theorists and educational practitioners themselves are increasingly having to deal. The introduction of entrepreneurial activity into aspects of the public realm which were previously taken care of via state provision has resulted in a number of uneasy changes. Public institutions are finding themselves restructured along business lines and in some sectors are finding themselves in sometimes uneasy relationships with private contractors. Their physical infrastructure, their information technology needs, their management and administrative support may well be in the hands of private contractors operating under the aegis of Private Finance Initiative (PFI) schemes (Higher Education Funding Council for England, 2005). This liberalization of markets and the opening up of public provision to competition, or as it is sometimes now called 'contestability', is worthy of exploration. Therefore, let us step back and examine what some of the key concepts here mean.

Neoliberalism: the apotheosis of competition and the erosion of the public sphere

Many of the economic and social changes of the last quarter of a century have taken place within a zeitgeist which has been described as neoliberalism. This term is widely used in discussions of contemporary economic, political and cultural life so it is perhaps useful to pause and explore what it means. Many authors on the subject are keen to distinguish it from classical liberalism (Olssen, 2006). In classical economic liberalism, the basis for governance is in terms of 'natural, private-interest-motivated conduct of free, market exchanging individuals' and for neoliberalism, 'the rational principle for regulating and limiting governmental activity must be determined by reference to artificially arranged or contrived forms of free, entrepreneurial and competitive conduct of economic-rational individuals' (Burchell, 1996: 23–4). Neoliberalism does not just happen by chance. It has to be carefully arranged such that people, firms and institutions are set up in a kind of competitive arena. From a neoliberal point of view, concepts such as freedom, choice, competition and individual initiative, as well as education, truth and rational argument, are constructed by and through the state so as to facilitate this competition. To secure these practices and values, as well as compliance and obedience, the state meticulously constructs the appropriate conditions through the development of techniques of auditing, accounting and management. The diligent application of these techniques enables

> the marketplace for services to be established as 'autonomous' from central control. Neo-liberalism, in these terms, involves less a retreat from governmental 'intervention' than a re-inscription of the techniques and forms of expertise required for the exercise of government. (Barry *et al.*, 1996: 14)

In both classical liberalism as well as neoliberalism, the common theme concerns the primacy of the market and the desirability of limiting state involvement in market mechanisms. In other words, both orientations seek to establish 'the limits of government in relation to the market' (Burchell, 1996: 22).

The inroads that private capital is making into public life have implications for the way that dialogues are possible in politics and in the management of public institutions – in other words, for how the public sphere operates. The major theorist of the public sphere, Jurgen Habermas (1991: 176) defined it as being 'made up of private people gathered together as a public and articulating the needs of society with the state'. Through activities such as assembly and dialogue, the public sphere is believed to generate opinions and attitudes that serve to affirm or challenge – therefore to guide – the affairs of state. In ideal terms, the public sphere is the source of public opinion needed to 'legitimate authority in any functioning democracy' (Rutherford, 2000: 18). The public sphere does not necessarily exist in one particular place. It is a virtual or imaginary community.

In its ideal form, the public sphere is, for Habermas, successful as a result of rational-critical discourse such that everyone is an equal participant and the supreme communication skill is the power of argument. The rise of neoliberalism corresponds to what Habermas would see as a deformation of the public sphere. Indeed he writes of recent years seeing a 'refeudalization' of power, whereby the illusions of the public sphere are maintained only to give sanction to the decisions of leaders and only certain economically powerful voices are listened to. In this case, we would anticipate that the incursions of private finance into the workings of the education system make certain kinds of policies more likely and dialogue and democracy less able to prevail. Accordingly, Dave Hill argues that:

> Education as a social institution has been subordinated to international market goals including the language and self-conceptualization of educators themselves ... Within Universities ... the language of education

has been very widely replaced by the language of the market, where
lecturers 'deliver the product', 'operationalize delivery' and 'facilitate clients' learning', within a regime of 'quality management and enhancement', where students have become 'customers' selecting 'modules' on a
pick 'n' mix basis, where 'skill development' at Universities has surged in
importance to the derogation of the development of critical thought.
(Hill, 2003: 7)

Later in this volume we will explore what this means for the content of
courses and how they are managed so as to secure maximal student satisfaction, but for the moment it is apposite to note that there are many concerns
about academic freedom itself. The current flurry of interest in the UK concerning those who hold unpopular views, those whose research may be supported by powerful commercial interests such as pharmaceutical companies
and those who fall foul of cherished government policies, has a long and dis-
tinguished pedigree. As veteran campaigner Noam Chomsky put it:

Early on in your education you are socialized to understand the need to
support the power structure, primarily corporations – the business class.
The lesson you learn in the socialization through education is that if you
don't support the interests of the people who have wealth and power, you
don't survive very long. You are just weeded out of the system or marginalized. And schools succeed in the indoctrination of the youth – borrow-
ing the Trilateral Commission's phrasing – by operating within a
propaganda framework that has the effect of distorting or suppressing
unwanted ideas and information. (Chomsky, 2000: 17)

Or, a little more recently, the situation was phrased even more starkly
by Zinn:

The boundaries for free expression in the university, though broader than
in the larger society, are still watched carefully. When that freedom is
used, even by a small minority, to support social change considered dangerous by the guardians of the status quo, the alarm goes out: 'The com-
munists are infiltrating our institutions'; 'Marxists have taken over the
curriculum.' ... The axes then get sharpened. Yes, some of us radicals
have somehow managed to get tenure ... but we have seen the axe fall
countless times on colleagues less lucky. (Zinn, 2005: 93)

Debate about academic freedom is riddled with these kinds of concerns.
They are aligned with a strong suspicion that some institutions and employers' bodies are apt to use a variety of clandestine and informal processes to

keep people perceived as troublemakers out of institutions. These kinds of coercive and exclusionary processes coexist alongside more insidious pressures. Harris (2005) and Brooks (2001) argue that there is increasing pressure on academics to pursue a correct professional identity. This is propelled by the use by universities of executive recruitment firms to attract and retain 'high-impact professors' as well as to create more deans in order to strengthen their profiles (Fazackerley, 2004). As Harris (2005) sees it, there is increasing pressure also for academic activity to contribute to the institution's overall strategy, and to secure its market position. This in turn places the onus on individuals to pursue and construct academic identities which are aligned with corporate identity.

This then is the picture in the economic and political sphere and the implications for the education system. There are further aspects of the process of modernization to which we would like to draw the reader's attention because they prefigure and enable a number of processes which we shall deal with later in this volume. To have a large body of young people who can be educated at university and allegedly equipped to thrive upon the demands of a technologically challenging, rapidly changing workplace, a number of aspects of society must already be in place. We need, at the very least, a large body of people who are relatively unconstrained by family or community ties so they can devote the several years necessary to further study. Of course, people do work and study and fulfil family commitments, but the very fact that we or our offspring can even contemplate doing so suggests that we are living in post-traditional societies. Many social commentators have pointed to a process of 'detraditionalization' that has characterized modernity and which makes investing in oneself through education a feasible, legitimate thing to do.

Detraditionalization and post-compulsory education

Traditions, it is claimed, have been dissolved or eroded in many developed societies. But what were traditions exactly? Perhaps if we were to examine what they did, we can see how the social practices and ways of enhancing one's identity that have replaced them have become popular. Thompson (1996) identifies four aspects of tradition. These are the 'hermeneutic aspect', the 'normative aspect', the 'legitimation aspect' and the 'identity aspect'. The hermeneutic aspect consists of a body of implicit norms or assumptions that are taken for granted in people's daily lives and are transmitted from one generation to the next. The normative aspect includes the beliefs and patterns of activity that are knowingly taken over from the past. The legitimation aspect involves the means by which power and authority are established and supported. Max Weber, for example, claimed that the legitimacy of a system of domination could be based on belief in the sanctity of traditional authority. The last aspect, concerned with identity, involves identity formation and how one perceives oneself in a social setting. According to Thompson (1996), there are two types of identity formation: 'self-identity' is the sense of oneself as an individual, while 'collective identity' is a sense of belonging to a particular social group.

Detraditionalization occurs when people stop creating their lives and identities according to social or community context and instead establish their identity based on their individual context. Heelas (1996) suggests that with detraditionalization, people lose their belief in established orders, and faith in the values, beliefs, or forms of behaviour inherited from tradition is undermined. Detraditionalization involves individuals becoming detached from the cultural contexts that they once belonged to and a shift in authority to the 'individual' through the acquisition of new individualistic values. In late modernity, individuals are charged with making for themselves a lifestyle (Featherstone, 1991) and it is increasingly claimed that individuals create and mould their identity or identities (Bauman, 1988; Maffesoli, 1988; Giddens, 1991; Beck, 1992) through the symbolic capacities of consumption (Lury, 1996) and the acquisition of personal cultural capital. According to this body of thought 'we have no choice but to choose' (Giddens, 1991: 81), due to 'detraditionalization', the weakening of traditional foundations of identity, such as class, the extended family and local settings – all consequences of geographical and social mobility. As Slater (1997: 85) describes, identities are no longer 'unproblematically assigned to us', but understood through the image we create of ourselves through education, occupation, lifestyle or consumption. We choose our self-identity and are required to 'produce and sell an identity to various social markets'. Education is one of the major instruments for producing and sustaining these identities.

In contrast, theories which prioritize the significance of social structure question such a strong focus on agency. Someone's proficiency in the education system is viewed as being connected with social reproduction and as a battleground for distinctions based on social class or gender (Douglas and Isherwood, 1979; Bourdieu, 1984), rather than as a means of individualization. As Warde (1994) argues, 'class matters' and monetary, social, cultural and educational resources are seen as being important to structural differentiation.

Despite detraditionalization there is thus still clearly a resonance between so-called middle-class values and educational ethos, of the kind that has long been recognized by researchers exploring issues of social inequality (Bowles and Gintis, 1976; Willis, 1977; Walkerdine and Lucey, 1989; Walkerdine *et al.*, 2001; Kehily and Pattman, 2006). The mutually reinforcing world of the middle-class home and the educational system is believed to have facilitated the development of a meritocratic ideology that hard work equals educational achievement (Power, 2000). As Kehily and Pattman (2006) note, among professionals there is a more complex dynamic at work in the form of a widely recognized yet under-analysed triad between family-education system-conformity which produces the middle-class educational success story (Hodkinson and Bloomer, 2000; Ball, 2003b). This alignment between ideas, ideologies and habits of conduct in the middle-classes and in the education system has yielded a great deal of research and theorizing which we shall explore later, particularly in the light of the changes which have been mooted in the post-compulsory education system so as to attract more students into it.

Power in the academy: Foucault and the shaping of academic identities

Earlier in this chapter we highlighted some of the concerns that academic freedom is being mitigated by the corporate and economic agendas of the institutions within which academic work is done. This friction between the sense of independence historically associated with academic life and the governmental and commercial goodwill upon which universities depend is a theme to which we shall return later. Control is at its most conspicuous when it yields this kind of turbulence. Equally, many of us who work in universities have become aware of more subtle processes whereby our thinking is shaped, our identities are moulded and our ideas about what is possible in our working and private lives are constrained. To explore this we need a rather different kind of analysis.

To this end, a number of scholars such as Stephen Ball (2003a) and Mark Olssen (1999; 2006) are examining the relevance of Foucault's ideas to the study of education. These notions have been under-explored in educational sociology so far, but in the light of the changes we have identified above are increasingly pertinent to understanding educational situations. In his early career, Foucault focused upon the more localized expressions of pastoral power and bio-power.

Pastoral power was for Foucault associated with the Church. Pastoral power rests on the Church's ability to secure individual salvation in the afterlife. There are links between pastoral power and individualism, in that

individuals can (in some theologies at least) help to secure their own salvation. In contemporary developed nations, as well as salvation in the next
life, we may be concerned with our salvation in the present. As well as the
usual concerns of scholars of Foucault with health, wellbeing and sexuality,
we might just as easily point to the way in which contemporary individuals
are encouraged to add value to themselves via the acquisition of skills, qualifications and the wherewithal to cope with the demands for flexibility in
the contemporary labour force (Dreyfus and Rabinow, 1982).

Foucault's notion of bio-power relates to the way many modern states
have attempted to govern their citizens through 'an explosion of numerous
and diverse techniques for achieving the subjugations of bodies and the control of populations' (Foucault, 1978: 140), in particular through the use of
statistics and probabilities. Bio-power might be particularly concerned with
statistics relating to public health, longevity, rates of infection, rates of success in education and the measurement of human capital in educational
institutions. Here we might be concerned with the involvement of staff in
further education and training to enhance their effectiveness, their efficient
disposition according to the needs of the student body and so on. Bio-power
can be detected in any conception of the social system, the education system
or the state as a 'body' and the use of state power as essential to its life.
Hence, attempts are made to measure the wellbeing of the system, according
to its budget, the proportion of the population being educated, the external
research funding earned and the like.

Under the conditions of neoliberalism and detraditionalization, a sense of
personal freedom is fostered, yet this is not necessarily quite as free as it
might at first appear. As Marshall and Marshall warn:

> because they have been constituted to think that they are free and auton-
> omous and that this very constitution has permitted the advance of
> power/knowledge and the subjugation of people as subjects to lead
> useful, docile and practical lives. (Marshall and Marshall, 1997: 137)

For example, as one colleague said, discussing the rewards of work in higher
education: 'At least you get to manage your own time'. Yet on subsequent
discussion it turned out that practically all his waking hours were spent in
work related to the university. 'Managing his own time' seemed to consist
of postponing holidays, not taking lunch breaks and spending his evenings
answering email. Thus, by imperceptible degrees, the self-managed work
had spread out to engulf what little was left of his personal life.

The way in which the practical activities of education, as well as its goals
and philosophies, exert a kind of subtle discipline upon its practitioners and

students make it fertile territory for analysis based upon Foucault's work. This kind of analysis draws on the full range of Foucault's scholarship and incorporates not only his earlier concerns with disciplinary power, but also the ideas of governance in his later writings.

Taking this kind of perspective in a strong form reveals that the moulding of academic life is not simply a matter of accommodating staff to an increased workload. According to Besley (2005a) and Marshall (1996) some of the key assumptions in liberal education and philosophy of education are susceptible to a Foucauldian rereading. For example, the aim of liberal education in the work of John Dewey and R. S. Peters is personal autonomy (Marshall, 1996: 213). However, liberal education's pursuit of personal autonomy and development of the mind serves a crucial function in masking the ways in which governmentality, authority and power relations operate.

Governmentality in higher education involves the linking of particular rationalities to specific technologies, enabling collective power to be exercised over individuals. This sounds rather abstract. To bring the idea to life, consider the process of 'appraisal' and 'staff development'. Staff development is often driven by contractual obligations and tasks proposed during appraisal processes which involve pursuing further credentials, such as higher degrees or teaching qualifications and to achieve these by a given date. As Smith (2005) notes, staff development might also involve end of year institutional events in which the 'reculturing' (Jephcote, 1996) of staff to ensure a better fit between corporate and individual goals can be engineered. Indeed, attendance at these meetings and the uptake of staff development may be interpreted as an indicator of the extent to which staff are 'embracing' (Yarrow and Esland, 1998) the required cultural change. Conversely, if it is less than expected, this might be taken as a measure of their 'dissent'. Now of course it is often taken as a mark of good management that objectives are agreed and staff are 'empowered' to develop their portfolio of experiences and qualifications. But this is exactly our point. The process of governance does not operate through ordering people around in any simple sense. It is instead effectively and persuasively formulated as one that appears to confer advantage on those who participate.

It is through attention to these processes that we can begin to answer some of Foucault's questions concerning power and governance, such as 'by what means is it exercised?' and 'What happens when individuals exert (as they say) power over others?' (Foucault, 1982: 217). Rather like the questions that we have just raised about the management process in higher education, Foucault was fascinated by the process of government, which he saw as a form of activity aimed to guide and shape conduct. To govern thus designates 'the way in which the conduct of individuals or of groups might be directed ... [it] is to structure the possible field of action of others' (1982: 221).

The exploration of knowledge through education and the kinds of goals to which students and educators bend themselves can be seen as a process of discipline or 'normalization' of the kind that Foucault described in *Discipline and Punish* (1977). The regulation and governance of conduct in schools and post-compulsory education has been assisted by the rise of what Nikolas Rose has called the 'psy' sciences and their role in constituting contemporary conceptions of the self (Foucault, 1977; 1988a; Rose, 1989; 1998; Dreyfus, 2002). The 'psy' disciplines include psychology, psychiatry and psychotherapy and have been most influential in opening up a space inside the heads of teachers, lecturers and students, filled with what Smail (2005) calls a 'luxuriant interior jungle'. This is where one can find constructs within students such as self-esteem, motivation to study, personal epistemological beliefs and, if we are fortunate, the results of our successfully implemented 'learning outcomes'. On the part of the teacher or lecturer too, appropriate forms of knowledge can be found, or if they are missing, staff development can be deployed to establish them. Appropriate attitudes to teaching, learning and assessment, the desired degree of 'flexibility', the residua of 'good practice' seminars and the panoply of skills that in many cases are demanded in discourses around teaching and learning in higher education can be located in the educator.

Arguably, Foucault himself and some of his followers may have concentrated 'too much on the technology of domination and power', and perhaps rather too much on notions of disciplinarity (Besley, 2005a: 313). The usual interpretation of Foucault engages more with *Discipline and Punish* and with images of circular prison buildings than with Foucault's later writing. Yet there are intimations of something altogether more subtle in Foucault's later works (Foucault, 1988b).

For Foucault both 'technologies of domination' and 'technologies of the self' help to constitute the self. We will return to these themes later in the volume but for the moment let us focus on the 'technologies of the self' that produce effects that constitute the self. Technologies of the self are a set of techniques through which people can work upon or change themselves. In classical antiquity, philosophers advocated a kind of stocktaking of the self. In mediaeval Christianity the notion that thoughts as well as deeds could lead to punishment in the hereafter encouraged introspection and confession, and notions of the self and consciousness developed by leaps and bounds. Technologies of the self define the individual and enable them to control their own conduct (Marshall, 1996; Besley, 2005a).

Foucault (1985: 29) in *The Use of Pleasure* describes technologies of the self as follows: they are 'models proposed for setting up and developing relationships with the self, for self-reflection, self-knowledge, self-examination, for deciphering the self by oneself, for the transformation one seeks to accomplish with oneself as object'.

To provide an example of this, consider the recent publication of 'The UK Professional Standards Framework for Teaching and Supporting Learning in Higher Education' (Higher Education Academy, 2006). This document lays out a neatly typologized system of desirable attitudes and practices that constitute professional standards. For instance, there are expectations of 'staff who have a substantive role in learning and teaching to enhance the student experience' (2006: 3). People in this position are expected to demonstrate

> an understanding of the student learning experience through engagement with all areas of activity, core knowledge and professional values; the ability to engage in practices related to all areas of activity; the ability to incorporate research, scholarship and/or professional practice into those activities. (2006: 3)

This seems simple enough. Indeed it is hard to disagree with. To show how commonsensical it is, imagine if the advice were reversed, and it was suggested that staff should show no understanding of the student learning experience and should not incorporate research, scholarship and professional practice into their activities. From the point of view of technologies of the self however, it is a much more significant document. It provides a set of criteria by which educators can scrutinize and judge their own and one another's activity. It expounds notions of 'professionalism', an enjoinment to 'enhance the student experience' and the obligation to infuse one's work with 'research, scholarship and/or professional practice'. These matters, which were once part of a realm of activities which were taken for granted and left to develop organically, are increasingly being specified so that we can see them and, presumably in the fullness of time, measure them.

Technologies of the self as applied to the higher education system refer to the ways in which its inhabitants are induced to perform various 'operations on their own bodies and souls, thoughts, conduct, and way of being', that people make either by themselves or with the help of others, in order to transform themselves to reach a 'state of happiness, purity, wisdom, perfection, or immortality' (Foucault, 1988b: 18). Thus, by diligent application of the kinds of criteria outlined by bodies such as the Higher Education Academy, a latter-day state of grace may be achieved.

Foucault also examined the 'arts of the self', which are designed to explore the 'aesthetics of existence' and to facilitate inquiry into the governance of self and others. Taken together, these technologies 'make the individual a significant element for the state' through the exercise of a form of power – governmentality – in becoming useful, docile, practical citizens (Foucault, 1977; 1988c; 1991: 153).

The technologies of the self and the internalized scrutiny of oneself as an educator or student are not the whole story in higher education, of course. There are elements of a more frankly coercive scrutiny apparent in many higher education systems. For example Baty (2006: 1) reports on 'an electronic monitoring system called Uni-Nanny, under which students identify themselves at every "learning event" with individual computer chips in their key rings', which is 'already in use at Glamorgan University' and with roll-out expected in other institutions in the near future. This initiative is prompted by concerns over student drop out rates and it is proposed that student drop out rates can be reduced by attendance monitoring. It is believed that in the UK one in six students drops out, costing the public purse an estimated £450 million a year. The commonsensical quality of this move to monitor attendance electronically is reflected in an editorial in *The Times Higher Educational Supplement* (2006) which intones solemnly 'The days when students could go their own way without anyone questioning regular absences are long gone at most universities. With drop-out rates creeping up, particularly in the first year, of course innovative responses should be welcomed.' The only demur is that the name – 'Uni-Nanny' – might hint at a 'condescending attitude'.

As Foucault reminds us, technologies of power 'determine the conduct of individuals and submit them to certain ends or domination, an objectivizing of the subject' (Foucault, 1988b: 18). The increasing use of technological means to monitor students and staff may be interpreted in line with Foucault's earlier work that emphasized the application of such technologies of domination and how they might be used in the process of producing 'docile bodies' in the grip of disciplinary powers that they lack the language or political muscle to resist. Here, the 'self' is produced by processes of objectification, classification and normalization in human practices and in the forms of knowledge we gain about people in the human sciences. Educationalists, for example, help us to construct an image of the disaffected non-attending student whose absence can be diagnostic of their imminent departure. Thus the logic of attendance monitoring becomes irresistible – it is aligned with appropriate pastoral care for the students and with saving the drain on the public purse.

These modes of governance are of great importance from a Foucauldian point of view. Technology and surveillance practices are seamlessly brought into alignment with forms of consciousness and thinking which are enabled to see them as beneficial. They form parts of a mosaic of 'governmentality'. This is a way of regulating and coordinating human social activities which might involve the latest technology, but whose emergence can be traced to the beginnings of liberalism itself. It is directed through processes of policing, administration and the governance of individuals (Foucault, 1977; 1997). Foucault drew attention to the complex of calculations, programmes, policies, strategies, reflections and tactics that shape the conduct of individuals, 'the conduct of conduct' for acting upon the actions of others in order to achieve certain ends. This, then, is the process of governmentality. It is, in Foucault's view applied to people 'not just to control, subdue, discipline, normalize, or reform them, but also to make them more intelligent, wise, happy, virtuous, healthy, productive, docile, enterprising, fulfilled, self-esteeming, empowered, or whatever' (Rose, 1998: 12).

These varieties of governmentality can be seen running through many initiatives in higher education. From getting a degree itself, with the implications that one is investing capital in one's future skilfulness and employability, through to the implication that as a member of staff one can add capital to oneself through further study and training and by assuming casts of mind that foreground self-monitoring and 'reflective practice'.

Within neoliberal economies and the kinds of institutions that flourish within them there have also been subtle yet important changes in personal autonomy. Rather than the sense of self-governance and being captain of one's own ship that might have previously prevailed, the idea of personal autonomy has been replaced by the notion of the 'autonomous chooser ... whose choices have been structured through the manipulation of needs and interests ... and that freedom *from* is the prime neoliberal emphasis' (Marshall, 1996: 213).

When we talk about the control and governance of societies, institutions and educational establishments in this way, we are not just talking about control in the negative sense of repression or oppression. We are also seeking to foreground a more positive sense in that the distinctive features of the forms of governmentality that we have been outlining encourage people to grow in particular directions. Towards, for example, not merely compliance with the regime but towards taking an active part, perhaps by becoming a 'champion of excellence' or a disseminator of 'best practice'. Thus individuals can develop themselves and extend their careers along pathways where the regime and the increasingly capitalized worker jointly construct opportunities. The award of a Higher Education Academy Teacher Fellow-ship can lead to promotion and advancement in one's host institution and liberates funds so as to facilitate further research and collaboration to develop teaching and learning processes.

In this kind of context Foucauldian theory enables us to pose questions about the *how* of government – 'how to govern oneself, how to be governed, how to govern others, by whom the people will accept being governed, how to become the best possible governor' (Foucault, 1997: 287). These are all ques-tions that people solve every day in the education system as students, educa-tors or administrators. In line with the perspectives popularized by Foucault and Rose, Ball (2003b) notes that changes in education systems bring about changes in 'our subjective existence and our relations one with another' (Rose, 1989: ix). Ball calls this the 'struggle over the teacher's soul', which invites concerns over who teachers are, in relation to students and colleagues.

The role of statistics is particularly well advanced in the UK, where a number of newspapers publish regular higher education guides within which institutions are marked upon a variety of criteria and arranged in a league table accordingly. In addition a variety of other bodies, publications and agencies survey and publish awards that institutions proudly display on their websites. They may for example identify themselves as the 'friendliest university', or courses may identify their ratings in their latest Higher Edu-cation Funding Council Quality Assurance visits. Such is the variety of awards that almost all can claim to have achieved something. The Univer-sity of Wales, Swansea's award for 'best student experience' was commemo-rated on a variety of university merchandise, including Frisbees.

This characteristic of neoliberalism has passed almost without comment. But thinking back to what we said earlier about the process of competition, it is clear that a more systematic process is at work. The public sphere is full of examples of competition. Institutions compete with each other for posi-tion in the various beauty contests arranged by statutory and commercial agencies. Researchers compete for research funding and public good works are funded partly through competition for Lottery funding. Gradually 'competition' has come to replace policy. Institutions compete not to offer rigour or academic detail, but friendliness and 'experience'.

The competitive strategies whereby colleges and universities challenge themselves against targets and compete with one another to gain awards results in a celebratory, almost carnivaslesque, quality to websites and pro-spectuses. At the time of writing (August 2006) the University of Leicester advertises that it has achieved '14 consecutive teaching quality inspec-tion scores of "excellent" – a feat matched by just one other UK university'. University of Wales, Bangor offers itself rather less specifically as a 'great place to study' and offers a series of laudatory 'graduation stories'. Lough-borough University identifies itself as being the 'students' favourite' having been voted the 'best liked university' in the 2005 national student survey. And so the pattern is repeated over the country. This celebratory tone looks innocent enough. Yet the strategy of masking activities and data that are susceptible to a more politically nuanced analysis behind an aesthetic appeal to the senses might be more sinister. Walter Benjamin (1970) writes about the transformation of the political into the aesthetic moment, and of how the political process is transformed into an aesthetic spectacle. This aestheticization of politics tends to make political critique difficult if not impossible. Instead, the participant is invited to 'think with one's blood' and to interact instead at an emotional level (Smith, 2005).

The use of statistics as a positivist justification for the implementation of policy has reached such proportions in advanced Western societies that Smith (2005) calls it an 'epistemological crisis'. In practice, many institutions collude with statutory bodies and inspection agencies to ensure that the fig-ures are favourable. Ball (2003a: 216) uses the Lyotardian notions of perfor-mativity and fabrication to describe these phenomena. The performances of individual participants or institutions serve to provide measures of produc-tivity, output, or displays of 'quality'. They are also at stake when visits are made to institutions by quality assurance bodies, which take on a curious pan-tomime quality. These performances stand for, encapsulate or represent the quality or value of an individual, a course of study or an organization within a field of judgement. As Smith (2005) says, in the context of a quasi-market, in these performances 'truth' is a representational gambit. In describing the figures created through audits of institutions, Ball (2003a: 224) puts it as follows: 'truthfulness is not the point; the point is their effectiveness, both in the market or for inspection or appraisal, and in the "work" they do "on" and "in" the organization, their transformational and disciplinary impact'.

This is why particular attention is devoted in this book to the work of Michel Foucault and Nikolas Rose as providing a means of understanding the regulatory and disciplinary functions in which colleges and universities are implicated and the modes of consciousness and public life that they pre-dispose in their students, staff and the wider public.

Neoliberalism revisited: the private self of the educator in a global business environment

Yet there is more to the picture even than this. So far we have explored the 'governance of the soul' and the 'shaping of the private self' (Rose, 1989) as

it occurs in the post-compulsory education sector, and explained the importance of the work of Foucault to understanding what goes on here. Now
that we have done this, we can turn a second time to some of the arguments
about neoliberalism and corporate agendas and see how an understanding
of Foucault's work can deepen them and add more to the picture of what
institutions of further and higher education are doing in the early twenty-
first century.

The combination of Foucault with accounts of neoliberalism will allow us
to grasp more fully the significance of education's role in human capital
development – effectively, the production of docile bodies (Cooper, 2002),
willing to adapt to whatever pathway the increasingly 'flexible' labour markets might follow.

Education is crucial for business if it wants to rely on a strategy of con-
tinuously changing the nature of work, consumption and remuneration.
Reorganization of the institutions of civil society has become a kind of
'permanent revolution'. Business has not only gained a foothold here, but is
also continually reorganizing its manufacturing and mercantile activities
to suit perceived changes in the market. Almost any working person in the
developed economies could say that part of their job is 'to facilitate change'.
Thus, an educated employee in today's economies is one who is 'adaptable'
or 'flexible' – who is able to take one job one day and another job the
next day. The ideal worker is engaged in a continuous process of investment
in themselves through lifelong learning (Beckmann and Cooper, 2004).
A model of the ideal person – whether as student or teacher – is emerging,
who is proactive in updating their 'skills' to suit the market. This process of
learning, updating, upskilling and human capital self-investment is essential
to maintain social cohesion in a world where there is continuous change in
working networks, in work itself and the process through which people are
prepared for life in the labour force. There is an important link, then,
between what is happening to us, the flexibilities and changes that are
demanded, the consciousness that this encourages and the international economic and political climate.

In Ulrich Beck's classic work on risk society (Beck, 1992) this link
between the changes involved in modernization and subjectivity is made
more explicit. Here, Beck argues that in order for societies to evolve
modernization must become *reflexive*. That is, people must reflexively and
proactively change themselves. In a now-famous aphorism he contends
that structural change forces social actors to become progressively increasingly free from structure. Through a process of detraditionalization of
the kind we outlined earlier, for modernization successfully to advance,
people are encouraged to release themselves from structural constraint

and actively shape the modernization process themselves, as if it were a kind of 'enlightened' self-interest.

We mentioned earlier that the remit of the neoliberal movement is global. Many of the larger companies involved in the provision of services such as education may well come to play a more prominent and interventionist role in the UK in the future. Rikowski (e.g. 2001; 2002a; 2002b), Hill (2003) and others (e.g. Coates, 2001; Mojab, 2001; Pilger, 2002) argue that the World Trade Organization (WTO) and other 'global clubs for the mega-capitalists' are setting this agenda up in education across the globe. This is possible through the developing, operationalizing and widening sectoral remit of the General Agreement on Trade in Services (GATS). As Hill (2003) reminds us, this is facilitating the international trade in services, as exemplified by the way that UK universities are providing educational services in a whole raft of other countries, either through a physical presence there or via distance learning. For-profit organizations such as Nord-Anglia and Global Education Management Systems have an international profile of activities and already educate many thousands of people worldwide.

Educational processes are not just constructed so as to be favourable to a neoliberal business culture. Already, they constitute neoliberal business culture inasmuch as globally mobile businesses have a growing stake in education. Equally, the state's role in regulating quality in education is apt to be implemented in a manner broadly congenial to business culture. Rikowski argues that there are two reasons why the state needs to control the process of education. First, to try to ensure that it occurs at all. Many systems of inspection and control in the UK higher education system are propelled by a curiosity to see whether the money that accompanies the students has indeed been spent on them. From Higher Education Funding Council for England Quality Assurance reviews to visits from professional and statutory bodies, the questions are as often about staffing levels and resources for student learning than as much about the content of the curriculum. Second, centralized regulation tries to ensure that modes of pedagogy are commensurate with the seamless, managed production of future labour power. In this point of view it is expected that the state would seek to destroy forms of teaching and learning that:

> attempt to educate students regarding their real predicament – to create an awareness of themselves as future labour-powers and to underpin this awareness with critical insight that seeks to undermine the smooth running of the social production of labour-power. (Hill, 2003: 10, drawing upon Rikowski, 2001)

Who, among the contemporary phalanxes of 'employability champions', 'key skills coordinators' and impeccably credentialed practitioners, would dare to suggest this as a 'learning outcome'?

The processes of bureaucratized regulation also, as Boxley (2003) points out, entail *strict regulation and self-regulation by teachers* such that they are aware of how the very ways in which they relate to their students are being constrained by the expectations of performative measurability. In the years of compulsory education, there is increasing reliance on tests for children. Whereas once these might have served a formative assessment or diagnostic function for children they are now a means of assessing teachers and schools, even sometimes education authorities as a whole. In this context, it may be that teachers, as Boxley (2003) argues, are 'becoming to their very hearts Standardized Assessment Task teachers'. In Fielding's terms, 'How many teachers of young children are now able to listen attentively in a non-instrumental way without feeling guilty about the absence of criteria or the insistence of a target tugging at their sleeve?' (Fielding, 1999: 280).

Equally, in higher education, pass rates, progression rates and measures of student satisfaction are yardsticks by which staff are measured, and, intriguingly, come to measure themselves. Problems associated with low pass rates are reflected back upon teaching teams as if they were responsible for them. A colleague faced with low pass rates in a module addressing individual differences and psychological assessment reported having a conversation with an external examiner in which the external examiner agreed that the standard of the examination papers was low but advised that it was better to set the students 'something that they could do' in future.

All of this is part of creating a seamless web of what Ainley (1999) calls 'learning policy', where learning is utterly desocialized and reduced to the production of a more globally competitive workforce assessed against tasks adjusted so as to flatter the student and the institution.

Conclusion: but what's the alternative?

So far, our account of what goes on in the post-compulsory education system might seem rather bleak. We have depicted a world in which a global business agenda pervades the once proud public institutions of education, where the people who work within the system are reshaping themselves to cope with the flexibility imposed and to play their parts within the carnival of quality assurance and accountability that demands ever more working hours in the academic year. Our intention here is to do what C. Wright Mills enjoined social scientists to do in his classic *Sociological Imagination*:

Know that many personal troubles cannot be solved merely as troubles, but must be understood in terms of public issues – and in terms of the problems of history making. Know that the human meaning of public issues must be revealed by relating them to personal troubles – and to the problems of the individual life. Know that the problems of social science, when adequately formulated, must include both troubles and issues, both biography and history, and the range of their intricate relations. Within that range the life of the individual and the making of societies occur; and within that range the sociological imagination has its chance to make a difference in the quality of human life in our time. (Mills, 1959: 226)

What we are doing then is placing the unease felt by ourselves and our colleagues and students about what is happening in post-compulsory education in a more systematic context. Our unhappiness within the education system, and that of our colleagues and students, is surely not merely some twitch of the hormones or a pharmacologically remediable depletion of some delinquent neurotransmitter. It is surely meaningful in terms of public issues, organizational practices and corporate strategies that have so far remained largely unexplored as they affect the 'souls' of educators and students, or as they are now retypified, 'learners'. Perhaps it is not too late to dream of something different:

a discursive public 'space' in which people can formulate, consider and debate the issues of the day . . . a space for 'public discourse', the function of which is other than the promotion of governmental aims, the pursuit of private interests or consumption; . . . the site for the nurturance of a critical language, a prime function of which is to make clear the assumptions, agency and power bases of other discourses; . . . an ideal site for the celebration of the diversity of opinions; . . . it can help people develop a 'public good' perspective, and help them interrogate issues transcending their own parochial concerns; . . . it can help people to recognize a necessary interdependency between responsibilities and liberties . . . (Bottery, 2000: 211)

References

Ainley, P. (1999), *Learning Policy*. London: Macmillan.

Ball, S. J. (2003a), 'The teacher's soul and the terrors of performativity', *Journal of Education Policy*, 18(2), 215–28.

Ball, S. J. (2003b), *Class Strategies and the Education Market: The Middle Classes and Social Advantage*. London: Routledge.

Barry, A., Osborne, T. and Rose, N. (1996), *Foucault and Political Reason: Liberalism, Neoliberalism and Rationalities of Government*. Chicago, IL: University of Chicago Press.

Baty, P. (2006), 'Uni-nanny is watching', *The Times Higher Educational Supplement*, August 4 2006.

Bauman, Z. (1988), *Freedom*. Buckingham: Open University Press.

Beck, U. (1992), *Risk Society: Towards a New Modernity*. London: Sage.

Beckmann, A. and Cooper, C. (2004), ' "Globalisation", the new managerialism and education: rethinking the purpose of education in Britain', *Journal for Critical Education Policy Studies*, 2(2). www.jceps.com/?pageID=article&articleID=31. Accessed 25/03/06.

Benjamin, W. (1970), 'The work of art in the age of mechanical reproduction', in W. Benjamin, *Illuminations*. London: Fontana, pp. 219–54.

Besley, A. C. (2005a), 'Jim Marshall: Foucault and disciplining the self', *Educational Philosophy and Theory*, 37(3), 309–15.

Besley, A. C. (2005b), 'Foucault, truth telling and technologies of the self in schools', *Journal of Educational Enquiry*, 6(1), 76–89.

Blair, T. (1996), Speech by the Leader of the Opposition. The Labour Party Annual Conference, Blackpool, October 1 1996.

Bowles, S. and Gintis, H. (1976), *Schooling in Capitalist America*. London: Routledge and Kegan Paul.

Bottery, M. (2000), *Education, Policy and Ethics*. New York: Continuum.

Bourdieu, P. (1984), *Distinction: A Social Critique of the Judgement of Taste*. London: Routledge and Kegan Paul.

Boxley, S. (2003), 'Performativity and capital in schools', *Journal for Critical Education Policy Studies*, 1(1). www.jceps.com/?pageID=article&articleID=3. Accessed 01/01/06.

Brooks, A. (2001), 'Restructuring bodies of knowledge', in A. Brooks and A. Mackinnon (eds), *Gender and the Restructured University*. Buckingham: Open University Press, pp. 15–44.

Burchell, G. (1996), 'Liberal government and techniques of the self', in A. Barry, T. Osborne and N. Rose (eds), *Foucault and Political Reason*. Chicago, IL: University of Chicago Press, pp. 19–36.

Chomsky, N. (2000), *Chomsky on Miseducation*. New York: Rowan and Littlefield.

Clarke, J. (2005), 'New Labour's citizens: activated, empowered, responsibilized, abandoned?', *Critical Social Policy*, 25(4), 447–63.

Coates, B. (2001), 'GATS', in E. Bircham and J. Charlton (eds), *Anti-Capitalism: A Guide to the Movement*. London: Bookmarks pp. 92–134.

Considine, M. (2006), 'Theorising the university as a cultural system: distinctions, identities, emergencies', *Educational Theory*, 56(3), 255–70.

Cooper, C. (2002), *Understanding School Exclusion: Challenging Processes of Docility*. Nottingham: Education Now/University of Hull.

Department for Education and Employment (DfEE) (1997), *The Learning Age: A Renaissance for a New Britain*. www.dfes.gov.uk/. Accessed 05/05/05.

Department for Education and Skills (DfES) (2003), *The Future of Higher Education*. London: The Stationery Office.

Douglas, M. and Isherwood, B. (1979), *The World of Goods: Towards an Anthropology of Consumption*. London: Allen Lane.

Downes, D. (2001), 'The "macho" penal economy: mass incarceration in the US – a European perspective', *Punishment and Society*, 3(1), 61–80.

Dreyfus, H. (2002), *Heidegger and Foucault on the Subject, Agency and Practices*. Berkeley, CA: Regents of University of California socrates.berkeley.edu/hdreyfus/html/paper_heidandfoucault.html. Accessed 23/02/06.

Dreyfus, H. L. and Rabinow, P. (1982), *Michel Foucault: Beyond Structualism and Hermeneutics*. Chicago, IL: The University of Chicago Press.

Evans, M. (2004), *Killing Thinking: The Death of the Universities*. London: Continuum.

Fazackerley, A. (2004), 'RAE triggers headhunt race', *The Times Higher Education Supplement*, October 22 2004.

Featherstone, M. (1991), *Consumer Culture and Postmodernism*. London: Sage.

Fielding, M. (1999), 'Target setting, policy pathology and student perspectives: learning to labour in new times', *Cambridge Journal of Education*, 29(2), 277–87.

Fisher, W. (2006), *The Metamorphosis of Higher Education in the UK – is there an Identity Crisis?* Paper presented at the conference of the Society for Research in Higher Education, Lancaster, July 2006.

Foucault, M. (1977), *Discipline and Punish: The Birth of the Prison*. London: Penguin.

Foucault, M. (1978), *The History of Sexuality, Vol. 1: An Introduction* (trans. Robert Hurley). New York: Random House Inc.

Foucault, M. (1982), 'The subject and power. Afterword', in H. L. Dreyfus and P. Rabinow, *Michel Foucault: Beyond Structuralism and Hermeneutics* (Second edn). Chicago, IL: University of Chicago Press pp. 208–9.

Foucault, M. (1985), *The Use of Pleasure: The History of Sexuality, Vol. 2*. New York: Vintage.

Foucault, M. (1988a), 'Truth, power, self: an interview with Michel Foucault', in L. H. Martin, H. Gutman and P. H. Hutton (eds), *Technologies of the Self: A Seminar with Michel Foucault*. Amherst: University of Massachusetts Press, pp. 9–15.

Foucault, M. (1988b), 'Technologies of the self', in L. H. Martin, H. Gutman and P. H. Hutton (eds), *Technologies of the Self: A Seminar with Michel Foucault*. Amherst: University of Massachusetts Press, pp. 16–49.

Foucault, M. (1988c), 'The political technology of individuals', in L. H. Martin, H. Gutman and P. H. Hutton (eds), *Technologies of the Self: A Seminar with Michel Foucault*. Amherst: University of Massachusetts Press, pp. 145–62.

Foucault, M. (1991), 'Governmentality', in G. Burchell, C. Gordon and P. Miller (eds), *The Foucault Effect: Studies in Governmentality*. Chicago, IL: The University of Chicago Press, pp. 87–104.

Foucault, M. (1997), 'The ethics of the concern for self as a practice of freedom', in P. Rabinow (ed.), *Michel Foucault: Ethics, Subjectivity and Truth, The Essential Works of Michel Foucault 1954–1984, Vol. 1* (trans. Robert Hurley and others). London: Penguin, pp. 281–301.

26 *Rethinking Universities*

Furedi, F. (2004), *Where Have All the Intellectuals Gone?* London: Continuum.

Furedi, F. (2006), 'Grumbling won't change a thing', *The Times Higher Education Supplement*, July 28 2006.

Giddens, A. (1991), *Modernity and Self-identity*. Cambridge: Polity.

Gioia, D. A. and Thomas, J. B. (1996), 'Identity, image, and issue interpretation: sense making during strategic change in academia', *Administrative Science Quarterly*, 41(2), 370–403.

Giroux, H. (2004), 'Critical pedagogy and a postmodern/modern divide: towards a pedagogy of democratization', *Teacher Education Quarterly*, 31(1), 31–47.

Giroux, H. and Giroux, S. S. (2003), 'Take back higher education', *Tikkun*, 18(6), 28–32.

Habermas, J. (1991), *The Structural Transformation of the Public Sphere: An Inquiry into a Category of Bourgeois Society* (trans. T. Burger and F. Lawrence). Cambridge, MA: MIT Press.

Harris, S. (2005) 'Rethinking academic identities in neo-liberal times', *Teaching in Higher Education*, 10(4), 421–33.

Heelas, P. (1996), 'On things not being worse, and the ethic of humanity', in P. Heelas, S. Lash and P. Morris (eds), *Detraditionalisation*. London: Blackwell, pp. 200–22.

Higher Education Academy (2006), *The UK Professional Standards Framework for Teaching and Supporting Learning in Higher Education*. York: Higher Education Academy.

Higher Education Funding Council for England (2005), *PFI Case Studies*. London: Higher Education Funding Council for England.

Hill, D. (2003), 'Global neo-liberalism, the deformation of education and resistance', *Journal for Critical Education Policy Studies*, 1(1) www.jceps.com/?pageID=article&articleID=7). Accessed 30/01/06.

Hodkinson, P. and Bloomer, M. (2000), 'Stokingham Sixth Form College: institutional culture and dispositions to learning', *British Journal of Sociology of Education*, 21(2), 187–202.

Jephcote, M. (1996), 'Principals' responses to incorporation: a window on their culture', *Journal of Further and Higher Education*, 20(2), 33–48.

Kehily, M. J. and Pattman, R. (2006), 'Middle-class struggle? Identity, work and leisure among sixth formers in the United Kingdom', *British Journal of Sociology of Education*, 27(1), 37–52.

Luhmann, N. (1990), *Essays on Self-Reference*. New York: Columbia University Press.

Lury, C. (1996), *Consumer Culture*. Cambridge: Polity.

Maffesoli, M. (1988), 'Jeux de masques: postmodern tribalism', *Design Issues*, 4(1–2), 141–51.

Marshall, J. D. (1996), *Michel Foucault: Personal Autonomy and Education*. Dordrecht: Kluwer Academic Publishers.

Marshall, J. D. and Marshall, D. (1997), *Discipline and Punishment in New Zealand Education*. Palmerston North: Dunmore Press.

McLaren, P. (2005), *Capitalists and Conquerors: A Critical Pedagogy Against Empire*. New York: Rowan and Littlefield Publishers.

Mills, C.W. (1959), *The Sociological Imagination*. Chicago: Aldine.

Mojab, S. (2001), 'New resources for revolutionary critical education', *Convergence*, 34(1), 118–25.

Morris, E. (2002), Speech by Estelle Morris, Secretary of State for Education. Labour Party Conference, Blackpool, October 2 2002.

Neave, G. (2006), 'Times, measures and the man: the future of British higher education treated historically and comparatively', *Higher Education Quarterly*, 60(2), 115–29.

Olssen, M. (1999), *Michel Foucault: Materialism and Education*. Westport, CT: Bergin and Garvey.

Olssen, M. (2006), 'Understanding the mechanisms of neoliberal control: lifelong learning, flexibility and knowledge capitalism', *International Journal of Lifelong Education*, 25(3), 213–30.

Pilger, J. (2002), *The New Rulers of the World*. London: Verso.

Power, S. (2000), 'Educational pathways into the middle class(es)', *British Journal of Sociology of Education*, 21(2), 133–45.

Rikowski, G. (2001), *The Battle in Seattle: Its Significance for Education*. London: Tufnell Press.

Rikowski, G. (2002a), *Globalisation and Education*. A paper prepared for the House of Lords Select Committee on Economic Affairs, Inquiry into the Global Economy. www.ieps.org.uk or rikowski@tiscali.co.uk. Accessed 20/12/05.

Rikowski, G. (2002b), 'Transfiguration: Globalisation, the World Trade Organisation and the national faces of the GATS', *Information for Social Change*, 14, 8–17.

Rose, N. S. (1989), *Governing the Soul: The Shaping of the Private Self*. London: Routledge.

Rose, N. S. (1998), *Inventing Our Selves: Psychology, Power, and Personhood*. Cambridge: Cambridge University Press.

Rutherford, P. (2000), *Endless Propaganda: The Advertising of Public Goods*. Toronto: University of Toronto Press.

Slater, D. (1997), *Consumer Culture and Modernity*. Cambridge: Polity.

Smail, D. (2005), *Power, Interest and Psychology: Elements of a Social, Materialist Understanding of Distress*. Ross on Wye: PCCS Books.

Smith, R. (2005), 'Grecian urns and yellow cards: quality and the internalisation of the quasi-market in the FE sector', *Journal for Critical Education Policy Studies*, 3(2). www.jceps.com/?pageID=article&articleID=54. Accessed 14/03/06.

Thompson, J. (1996), 'Tradition and self in a mediated world', in P. Heelas, S. Lash and P. Morris (eds), *Detraditionalisation*, London: Blackwell, pp. 89–108.

Times Higher Education Supplement (2006), 'Shame about the name', *The Times Higher Educational Supplement*, August 4 2006.

Trow, M. (1976), 'The public and private lives of higher education', *Daedalus*, 104, 113–27.

Trowler, P. (2005), *Reinventing the University: Visions and Hallucinations*. www.ru.ac.za/academic/adc/conference/docs/PaulTrowler.pdf. Accessed 22/12/05.

Touraine, A. (1995), *Critique of Modernity*. Cambridge, MA: Blackwell.

Tysome, T. (2006), 'Community of scholars crumbling', *The Times Higher Education Supplement*, July 28 2006.

Walkerdine, V. and Lucey, H. (1989), *Democracy in the Kitchen: Regulating Mothers and Socialising Daughters*. London: Virago.

Walkerdine, V., Lucey, H. and Melody, J. (2001), *Growing Up Girl: Psychosocial Explorations of Gender and Class*. Basingstoke: Palgrave.

Warde, A. (1994), 'Consumers, identity and belonging: reflections on some theses of Zygmunt Bauman', in R. Keat, N. Whiteley and N. Abercrombie (eds), *The Authority of the Consumer*. London: Routledge, pp. 58–74.

Willis, P. (1977), *Learning to Labour: How Working Class Kids Get Working Class Jobs*. Farnborough: Saxon House.

Yarrow, K. and Esland, G. (1998), *The changing role of the professional in the new FE*. Unpublished Conference Paper, BERA Conference, Queen's University, Belfast.

Zinn, H. (2005), *Howard Zinn on Democratic Education*. London: Paradigm Publishers.

Chapter 2

Education, Society, Economy and Culture

Preamble: social power and educational experience

There have been many attempts to develop ideas about how education serves a particular economic interest, or how it imparts a hidden curriculum that leads to a docile workforce. These have been the stuff of radical education for many years. In this chapter, rather than tread the well-worn furrows of the last half century of radical educational writings, let us attempt something a little different. Rather than the operations of a distant state or political power upon educational processes, we will examine the extent to which the operations of social power in the education system manifest themselves in the subjective worlds of students and lecturers, and explore how this has been transformed in the world's developed economies.

As in the quote from Mills towards the end of the previous chapter, it is in doing this that we can see the link between social and political power and educational processes most clearly reshaping staff and students. When we talk of the 'stress' faced by university staff or the characteristics of students in terms of 'skills' and 'employability', it is important to grasp how they came to be conceptualized in this way in the first place.

Educational researchers may choose different 'ladders' (Silverman, 1993), or different 'processes of engagement' (Morgan, 1983), to better conceptualize the world around them. For those doing radical or critical educational studies that choice often means using frameworks derived from the works of 'modernist' and Marxian-inspired critical theorists, as we might see for example in the classic work by Bowles and Gintis (1976), who most famously advanced the argument that schooling reflected the needs of the American capitalist system. Equally, this strand of work owes something to Habermas and the members of the Frankfurt School, and in the last couple of decades, workers in the field have drawn heavily upon the work of Pierre Bourdieu to understand education in terms of culture and the acquisition of cultural capital. Accordingly, inasmuch as a theoretical perspective is explicit in much of the analysis of people's relationship to higher education in the existing literature, it draws upon Bourdieu. This kind of theoretical perspective has proved extremely popular among researchers in the field of educational studies and its deployment has achieved the status of an ortho-doxy in the discipline (Reay, 2004).

It is noteworthy that in the vast body of writing about post-compulsory education there are only a few hints as to how the study of educational matters could draw upon the so called 'post' theorists, such as Baudrillard, Barthes, Derrida, Lyotard and Foucault. However, as we hope to have established in Chapter 1, these theorists might be thought to be especially valuable to researchers looking for a way of making sense of the educational process and its role in society. They could not only help critical researchers focus on voices that have been marginalized or that cannot be heard (Alves-son and Willmott, 1992), they could also help researchers and theorists of education to be 'reflexive', in grasping how they may be raising themselves above those marginalized voices (Platt, 1989).

Pierre Bourdieu's work provides well-developed pathways for those wishing to consider how education forms a kind of cultural capital and how a nexus of ideological and practical factors may constitute a 'habitus' for a particular group of people. Thus, those who grow up into the middle classes – or, what is nearly the same thing, among those with a good deal of cultural or social capital – are apt to succeed in the education system, are more likely to gain at least degree level qualifications and enjoy favourable economic and social positions in later life. Moreover, they are more likely to be able to afford to buy houses in the catchment areas of 'good' schools, afford private education, enable their children to enjoy the best educational resources and so on, thus perpetuating their lineage's cultural capital. Indeed, as we learn from research such as that of Blanden *et al.* (2005), social mobility has declined in Britain and expansion in higher education has dispropor-tionately benefited the more affluent sectors of the population. Therefore, it is tempting to believe that Bourdieu must have got something right.

However, this is not the end of the story. Bourdieu is not without his critics. Some see his work as perpetuating an overly reductionist view of human social activities. As Rojek and Turner (2000) argue, his work con-tains a residue of Marxist theory, which means that a good deal of his analysis maps back onto social class categories. In his famous study of taste (Bourdieu, 1984), the communities of taste he discovers – in terms of prefer-ences for foodstuffs, music and so on – map neatly onto socio-economic categories. Rojek and Turner comment that this leaves little opportunity for theorizing change, regional variation or social struggles over consump-tion. By the same token, cultural capital tends to comprise pretty much the same things from one generation to the next as it is passed down from generation to generation. We have, within this perspective, very few ways of accounting for the voracious cultural appropriation of new styles, tastes, activities and values; how fashions move from one class or subcultural niche to another, or how education and the experiences within it might change as it adapts to serve new markets. If we find now that teaching and learning experiences can be delivered to students via their handheld devices, or that lectures are 'podcast' we might need to look elsewhere to find a theoretical framework to assimilate these new manoeuvres.

A further strand of enquiry which is difficult to open up using Bourdieu's ideas concerns consciousness itself. By the time someone has assimilated the ways of doing, thinking and being that comprise one's 'habitus', they have pretty much become automatic. Reflexive awareness of the process is exceptional (Adams, 2006): 'principles embodied in this way are placed beyond the grasp of consciousness, and hence cannot be touched by voluntary, deliberate transformation' (Bourdieu, 1977: 94). Consequently, the reproduction of culture, habitus and identity itself happens unwittingly: 'what they do has more meaning than they know' (Bourdieu, 1977: 35). Latour says that Bourdieu 'subjugates the multiplicity of expressions and situations to a small number of obsessively repeated notions which describe the invisible forces which manipulate the actors behind their backs' (Latour, cited in Boyne, 2002: 119).

Thus, says Adams (2006), despite Bourdieu's attempts to account for change, reflexivity and his attempt to find a place for the generative capacities of habitus, he could still be charged with being excessively deterministic (Lamont, 1992; Halle, 1993; Alexander, 1994; Widick, 2003). Habitus and social structure delimit the possibility of free will or agency. Indeed, 'cognitive structures which social agents implement in the practical knowledge of the social world are internalized, "embodied", social structures ... which function below the level of consciousness and discourse' (Bourdieu, 1984: 468). Therefore 'it is difficult to know where to place conscious deliberation and awareness in Bourdieu's scheme of things' (Jenkins, 1992: 77).

While we are aware that there are myriad things that students and staff in post-compulsory education do every day so as to sustain the patterns of tradition, ways of working and even 'academic standards', there is still a need to explore how consciousness may be shaped by powers, ideologies and institutions. This is why we made such play of Foucault's work in Chapter 1 and why we will make further use of it here to establish our distinctive perspective upon post-compulsory education.

Consequently, this chapter will attempt to consolidate the hints we have given so far as to how Michel Foucault's ideas could be incorporated into this body of scholarship. His ideas have been much utilized by scholars such as Nikolas Rose in analyses of 'governmentality' in policy, health and social care. However there have been relatively few attempts to apply these ideas in education. Some exceptions to this trend can be seen in works such as Ball (1990); Marshall (1996); Olssen (1999) and Baker (2001).

Power is central to Foucault's work. He famously analysed topics such as power relations in the penal system (1979), the way in which power is exerted over those deemed insane (1973), the exertion of power over the individual in other areas of medicine (1989), and also the way in which the individual may exert power over, or discipline, themselves, by reference to ancient civilizations (Gauthier, 1988; Foucault, 1990). Foucault interpreted changes in penal systems as efforts to ensure that power operated more efficiently, and saw the overall aim of post-enlightenment penal processes to be the reform of the soul. In many nations, prisons became 'penitentiaries' where the purpose became repentance as well as containment. Foucault viewed the development of the 'human sciences' as closely entwined with the birth of a form of social domination that led to systematic and bureaucratic forms of organization in Western societies in the nineteenth century (Mourad, 2001). He also elaborated upon the insight that the knowledge gained from the human sciences was used to make individuals productive, cooperative participants in modern social systems. The production of knowledge, then, is implicated in the exercise of power.

Keeping the customers happy: epistemological sequelae of student satisfaction

A small vignette should suffice to illustrate the processes of power at work in the education system. Douglas and Douglas (2006) describe how 'mystery students' can be employed to evaluate the quality of a university course, in a manner analogous to how mystery customers who are confederates of the employer can evaluate standards of service in hotels, retail businesses and restaurants. Douglas and Douglas counsel that:

> they should not be thought of in terms of management 'spies'. Indeed, within the limited literature available on this subject, the general consensus is that operating mystery customer programmes provides a positive method of service performance measurement that is welcomed by 'good' employees. (Douglas and Douglas, 2006: 112)

Thus, the teaching and learning process is subject to ever further processes of observation and scrutiny, hand in hand with the development of professional standards and upfront tuition fees, so as to consolidate the move towards a system where 'standards of service' can be monitored.

These developments of monitoring processes can, from a Foucauldian perspective, be seen as incursions of power into the lives of university staff. Yet for Foucault himself this concern with power was motivated by a broader concern with how we come to see ourselves as human beings. Perhaps the clearest statement of his position was provided in an interview with Paul Rabinow in 1983:

> My objective ... has been to create a history of the different modes by which, in our culture, human beings are made subjects. My work has dealt with three modes of objectification which transform human beings into subjects ... The first is the modes of inquiry which try to give themselves the status of the sciences ... In the second part of my work, I have studied the objectivizating of the subject in what I shall call 'dividing practices' ... Finally, I have sought to study – it is my current work – the way a human being turns him – or herself into a subject. For example, I have chosen the domain of sexuality ... Thus it is not power, but the subject that is the general theme of my research. It is true that I became quite involved with the question of power. It soon appeared to me that, while the human subject is placed in relations of production and of signification, he is equally placed in power relations that are very complex. (Foucault, 1982: 208–9)

As a result of this interest in the question of consciousness or subjectivity, Foucault did not only conceive of power in terms of sovereignty and overt coercion, but also in terms of the management, organization, orchestration and shaping of people, with the subsequent determining of their conduct, believing that the construction and ordering of groups was central to power (Moss *et al.*, 2000). He talked of the use of 'observation' and 'gaze' (Foucault, 1973) during the exertion of power. Although in some situations Foucault saw power as productive (Foucault, 1980), he also believed that one effect of disciplinary power was to produce 'docile' bodies (Foucault, 1979), citizens that were useful for practical, productive labour.

Thus, the regular processes of evaluation and review, along the lines of those in commerce, can be seen as part of these mechanisms which secure docility. As Emanuel and Adams (2006) say in their account of the development of a 'quality of instructor service to students' questionnaire:

> The preferences students identified coincide with the dimensions of service quality as advanced by Garvin (1984) and with previous customer service assessments compiled by Zeithaml *et al.* (1990). According to their investigations, the attributes of quality service are: *Tangibles, Reliability, Responsiveness, Assurance* and *Empathy*. Tangibles include appearance

of the classroom, student seating and the like. Reliability is the instructor's ability to instruct the course dependably and accurately. Responsiveness addresses the instructor's willingness to respond to students' questions and concerns. The instructor's knowledge and ability to convey trust and confidence to students define the Assurance dimension. Empathy is the caring and individual attention the instructor provides his/her students. (Emmanuel *et al.*, 2006: 538)

Thus not only are staff and institutions evaluated as if it were possible to do so along the lines of generic 'service quality', the dimensions themselves are subject to itemization. Notice that this approach privileges the subjective dimensions of the instructor's knowledgeability, rather than whether it is indeed anchored in the discipline being taught. For example, a colleague regularly commences his teaching of statistics and research methods with a preamble where he expresses scepticism about whether such methods are indeed suitable for the social sciences. This, as those familiar with the disciplines concerned will know, represents a longstanding dilemma in these forms of inquiry. We may doubt the suitability on epistemological grounds and we may be concerned as to whether human data can ever meet the mathematical requirements of the statistical procedures used. Yet to undertake many kinds of research in the social sciences, or even to understand them, we need to be familiar with the language of variables, and with a range of descriptive and inferential statistics which might be applied. But our acquaintance's avowal of this dilemma, far from demonstrating his understanding of the situation, was taken by some students as undermining his fitness for purpose. 'He said he didn't believe in statistics. What kind of an attitude is that?' exclaimed one of them. Likewise, Fernandez-Armesto (2006) recalls being advised by a publisher to keep unresolved questions out of a history textbook he was writing, because it would 'undermine the book's authority' and teachers would not be able to set tests on these issues.

Expressing uncertainty, scepticism and critique, then, may not be preferred by students and publishers. An overriding concern with satisfaction and acceptability might lead to the kinds of viewpoints we have just described being muted or might lead to those who expressed them being replaced in due course by others more willing to teach a class or write a book which expressed no such uncertainty.

To make sense of these phenomena, we were reminded of the work of Rose (e.g. 1990; 1999) whose interest in 'governmentality' focuses on the process by which selves and subjectivities are made governable, often through the development of theories about an interior landscape inside the head, and new social phenomena such as public opinion. Rose (1999: 60) maintains that in advanced liberal democracies the citizen is hailed on every side by solicitations seeking their 'engagement in a whole array of programmes for their ethical reconstruction as active citizens'. He also argues that the concern of liberal governments has been to 'modulate events, decisions and actions in the economy, the family, the private firm, and the conduct of the individual person, while maintaining their autonomy and self-responsibility' (Rose, 1996: 46).

These ideas, which we introduced in Chapter 1, can help us extend our understanding of the kinds of experiences which are increasingly commonplace in the higher education system. Consider the following account from an educator involved in teaching trainee teachers in institutions in the United States. Despite the geographical distance from the UK and the highly specific nature of the course, this may well resonate with experiences in the UK. The account, which we shall quote at length, comes from Porfilio and Yu (2006):

> Over the past four years, I have educated over a thousand students, within various teacher education programs, located in the Northeastern United States. Although I enjoy mentoring students and sharing my ideas in relation to teaching, schools, and society, I have found myself struggling with commercial ideologies structuring life inside the classroom. Like many graduate students, I entered the university setting as part of the growing pool of 'contingent members,' individuals who serve as a cheap source of labor for colleges that are seeking flexible employees as they believe 'cheaper is always better' (Bradley, 2004; Hess, 2004). For over two years, I remained at the beck and call of administrators, filling in courses that were created particularly by market demands. Very often, I was called upon just a week before the start of a semester to teach courses I was not fully prepared for.
>
> Through my experiences as a 'temporary' worker, I gained a better perspective as to how corporate culture operates in academic institutions to position students to play a powerful role in the learning process. The college reinforces students' pre-existing commercialized notions surrounding education, teaching and learning by conditioning them to accept 'the market' as the solution to all our problems and to view education as purely a commodity. In essence, this translates into the idea that 'paying' tuition provides them with the entitlement of determining what should be taught and how they should learn. Thus, the 'consumer is always right' mentality is intruding our classroom and dismantling the democratic and moral dimensions of higher learning.

This mentality is born out in my first set of student evaluations. While I valued students' opinion on my teaching performance, I was perplexed at many of their views. Several students, who were dissatisfied with the course, evaluated it through the eyes of a consumer. The course would be considered valuable if it satisfied their market-related personal needs, not as to whether it helped them become more thoughtful educators or critical citizens. For instance, they even drew a conclusion about my teaching performance based upon the fact that they were requested to purchase textbooks, which they thought were too many and too costly.

Other students suggested that this foundations of education course was too rigorous and should never be taught. Apparently, doing that type of critical, intellectual work puts a cramp into students' busy schedules. The clinical nature of the program made it arduous for my students to interrogate the social, historical, and economic forces that create hate, hostility and violence inside and outside the schools. The required course readings along with the critical in-class discussions challenged many of their entrenched beliefs surrounding North American schools and the wider society. For many students, it was the first time they were compelled to examine the unearned privileges they, as other White, middle class citizens, acquire merely from their racial status. A few students went so far to state that the course should be dismantled entirely and I should go along with it. In its place, the pre-service teachers suggested a more 'practical' course be offered, implying that teacher education institutions should merely operate as breeding grounds to train compliant teachers, individuals who lack the critical insight and courage to 'deflect and transform the invasive power of capital' within their schools as well as within their own social worlds (McLaren, 2005: 92).

Although I was troubled by these comments, as every teacher wants their students to grow intellectually in the classroom, I became truly disenchanted when I found the college often sided with the students and engendered a corporate way of teaching and learning. The administration examined my teaching performance solely by whether it created happy customers. As a result, I was not invited to teach again at this institution because of the chairperson's 'bottom line' mentality – good teaching is characterized by producing happy students. By treating teaching as a commercial relationship, the institution overlooked that my intellectual labour may have left positive marks on many students. My critical role in helping future teachers understand the nature of education and become critical teachers themselves was eradicated.

This account is worth quoting at length because it shows some of the relationships between students, teachers and organizational processes that secure the curriculum. This is borne out also in the UK among some of us who have sought to introduce more challenging or philosophically sophisticated material into curricula in the UK. Students may object and may not succeed in their assessments. We are told that such an approach is inadvisable because it 'impacts negatively upon the student experience'.

In tandem with this, education is being seen as a set of skills that can be acquired so as to pass the relevant assessments and to facilitate access to a subsequent career. This quotation also highlights the difficulty in bringing material into the curriculum which might challenge or offer an alternative to students' existing preconceptions, or if we attempt to suggest that theirs is not the only way of looking at the situation.

In teaching about child development to psychology students, for example, one of us (BB) was minded to challenge students' implicit belief in such things as 'maternal instincts' and 'mother infant bonding' by introducing ideas from the work of Elisabeth Badinter (1981) on practices such as wet nursing. This suggests that at certain times in European history the contact between mother and infant was not valued as it is at present, and Badinter holds to a theory of 'maternal indifference'. Add to this the 'emotional indifference' of medieaval parents to their children proposed by Philipe Ariès (1979) and the activities catalogued in a collection edited by de Mause (1974), a picture begins to build up of contemporary emotional attachments between adults and children which suggests that the love which children presently enjoy is a relatively recent phenomenon. However, for some students such notions are sufficiently distasteful for them to refuse to participate, and to say that such writings are 'not natural' and 'irrelevant'. Now this is not to say that these historical accounts are literally true, any more than one would say that late twentieth-century infant attachment theories are true in any simple sense. The point is to highlight the difficulty of introducing ideas that go beyond the common sense or folkways of the present time. Even more damningly, as some pointed out to me, this would apparently not help them become educational psychologists or clinical psychologists. Under such circumstances the idea that thinking about issues in a historical or cultural context might improve the clinical or educational judgements made by future professionals can make little headway.

A number of authors such as Furedi (2006) see an over-reliance on student satisfaction and the incursion of business values into education as being antithetical to the need for education to challenge and stimulate rather than satisfy.

What is even more interesting is what happens to reduce students' dissatisfaction in the event of this turbulence between what university staff try to do and the demands of the student 'customers'. In the case of Porfilio and Yu (2006) this resulted in the termination of employment. In our case, next year the more challenging material was assigned a more peripheral place in the last ten minutes of the lecture and excited no comment. Other experiences reported include being subject to 'performance review' (Shepherd, 2006) or the sudden discovery of regulations that prevent one continuing in one's erstwhile teaching job (Mallot, 2006).

In some cases students are seen seeking an education which they find most congenial. Franz describes how

> we find students buying their education and shopping around for classes and majors; our goal as educators becomes attracting and retaining students for our courses. What the students desire out of their college experience starts driving programs. Resources follow students, and departments are rewarded in direct proportion to the number of students (customers) who choose to attend (buy) their classes ... classes become popularity contests. Pedagogy becomes entertainment ... (Franz, 1998: 63)

In the same way that many current higher education students are rather different to those of previous generations, higher education institutions are now charged with interacting with them in new ways, inspired by the growth of consumer culture, and to produce a different sort of graduate. Traditionally, universities were expected to produce well-educated, cultivated people, yet this agenda is now rather different (Harvey, 2000). The people whom we are now encouraged to think of as our 'customers' are, at the end of the process, supposed to be good 'employees' too. The people who leave with qualifications are supposed to have 'skills' and 'competencies', and to have been enabled to be responsible for their own 'employability'.

In this way we can see tensions in the disciplinary process of higher education. The 'customer's' satisfaction must be secured, but at the same time colleges and universities are enjoined to mould their 'customers' so as to produce a certain sort of citizen, or perhaps more accurately, a certain sort of employee. Just as Foucault saw the reform of the 'soul' as the aim of the penal process, it can be argued that the aim of the contemporary higher education system is the reform of the souls of students, and, as was argued in Chapter 1, the socio-political reconstruction of higher education involves the reform of the educator as well.

In the UK, the New Labour government's vision of the higher education system progressively including ever greater swathes of the 'socially excluded' also echoes Foucauldian notions. Besley (2002), in interpreting Foucault (1988), describes how the disciplinary technologies pioneered through the enlightenment and into the nineteenth century would not allow anybody to stand outside society as 'outcasts'. Those who deviate from the norm would be reconstituted as 'docile' bodies, thus conforming and contributing to a productive economy under advanced liberalism. Clearly, one way of gaining control over the outcasts, the 'excluded', is to rein them in to an education system interpenetrated with the discourses of a new professional class of educationalists, employability champions and widening access specialists whose powers intersect with those of the state. Foucault (1988) noted that at the end of the eighteenth century, an administrative technology of government simultaneously took care of individuals while fostering the state's strength. The same philosophy is thus evident in the contemporary higher education system itself.

Power, policy and the shaping of the private self

Foucault argued that some forms of power operate as enabling, encouraging and authorizing. The Australian higher education system has recently undergone similar changes to those in the UK and Luke (1997) analysed one such aspect, the imposition of Quality Assurance, and demonstrated how the Quality Assurance system imposed on a small Australian institution had resulted in an improved situation for women in the university. She argued that the QA system was a panoptic mechanism of 'making visible', but that this had led to more accountability, and new opportunities for women and other marginalized groups, who had previously experienced 'invisible' oppressions and disadvantages. Luke (1997: 438) agreed that the QA system as a whole encompasses a host of patriarchal assumptions and processes that disadvantage women and that QA constitutes an example of the mechanisms of governmentality and techniques of disciplinary society (1997: 441). Foucault maintained that institutionalized processes and social subjects are regulated, surveyed and disciplined through the mechanisms of accountability. But as Luke demonstrates, such panoptic power also brings marginalized groups into the disciplinary gaze. Thus there is a productive dimension to power/knowledge regimes.

Luke observes that global systems can have very different interpretations, practice applications and outcomes at institutional and departmental level (1997: 441) and shows how QA had a positive emancipatory effect on the systematically disenfranchised groups in the university (1997: 442) by, for example, causing the collection of data which demonstrated the inequalities experienced by these groups. Luke (1997: 446) concedes that QA is a form of governmentality and a social discipline regulating social subjects and practices, but argues that panoptic mechanisms of 'making visible' brought previously invisible and marginalized groups to light in ways that made them part of a new standard and set of norms. She concludes that the panoptic and internalized gaze broke an hegemonic forced consent on the part of people who were previously victims of sovereign, individual power and exclusionary systems of formal governance.

In this sense, the processes of surveillance and scrutiny are transformative in thoroughgoing ways. They do not merely leave structures and processes intact, but can facilitate fundamental changes in patterns of discrimination and inequality in the organizations and institutions of higher education.

Drummond (2003) applied Foucault to nurse education in the present day 'knowledge economy'. In line with increasing the role of government in the standards and content of higher education, Drummond discerns parallels between the present day and the ancient Greeks and the ways in which they constituted themselves as moral subjects (Gauthier, 1988). Of particular relevance is Foucault's (1986: 352) idea of '*rapport a soi*', the kind of relationship that you ought to have with yourself, which resulted in Foucault's use of the term 'ethics' to refer to the implications of the moral codes followed to establish this relationship. Foucault identified four dimensions to '*rapport a soi*', and Drummond relates them all to aspects of the nurse higher education system.

Foucault (1986: 353) argued that regimes and institutions have a characteristic 'mode of subjection', which was 'the way people are invited or incited to recognise their moral obligations'. Drummond observes that, in the field of higher education, this comes under the 'lifelong learning' remit. As human units, students are now obliged to carry out work on themselves and this is manifested by the interest in evidence-based practice, accumulation of credits, reflective diaries, accreditation of prior learning, learning outcomes and continual professional development, resulting in a continual training and retraining of people via these concepts which make visible aspects of the lifelong learning and educative process and thus represent a new way in which both they, and those whose job it is to assess them, can be made not only visible but manageable. Although Drummond specifically refers to nurse education, the phenomena that he writes about are now present, to varying degrees, throughout most of the higher education system in many subject areas.

Foucault's notion of 'ethical substance' is an aspect which is targeted by the 'modes of subjection', or that aspect of the self that is to be worked upon in relation to moral conduct. Drummond likens this to standard of performance; creative output; indeed, 'the commodification of the self' (Drummond, 2003: 61).

In Foucault's theory, technologies of the self were the means by which one changes oneself to become an ethical subject (1986). Drummond suggests that the equivalent in higher education in what he calls the 'knowledge economy' is the labour performed for the solvency of the economic enterprise. The activities encouraged in the higher education system of today have some striking parallels with these technologies of the self, in that they comprise a set of techniques that allow individuals to work on themselves by regulating their bodies, their thoughts and their conduct.

Another classical idea which fascinated Foucault was the concept of *telos* which related to the perfection or the end point of a process. In the case of education this relates to the kind of being the students aspire to be, or indeed the kind of institution we aspire to educate them in. In Drummond's view, in the knowledge economy, the kind of being we aspire, or are incited to become involves a disposition to sustain the cash-flow, as well as complying to 'outcomes', 'competencies' or other standardizations of the desired outcome model.

As we have seen, Foucault questioned the foundational 'truths' of disciplines and was interested in the means by which some statements, rather than others, are understood as 'true'. One recent change in the higher education system which has involved the creation of new discursive spaces and the formulation of new 'truths' has been the enormous current focus on 'skills', 'competencies' and 'learning outcomes'. For example, in the formulation of curricula, the design of syllabi and teaching practices, universities, their staff and students are encouraged to attend to the assessment and development of 'key skills'. Arguably, it is an effect of power to see the 'skills' putatively possessed by students as cognitive entities. One's 'skills' are in many respects related to one's ability to exercise power over the social and physical world (Smail, 1999). However, once one defines 'skills' as intra-psychic cognitive proficiencies, people perceived to be without them are usually members of less powerful groups.

This is most clearly manifested by those individuals in our culture who are deemed to be in need of some sort of compensatory education and training (Hyland, 2006). In some writings on post-compulsory education and training, commentators describe what they see to be a 'therapeutic turn' in educational developments. Some post-compulsory education and training programmes are concerned with personal and social skills, emotional intelligence and the enhancement of self-esteem, confidence and motivation in learners. Some critics such as Furedi (2003) see such strategies as encouraging a 'victim culture', which marginalizes learners and replaces the pursuit of knowledge with the development of personal qualities required for a life of social and economic risk and uncertainty (Furedi, 2003). Ecclestone (2004a: 113) asks 'why many educators regard the conferring of recognition and esteem on people deemed to be marginalized as a fundamental educational goal'. Concepts of 'self-esteem' and 'emotional intelligence' are seen by some authors to be growing in popularity and leading to 'new professional activities in emotional management, life coaching, mentoring, counselling and interventions to build self-esteem and make people feel good emotionally in the pursuit of motivation, educational achievement and social inclusion' (Ecclestone, 2004b: 11). This is part of a process where a person's ability to manage themselves is seen as a skill in post-compulsory education, and 'skill' has now been opened up as a pedagogic and cognitive object.

The discourse of skills: upskilling for the neoliberal workplace

The topic of skill is worth pausing over because it illustrates some of the shifts we are seeking to explicate. A colleague nearing the end of his career commented upon this acerbically, while biting the stem of his pipe on the steps of our no-smoking faculty buildings: 'When I was young skills were what you had if you were a lathe operator or a footballer. Now we've all got to have them, students, you, me, the whole bloody lot of us.'

This comment essentially replicates the historical analysis of skills provided by Payne (2000). Half a century ago, the 'Carr Report' of 1958 (HMSO, 1958: 10) could still talk of 'skilled craftsmen' as being the 'backbone of industry'. More recently, early in the UK's New Labour administration in 'The Learning Age' (DfEE, 1998: 65), there was deployed a much wider discourse of 'basic skills', 'employability skills', 'technician skills', 'management skills', and 'key skills'. The notion of skills, as Payne remarks, has expanded to include a whole range of 'soft', 'generic', 'transferable', 'social' and 'interactional' skills. These are frequently hard to distinguish from personal characteristics, behaviour and attitudes, which in the past would rarely have been thought of as skills (Keep and Mayhew, 1998).

It is possible to see parallels between 'key skills' and Foucault's technologies of the self. Foucault described the Stoics developing their technology of 'taking care of oneself' (Foucault, 1990). Once that was achieved, they could begin 'knowing oneself'. Ways of doing this included self-disclosure and examination of the self. The process was long and involved, taking years of reflection. There is thus a parallel with 'key skill number three' – 'improving own learning and performance'. This too requires the development of a Stoic consciousness, leading to an individual that is self-monitoring, self-creating, disciplined and who is responsible for their own education, employability and professional development. This in turn mirrors Drummond's (2003) discussion of 'continuing professional development', which many of today's students will find themselves exposed to, particularly those entering teaching or health and social care professions. Indeed, more pervasively in the current higher educational climate, the idea of Personal Development Planning where the subject is supposed to scrutinize themselves and identify skills that need improvement. In this regime it is no coincidence that when skills are mentioned they are often adjectivalized with terms like 'personal' or 'transferable', as if they were somehow internal to the individual and could be carried from one situation to another.

Studies of work for students and graduates in places such as trendy wine bars, hotels and boutiques, suggest that parts of the up-market service sector may be looking to recruit 'aesthetic labour'. That is, people endowed with, or prepared to undergo, makeovers so as to acquire the requisite voice-quality, demeanour, image and physical appearance for the organization (Witz *et al.*, 2003). Lloyd and Payne. (2006) note that working practices that require high levels of 'skill' are still relatively unusual in UK workplaces and that the proposed 'knowledge economy' is still largely a matter of rhetoric on the part of policymakers. In connection with this, the 'softening of skills' that has taken place, the term has expanded to include more interpersonal and aesthetic features of the employee. It has instead meant that these aspects of the person are features that can legitimately be manipulated in line with the requirements of employment. Over a decade ago, Ainley presciently argued that calls for the introduction of personal, transferable key skills into higher education would be problematic for, as he saw it, they were:

> neither personal, transferable, nor skills; they are social and generic competencies ... To present attitudes and habits detached from their cultural context as technical abilities that can be acquired piecemeal in performance not only divorces them from the cultural context that gave them their original meaning but represents them as equally accessible to all students whatever their class, cultural background, gender or race ... It ignores the fact that middle class students already possess these competencies as a result of previous education and family socialisation ... For at rock bottom, the real personal and transferable skills required for preferential employment are those of white maleness and traditional middle classness. (Ainley, 1994: 57)

A number of authors such as Payne (2000) and Avis (1996: 117) have suggested key skills function as a 'form of closure, deepening middle-class forms of social and cultural reproduction'. The more skill overlaps with attitudes, behaviours and character traits, the more it becomes bound up with the cultural capital of certain social groups, and acquires elitist connotations.

Payne says that:

> the new totalizing language of skill allows policy makers to claim that we are all being 'up-skilled', when in reality very little may be changing in terms of the actual quality of jobs many people do, with large swathes of often low waged, casualized service sector employment still only requiring enough 'skill' to fill shelves, swipe bar-codes, follow instructions and smile pleasantly at the customer. (Payne, 2000: 362)

Thus, however skills are developed among the students in the education system, there remain structural issues in the economies of many nations which ensure that the kinds of skills demanded remain stubbornly fixed at the level of servile interpersonal behaviour (Lloyd and Payne, 2006).

In Britain, according to Strathdee (2005) and Felstead *et al.* (2002: 11) there are:

> 6.4 million people qualified to the equivalent of NVQ level three in the workforce, but only 4 million jobs that demand this level of highest qualification ... there are 2.9 million economically active people aged 20–60 who possess no qualifications [and there] remains 6.5 million jobs for which no qualification would be required to obtain them.

Likewise, the Performance and Innovation Unit (2001) reports that 57 per cent of jobs required less than three months training and 29 per cent required more than two years. Thus we have an economy which has, apparently, little place for the skills with which workers in the education system are assiduously equipping students. We can agree with Olssen (2006) and Hirst that:

> What is supposed to be an inevitable market-driven global process is actually substantially a product of public policy ... It was influential economic policy elites and state officials in advanced states that shaped the deregulatory free market vision of world trade. (Hirst, 2000: 179)

Hence, we could go even further than Lloyd and Payne (2006). Inspired by Foucault's writings, perhaps the 'skills' we inculcate through further and higher education and the orientation to employment that we inculcate through the recently introduced 'Personal Development Planning' are a way of smuggling this kind of behaviour into the educational curriculum. In this way, it becomes learnable, something that both staff and students can 'see' as adding to the educational experience, the students' employability and the economy itself. It becomes a suite of demeanours and behaviours that one can instruct, learn, practice and display at interview; something one can exercise on the job, something that is implicitly aligned with the improved employment prospects allegedly consequent on being a graduate.

It is thus not surprising that Gore (1998: 234) noted that the 'techniques of power that Foucault elaborated in prisons (are) applicable to contemporary pedagogical practice'. An emphasis on the acquisition of skills is, in this view, clearly compatible with techniques of surveillance, normalization, exclusion, classification, distribution, individualization, totalization and regulation. Such techniques have increasingly entered the higher education workplace and have made incursions into the lives of staff and students alike. Gore (1998: 237) observes that 'educating is about the teaching of norms – norms of behaviour, of attitudes, of knowledge'. It could be argued that this has always been true of the education given to children at school, but in previous times, the higher education system has been perceived as existing somehow beyond those norms. By contrast the contemporary higher education system continues to embrace norms in an ever-increasing way. Moss *et al.* (2000) maintain that a climate which prioritises technical and managerial discourses and values, as higher education increasingly does, is unfavourable to critical thinking. Once more, we see a substantial shift in the perceived purpose of higher education, as it becomes increasingly driven by protocols and manuals and its students and practitioners are evaluated in tick-box exercises.

The construction and ordering of groups in this way is, in our view, central to the operation of power. Foucault believed that 'dominant discursive regimes' and 'regimes of truth' had a disciplinary or regulatory function. They help organize experience and influence ideas, thoughts and actions, excluding other understandings and interpretations:

> power is embedded in the governing systems of order, appropriation and exclusion by which subjectivities are constructed and social life is formed ... available systems of ideas discipline individuals as they act, see, think and see themselves in the world. (Popkewitz and Brennan, 1998: 19)

The pervasive power of the 'dominant discursive regime' in higher education was illustrated when Baker (2005) asked undergraduates at her host institution why they had come to university. All of them, across a range of subject areas, responded that it was to get a 'good job'. She then asked what they thought of the idea of someone going to university to study something in which they were interested. A number of them had clearly not encountered such a notion before and thought it extraordinary, but the dominant response was that it would be a waste of time and money. One student remarked that it would be nice, but nobody would ever be able to afford to do it. These students had all grown up in an era in which the 'dominant discursive regime' maintains that higher education has the instrumental purpose of improving one's employment prospects. This discourse is sufficiently predominant that the suggestion of anyone doing anything else is met with incredulity. It seemed to be the only one that these students were aware of, even though they must have had older relatives who had been exposed to previously dominant discourses regarding the purpose of higher education.

The 'good job' discourse very effectively excluded other understandings or ways of thinking. In line with Lloyd and Payne's (2006) predictions, the 'good job' discourse is itself a fragile construction. Whereas a narrowly defined set of graduate careers can boast average starting salaries of £22,000 a year (Taylor, 2005b), it is clear that relatively few will earn this much. The Higher Education Statistics Agency was reported in January 2005 to have revealed that 38 per cent of graduates are working in non-graduate jobs (Taylor, 2005a) and only 12 per cent were in 'traditional' graduate employment. Despite the high average salaries reported in the press at the start of 2005 other evidence suggests that wages may be lower, even averaging as little as £12,000–13,000. A university education no longer guarantees higher earnings and a middle-class lifestyle (Williams, 2003; Barr, 2004; O'Reilly, 2004). The progression to a 'good job' looks increasingly precarious, yet what is significant is the conviction with which people believe they are on the path towards one.

This highlights the importance of examining higher education's purpose, and exploring how the individual's consciousness has been successfully configured to privilege the notion of a 'good job'. The high-paying good job is the warrant for acquiring the kinds of skills that will equip the person for a low-paying casualized one. In the meantime the curriculum is being increasingly eviscerated of the kinds of thinking that will accommodate ambiguity, conflict and ambivalence, the ability to think outside the box, and the more rigorous methodological techniques which 'impact negatively' on student experience and progression rates.

Power in post-compulsory education

Foucault saw power as articulations of force circulating throughout the social body, shaping people's understandings of themselves and their relations to the world, especially in the penal and health care systems. As we have argued here, the education system can be seen in much the same way. Power as a force can be fluid and productive, not merely coercive. Mass education has entailed the articulation of the mechanics of disciplinary and bio-power within assorted forms of knowledge. Disciplinary power moulded subjects fit for productive labour. This has found expression in the emergence of disciplines of knowledge, the mastery of which credentials puts certain individuals into privileged and influential positions within the system. Yet the credentials are not necessarily those which are inculcated through the teaching and learning of 'skills' or even the acquisition of a degree itself. Strathdee (2005) notes that candidates applying for 'blue chip' graduate jobs who had attended the University of Oxford were 29 times more likely to be appointed than a graduate from a new (post-1992) university (Brown and Hesketh, 2004). Indeed, by continuing to capitalize the traditional universities and in concentrating research and development efforts in relatively few institutions, governments may be creating a two-tier system of higher education. In a sense, they may be perceived as presiding over the introduction of new forms of selection into higher education as applicants are sorted into the institutions for which they are deemed suitable.

Following this line of argument, we can see that the increasing 'need' for qualifications extends the state's power, aspects of which can be detected in the current higher education system. Whereas the economic case for higher level qualifications is not fully established, and will not match the output of qualified people without substantial structural change, there are increasing numbers of people demanding higher education qualifications. To achieve these they have to be processed through the higher education system and become subject to the associated disciplinary technology, government-inspired discourses and personal record keeping. This enmeshment in the mechanisms of the field of education recollects what has been termed 'linguistic entrapment' (Crawford *et al.*, 1995) in the field of health care. Like the health care system over the last quarter century, education too has been characterized by unstable relations of power and shifting forms of knowledge which are subject to provisional realignments, as discourses such as social justice and economic rationalism struggle for dominance. Thus, an understanding such as Foucault's where power is seen in this way is apposite to making sense of the state of near-permanent revolution in which universities find themselves.

The virtue of Foucault's work is that through it we can attempt to make visible 'workings of institutions which appear to be both neutral and independent' (Chomsky and Foucault, 1997: 130). Here, the productiveness of power would seem to be a 'fundamental precept of pedagogical endeavour'

(1974:237). Yet the 'functioning of power remains largely invisible in our daily practices, unless we are looking for it' (1974:248). In a sense it is the largely bureaucratic exercises of external examining, quality assurance reviews, research assessment exercises and other internal, statutory and professional processes which monitor the institutions and individuals within them. In some senses the rewards for compliance are quantifiable in that it affects how much money the institution gets, and in others there are more ineffable constituencies to be satisfied, such as matters of 'reputation', 'prestige', 'profile' or 'institutional brand management'. Power is 'a productive network which runs through the whole social body' (Foucault, 1980: 119). The techniques by which power is applied is not a monolithic or universal system – techniques and procedures affecting individuals are adapted and applied differently in diverse situations. Power 'applies itself to immediate everyday life which categorizes the individual' (Rabinow and Dreyfus, 1983: 212). 'One may have a hold over others' bodies ... so that they may operate as one wishes, with the techniques, the speed and the efficiency that one determines. Thus discipline produces subjected and practised bodies, "docile" bodies' (Foucault, 1979: 137–8).

Central to Foucault's work is the notion of technology – the practice of power involving 'the government of individuals, the government of the souls, the government of the self by the self, the government of families, the government of children, and so on' (Foucault, 1984: 256). The operation of power can be seen in the foregoing examples that we have described. Sometimes it is overt, through the operation of hiring and firing policies that favour staff who are less troublesome. Sometimes it is more subtle and involves getting people to think about themselves as staff or students in new ways as they fill in audits of quality, skill or personal development. Besley (2002) highlights the parallels that can be drawn between social and educational interventions in education, mental hygiene and disciplinary technologies, including technologies of the self which can result in useful, docile, practical citizens through a process of identification, typification and professional practice. While these are almost never successful in remedying the abnormality that they were set in place to address, they are more usually successful in neutralizing subversive potentials and domesticating possible tools of critique.

From Foucault's point of view, the educational enterprise as it is presently constituted would represent a new technology of power. As Olssen (2006: 223) says, it is a discourse 'which aims at resolving the individual and the general; *omnes et singulatum*, in the interests of the smooth functioning of the whole'. Thus education, especially where it involves a commitment to lifelong learning on the part of the individual, is part of the mechanisms of

control operating in contemporary societies. Education represents a strategy of governance at the policy level, but also represents a form of bio-
power that disciplines the educated subjects and offers a way of typifying
those who have not been included in the education system, by enabling
them to be identified as not having qualifications. Marshall proposes a new
variant of bio-power which he calls *busno-power* which:

> Is directed at the subjectivity of the person, not through the body but
> through the mind, through forms of educational practices and pedagogy
> which, through choices in education, shape the subjectivities of autono-
> mous choosers ... this busno-power also impinges upon the population
> as a whole, as individual consumer activity 'improves' both society and
> economy. (Marshall, 1995: 322)

As Olssen notes, busno-power constitutes a distinctively neoliberal form of
power which represents individuals as autonomous 'choosers' of their own
lives and thus as somehow responsible for their own destinies. In this
model, education, complete with its perfusion of 'transferable', 'personal'
or 'key' skills involves new techniques of self-regulation. It attempts to link
more directly the individual development of skills and economic and technological change (Kraus, 2001: 117; Tuschling and Engemann, 2006).

Conclusions and limitations

In this chapter therefore, we have attempted to lay out the grounds of an
appreciation of the contribution of the work of Michel Foucault to the discipline of educational studies, and its usefulness in making sense of the
educational experience. There are of course some criticisms of Foucault's
work. Many of these have been well-rehearsed elsewhere (Baudrillard,
1988; Kelly, 1994), so we will concern ourselves with those issues which
will have the most impact upon educational studies of the kind we describe
in this volume.

Of the critiques which could be levelled at Foucault's work, many can be
remedied by judicious incorporation of ideas from Bourdieu, suggesting that
some merits lie in working with a combination of the two. First, Foucault's
work is rarely based on the actual accounts and practices of social agents,
unlike that of Bourdieu's (e.g. 2000), so Foucault's abstraction and tendency to paint in broad brush-strokes can be remedied. Second, Foucault is
alleged to make certain relations and aspects of relations disappear (Alves-
son, 1996), such as gender, race and class. This is certainly not the case with
Bourdieu, although he may ultimately obscure them (McCall, 1991; Moi,

1991). It is clear that these are terms that infuse the current widening-participation debate, from researchers, policymakers and participants in the education system themselves. Third, Foucault, through his less than precise references to the 'state', fails to give us any clues as to how to untangle the operation of specific central agencies, which are often articulated in Bourdieu's work (1988; 1998). However, that aspect has been addressed by a number of other authors such as Rose (1990) who has documented through his career how agencies in government, commerce and the professions have helped to create the circumstances under which the delivery of services and the private self can be shaped.

References

Adams, M. (2006), 'Hybridizing habitus and reflexivity: towards an understanding of contemporary identity?', *Sociology*, 40(3), 511–28.

Ainley, P. (1994), *Degrees of Difference*. London: Lawrence and Wishart.

Alexander, J. (1994), *Fin de Siècle Social Theory*. London: Verso.

Alvesson, M. (1996), *Communication, Power and Organization*. Berlin: Walter de Gruyter.

Alvesson, M. and Willmott, H. (eds) (1992), *Critical Management Studies*. London: Sage.

Ariès, P. (1979), *Centuries of Childhood*. Middlesex: Penguin.

Avis, J. (1996), 'The enemy within: quality and managerialism in education', in J. Avis (ed.), *Knowledge and Nationhood*. London: Cassell, pp. 105–20.

Badinter, E. (1981), *Mother Love: Myth and Reality: Motherhood in Modern History*. New York: Macmillan.

Baker, B. (2001), *In Perpetual Motion: Theories of Power, Educational History, and the Child*. New York: Peter Lang.

Baker, S. (2005), *Like a Fish in Water: Aspects of the Contemporary UK Higher Education System as Intended and as Constructed*. PhD thesis, University of Wales.

Ball, S. (1990), *Foucault and Education: Disciplines and Knowledge*. London: Routledge.

Barr, D. (2004), 'Crying on the inside', *The Times*, May 1 2004.

Baudrillard, J. (1988), *Forget Foucault*. Paris: Semiotexte.

Besley, T. (2002), 'Social education and mental hygiene: Foucault, disciplinary technologies and the moral constitution of youth', *Educational Philosophy and Theory*, 34(4), 419–33.

Blanden, J., Gregg, P. and Machin, S. (2005), *Intergenerational Mobility in Europe and North America: A Report Supported by the Sutton Trust*. London: London School of Economics Centre for Economic Performance.

Bourdieu, P. (1977), *Outline of a Theory of Practice*. Cambridge: Cambridge University Press.

Bourdieu, P. (1984), *Distinction: A Social Critique of the Judgement of Taste*. London: Routledge.

Bourdieu, P. (1988), *Homo Academicus* (trans. P. Collier). Stanford, CA: Stanford University Press.

Bourdieu, P. (1998), *Acts of Resistance: Against the Tyranny of the Market* (trans. R. Nice). New York: New Press.

Bourdieu, P. (2000), *Pascalian Meditations* (trans. R. Nice). Stanford, CA: Stanford University Press.

Bowles, S. and Gintis, H. (1976), *Schooling in Capitalist America*. New York: Basic Books.

Boyne, R. (2002), 'Bourdieu: from class to culture', *Theory, Culture and Society*, 19(3), 117–28.

Brown, P. and Hesketh, A. (2004), *The Mismanagement of Talent: Employability and Jobs in the Knowledge Economy*. Oxford: Oxford University Press.

Chomsky, N. and Foucault, M. (1977), 'Human nature: justice versus power', in A. I. Davidson (ed.), *Foucault and his Interlocutors*. Chicago, IL: University of Chicago Press, pp. 107–45.

Crawford, P., Nolan, P. and Brown, B. J. (1995), 'Linguistic entrapment: medico-nursing biographies as fictions', *Journal of Advanced Nursing*, 22(11), 1141–48.

de Mause, L. (ed.) (1974), *The History of Childhood*. London and New York: Harper and Row.

DfEE (1998), *The Learning Age*. London: HMSO Cm3790.

Douglas, A. and Douglas, J. (2006), 'Campus spies? Using mystery students to evaluate university performance', *Educational Research*, 48(1), 111–19.

Drummond, J. (2003), 'Care of the self in a knowledge economy: higher education, vocation and the ethics of Michel Foucault', *Educational Philosophy and Theory*, 35(1), 57–69.

Ecclestone, K. (2004a), 'Learning or therapy? The demoralisation of education', *British Journal of Educational Studies*, 52(2), 112–37.

Ecclestone, K. (2004b), 'Developing self-esteem and emotional well-being – inclusion or intrusion?', *Adults Learning*, 16(3), 11–13.

Emanuel, R. and Adams, J. N. (2006), 'Assessing college student perceptions of instructor customer service via the Quality of Instructor Service to Students (QISS) Questionnaire', *Assessment & Evaluation in Higher Education*, 31(5), 535–49.

Felstead, A., Gallie, D. and Green, F. (2002), *Work Skills in Britain 1986–2001*. Leicester: Centre for Labour Market Studies.

Fernandez-Armesto, F. (2006), 'Only once did I find a book so repulsive that I simply threw it away. It became a bestseller'. *The Times Higher Education Supplement*, August 4 2006.

Foucault, M. (1973), *The Birth of the Clinic: An Archaeology of Medical Perception* (trans. A. M. Sheridan). London: Tavistock.

Foucault, M. (1974), *The Order of Things*. London: Tavistock.

Foucault, M. (1979), *Discipline and Punish: The Birth of the Prison*. New York: Vintage/Random House.

Foucault, M. (1980), *Power/Knowledge: Selected Interviews and Other Writings 1972–1977* (ed. C. Gordon). London: Harvester Wheatsheaf.

Foucault, M. (1982), 'The subject and power: afterword', in H. L. Dreyfus and P. Rabinow (eds), *Michel Foucault: Beyond Structuralism and Hermeneutics*. Chicago, IL: University of Chicago Press, pp. 208–9.

Foucault, M. (1984), 'Space, knowledge and power', in P. Rabinow (ed.), *The Foucault Reader*. New York: Pantheon Books, pp. 239–56.

Foucault, M. (1986), *The Care of the Self: The History of Sexuality, Vol. 3*. New York: Pantheon Books.

Foucault, M. (1988), 'Technologies of the self', in L.H. Martin, H. Gutman and P. H. Hutton (eds), *Technologies of the Self*. Amherst, MA: University of Massachusetts Press, pp. 16–49.

Foucault, M. (1989), *The Birth of the Clinic*. London: Routledge.

Foucault, M. (1990), *The Care of the Self: The History of Sexuality, Vol 3*. London: Penguin.

Franz, R. S. (1998), 'Whatever you do, don't treat your students like customers', *Journal of Management Education*, 22(1), 63–9.

Furedi, F. (2003), *Therapy Culture: Creating Vulnerability in an Uncertain Age*. London: Routledge.

Furedi, F. (2006), 'In pursuit of the happy bunnies', *The Times Higher Education Supplement*, January 27 2006.

Garvin, D. A. (1984), 'What does product quality really mean?', *Sloan Management Review*, 26(1), 25–8.

Gauthier, J.D. (1988), 'The ethic of the care of the self as a practice of freedom: an interview', in J. Bernauer and D. Rasmussen (eds), *The Final Foucault* (trans. J. D. Gauthier). Cambridge, MA: MIT Press pp. 1–20.

Gore, J. (1998), 'Disciplining bodies: on the continuity of power relations in pedagogy', in T. Popkewitz and M. Brennan (eds), *Foucault's Challenge: Discourse, Knowledge and Power in Education*. New York: Teachers College Press pp. 231–51.

Halle, D. (1993), *Inside Culture: Art and Class in the American Home*. Chicago, IL: University of Chicago Press.

Harvey, L. (2000), 'New realities: the relationship between higher education and employment', *Tertiary Education and Management*, 6(1), 3–17.

Hirst, P. (2000), 'Globalization, the nation-state and political theory', in N. O'Sullivan (ed.), *Political Theory in Transition*. London and New York: Routledge, pp. 172–89.

HMSO (1958), *Training for Skill (The Carr Report)*. London: HMSO.

Hyland, T. (2006), 'Vocational education and training and the therapeutic turn', *Educational Studies*, 32(3), 299–306.

Jenkins, R. (1992), *Pierre Bourdieu*. London: Routledge.

Keep, E. and Mayhew, K. (1998), 'Was Ratner right? Product market and competitive strategies and their links with skills and knowledge', *EPI Economic Report*, 12(3), 1–14.

Kelly, M. (1994), *Critique and Power: Recasting the Foucault / Habermas Debate*. Cambridge, MA: MIT Press.

Kraus, K. (2001), *Lebenslanges Lernen. Karriere Einer Leitidee*. Bielefeld: W. Bertelsmann.

Lamont, M. (1992), *Money, Morals and Manners: The Culture of the French and American Upper Class*. Chicago, IL: Chicago University Press.

Lloyd, C. and Payne, J. (2006), 'Goodbye to all that? A critical re-evaluation of the role of the high performance work organization within the UK skills debate', *Work, Employment and Society*, 20(1), 151–65.

Luke, C. (1997), 'Quality assurance and women in higher education', *Higher Education*, 33(4), 433–51.

Mallott, C. (2006), 'Schooling in an era of corporate dominance: Marxism against burning tires', *Journal for Critical Education Policy Studies*, 4(1). www.jceps.com/?pageID=article&articleID=58. Accessed 07/11/06.

Marshall, J. D. (1995), 'Foucault and neo-liberalism: biopower and busno-power', in A. Neiman (ed.), *Philosophy Of Education 1995, Proceedings of the Philosophy of Education Society*. IL: Philosophy of Education Society, pp. 320–9.

Marshall, J. D. (1996), *Michel Foucault: Personal Autonomy and Education*. London: Kluwer Academic.

McCall, L. (1991), 'Does gender fit? Bourdieu, feminism, and conceptions of social order', *Theory & Society*, 21(6), 837–68.

McLaren, P. (2005), *Capitalists and Conquerors: A Critical Pedagogy Against Empire*. New York: Rowan and Littlefield Publishers.

Moi, T. (1991), 'Appropriating Bourdieu: feminist theory and Pierre Bourdieu's sociology of culture', *New Literary History*, 22, 1017–49.

Morgan, G. (ed.) (1983), *Beyond Method: Strategies for Social Research*. Newbury Park, CA: Sage.

Moss, P., Dillon, J. and Stathem, J. (2000), 'The "child in need" and the "rich child": discourses, constructions and practice', *Critical Social Policy*, 20(2), 233–54.

Mourad, R. (2001), 'Education after Foucault: the question of civility', *Teachers College Record*, 103(5), 739–59.

Olssen, M. (1999), *Michel Foucault: Materialism and Education*. Westport, CT and London: Bergin and Garvey.

Olssen, M. (2006), 'Understanding the mechanisms of neoliberal control: lifelong learning, flexibility and knowledge capitalism', *International Journal of Lifelong Education*, 25(3), 213–30.

O'Reilly, J. (2004), 'Gulf widens in market for graduate jobs', *The Sunday Times University Guide*, September 12 2004.

Payne, J. (2000), 'The unbearable lightness of skill: the changing meaning of skill in UK policy discourses and some implications for education and training', *Journal of Educational Policy*, 15(3), 353–69.

Performance and Innovation Unit (2001), *In Demand: Adult Skills in the Twenty-first Century*. London: Cabinet Office.

Platt, R. (1989), 'Reflexivity, recursion, and social life: elements for a postmodern sociology', *Sociological Review*, 37(4), 636–67.

Popkewitz, T. and Brennan, M. (1998), 'Restructuring of social and political theory in education: Foucault and a social epistemology of school practices', in T. Popkewitz and M. Brennan (eds), *Foucault's Challenge: Discourse, Knowledge and Power in Education*. New York: Teachers College Press, pp. 3–37.

Porfilio, B. J. and Yu, T. (2006), ' "Student as consumer": a critical narrative of the com-
    mercialization of teacher education', *Journal for Critical Education Policy Studies*, 4(1).
    www.jceps.com/?pageID=article&articleID=56. Accessed 05/11/06.

Rabinow, P. and Dreyfus, H. L. (1983), *Michel Foucault: Beyond Structuralism and Herme-
    neutics* (Second edn). Chicago, IL: University of Chicago Press.

Reay, D. (2004), ' "It's all becoming a habitus": beyond the habitual use of habitus in
    educational research', *British Journal of Sociology of Education*, 25(4), 431–44.

Rojek, C. and Turner, B. (2000), 'Decorative sociology: towards a critique of the cul-
    tural turn', *The Sociological Review*, 48(4), 629–48.

Rose, N. (1990), *Governing the Soul: The Shaping of the Private Self*. London: Routledge.

Rose, N. (1993), 'Government, authority and expertise in advanced Liberalism', *Econ-
    omy and Society*, 22(3), 283–98.

Rose, N. (1996), *Inventing Ourselves: Psychology, Power and Personhood*. London: Routledge.

Rose, N. (1999), *Powers of Freedom: Reframing Political Thought*. Cambridge: Cambridge
    University Press.

Shepherd, J. (2006), 'Blame piled on managers', *The Times Higher Education Supplement*,
    August 4 2006.

Silverman, D. (1993), *Interpreting Qualitative Data: Methods for Analyzing Talk, Text and
    Interaction*. London: Sage.

Smail, D. (1999), *The Origins of Unhappiness*. London: Constable.

Strathdee, R. (2005), 'Globalization, innovation, and the declining significance of qua-
    lifications led social and economic change', *Journal of Education Policy*, 20(4), 437–56.

Taylor, M. (2005a), 'Research reveals harsh reality of life after college', *The Guardian*,
    January 3 2005.

Taylor, M. (2005b), 'Graduates turn back on buoyant jobs market', *The Guardian*,
    February 10 2005.

Tuschling, A. and Engemann, C. (2006), 'From education to lifelong learning: the emer-
    ging regime of learning in the European Union', *Educational Philosophy and Theory*,
    38(4), 451–69.

Widick, R. (2003), 'Flesh and the free market: (on taking Bourdieu to the options
    exchange)', *Theory and Society*, 32(5–6), 679–723.

Williams, D. (2003), 'Real little earner', *The Guardian*, November 15 2003.

Witz, A., Warhurst, C. and Nickson, D. (2003), 'The labour of aesthetics and the
    aesthetics of organization', *Organization*, 10(1), 33–54.

Zeithaml, V. A., Parasuraman, A. and Berry, L. L. (1990), *Delivering Quality Service:
    Balancing Customer Perceptions and Expectations*. New York: Free Press.

Chapter 3

Education as Power

In this chapter we will critically interrogate the notion of 'knowledge as power' in the context of contemporary higher education. This investigation will range over issues concerned with how knowledge has come to be positioned in the post-compulsory education economy; a discussion which intersects with notions of what counts as knowledge itself. In this debate we can see the material powers of the state, the institutions and of the knowledge itself. Moreover, we can see how within the education system the concern with what knowledge is has yielded some shifting policies and positions as competing ideas about knowledge and who should possess it have jostled for legitimacy in the contemporary policy field.

The now-famous statement, that 'knowledge is power' (*scientia potestas est*), originates with Francis Bacon in 1597. Since then it has informed the thinking of a great many intellectuals, from Thomas Hobbes to Michel Foucault. Indeed, the idea that regimes of truth are enforced through the operations of power has become a central feature of twentieth and twenty-first-century thought.

Therefore in this chapter we will consider what power means, especially in the context of universities in the early twenty-first century and explore how an awareness of power relations in the post-compulsory education system can give us a potentially more enlightening and insightful grasp of some of the experiences of staff and students. Rather than being the individual consequences of idiosyncratic causes, these may well turn out to be systematically structured and patterned. The situation, as we shall argue, is not a simple matter of powerful people ordering around their underlings. Nor is it simply a matter of overt oppressions, although of course a bullying, blame-oriented and punitive culture may obtain in some establishments. The operation of power may be more complex. As Foucault put it:

If power were never anything but repression, if it never did anything but to say no, do you really think one would be brought to obey it? What makes power hold good, what makes it accepted, is simply the fact it doesn't only weigh on us as a force that says no, but that it traverses and

produces things, it induces pleasures, forces knowledge, produces discourses. (Foucault, 1980: 119)

This then was the way some intellectuals were thinking about power at
the end of the twentieth century. To anyone who has participated in the
UK's system of quality assurance in the late twentieth and early twenty-
first century this might make sense. There are often palpable memories
of the frenetic toil in preparation for a visit, as well as the jubilation and
sense of relief on receipt of a favourable rating. The operations of power
thus yield a whole range of emotions and – curiously – more rarely lead
to a sense of injustice than might be imagined commensurate with the
burdens they impose.

From knowledge to empowerment through education

This sense that power suffuses educational activity, knowledge and scholarship, and that power can somehow be derived from becoming educated, has
a pedigree over a century old. Foucault, though he is widely quoted on the
subject, was clearly not the first to generate such insights. Therefore it is
appropriate to examine the background to the idea and understand how
this indivisibility of knowledge and power came to be thought of the way it
is in the present. From early intimations by Francis Bacon to the late nineteenth century we can see little change in the notion. Political and educational theorists from Karl Marx to John Dewey appear to have been
convinced of the emancipatory role that education could play. As far as the
former was concerned:

> historically, Marx viewed public education not as an insignificant factor
> in the struggle for socialism ... [he] believed that an ignorant population
> was more easily mystified and mislead than an educated one ... Suffice it
> to say that within the Marxist framework, educational arrangements,
> while certainly no antidote for the degradation resulting from capitalism,
> can contribute to its transformation. (Liston, 1988: 146)

Similarly, Dewey believed that the school could be a means for social progress and the gradual improvement of society. The idea that education,
appropriately applied, can yield liberation has its echoes in the more recent
past too. In the inter-war years in Europe the Frankfurt School (1923–1933)
developed a form of dialectical social criticism that inspired the work of the
diverse scholars who comprised the school. Following the migration of many

of the Frankfurt School's members to the United States their ideas gained greater credence there. One important notion in their brand of critical theory is that education, consciousness raising and the critique of ideology can eliminate 'false consciousness' and allow individuals and groups to unmask and resist oppressive regimes of power. For example, Herbert Marcuse had considerable faith in the power of critical thinking to break the historical repetition of domination and submission, for knowledge of the genesis and reproduction of socio-historical processes could enable those who had such knowledge to subvert them.

These ideas informed the thinking of critical educator Paulo Freire (1974) who made a great deal of the notion of 'conscientization', or the coming to critical consciousness, which was possible through appropriate education. This was seen to involve learning to perceive social, political and economic contradictions – developing a critical awareness – with a view to enabling individuals to take action against the oppressive elements of that reality.

This then comprises a picture of education which has an enduring appeal for progressives and educators, and casts them so that a favourable image of the craft of the pedagogue can be sustained. In this view, educators are involved at the very cutting edge of social progress, in pushing back the frontiers of ignorance and socially conservative tradition and in engaging democratically with learners so as to foreground the learners' interests and enable the pedagogy itself to enlighten the teachers. Knowledge is power in the sense that knowledge empowers people.

Power and education: the tyranny of emancipation

This picture of education liberating the individuals who participate in it is not the whole story however. There is an equally potent tradition of seeing education as a process of imposing power upon those who are being educated. This is hinted at in the work of some of the theorists above, for example where education is seen as akin to indoctrination, or where it is simply a matter of transferring knowledge from teacher to student in what Freire disparaged as the 'banking model' of learning. Our concern however is with something more fundamental than that. It is not as if education can simply be divided into the sort that is emancipatory and the sort that is oppressive. Let us try to understand why.

In the later part of the nineteenth century, Friedrich Nietzsche began a tradition of analysis which was to transform the analysis of power relations for the next hundred years. Among his concerns lay the idea that an intractable problem of coercion lies with the very nature of knowledge itself. Thus, his analyses of knowledge invariably drew attention to the way it is not simply a collection of facts or set of procedures for adjudicating between competing theories. Power was crucial to Nietzsche's understanding of systems of knowledge – they are enforced through power relations. The scientific tradition, from the eighteenth-century Enlightenment to the present day, would have it that truth claims can be verified at 'the tribunal of reason'. This however, is for Nietzsche a kind of bureaucratic ruse – a way of masking the powerful interests at stake in establishing a course of action as desirable (Nietzsche, 1886/1973; 1888/1968; Lovibond, 1994). This has parallels with Foucault's recurrent themes, but it has also been noted by many others. Paul Feyerabend, who said 'helping people does not mean kicking them around until they end up in someone else's paradise' (Feyerabend, 1987: 305) and from a feminist perspective too, Marion Young (1987) also condemns the idea of an apparently impartial reason as an authoritarian construct.

Importantly for scholars of education who have drawn upon his work, Bourdieu too makes use of this insight:

> It is as structured and structuring instruments of communication and knowledge that symbolic systems fulfil their political function, as instruments which help to ensure that one class dominates another (symbolic violence) by bringing their own distinctive power to bear on the relations of power which underlie them and thus by contributing ... to the domestication of the dominated. (Bourdieu, 1991: 167)

Now, these aspects of the educational process are not easily avoided. It is not as if through a more enlightened curriculum or a more democratic approach we can circumvent them. The problem is not so easily resolved. Any claim to truth has to fight its corner and vanquish other forms of 'truth' that have less epistemological authority. Equally, the practicalities of delivering learning experiences may mean that teachers and learners are refashioned. Students may readily assent to be lectured, yet often have to be coerced to 'participate' in discussion.

To Foucault of course power was central. In *Discipline and Punish*, he writes:

> power produces knowledge (and not simply by encouraging it because it serves power or by applying it because it is useful) ... power and knowledge directly imply one another ... there is no power relation without the correlative constitution of a field of knowledge, nor any knowledge that does not presuppose and constitute at the same time power relations. (Foucault, 1978a: 27)

The implicit corollary of this statement is that one may be free to know, but this very knowing also defines one's freedom (Garcia, 2001: 114).

The attractiveness of Foucault's formulation of knowledge for making sense of post-compulsory education experiences is manifold. Chiefly, for us it is appealing because it enables us to see how a relatively chaotic system like education, with many competing individuals, interest groups and agendas can be host to multiple sites of power. There are many examples from our own experience which suggest curiosities inherent in the operation of power. Often, changes for the worse in the working conditions of academic staff are announced to them not by their line managers but by relatively junior administrative colleagues. The news that one is no longer allowed to apply for research council funding, or that one has to undertake clearing duties from a call-centre style communal workspace rather than one's own office has been disclosed in chance remarks from temporary administrative assistants. Equally, there are demarcations of status inherent in who has keys, whose signature is required for budgets and in some instances, who has metal versus plastic cutlery in the dining area, with metal knives and forks being reserved for staff. One of us (BB) persisted with the bendy plastic variety out of a sense of solidarity with the student body, despite the tendency of the fork prongs to snap on some of the more robustly-fried chips. Yet this demarcation was enforced by some of the university's least well-paid workers. In other words, the relationship between the guards in the prison and the prisoners themselves is not straightforward. In the famous Panopticon analogy, the behaviour of the guards in the central guard tower is regulated by the demands of their task just as surely and completely as the prisoners.

Many classic conceptions of power and authority are rather clumsy when it comes to making sense of such peculiarities. Erving Goffman (e.g. 1961), in his famous work on institutions such as prisons and hospitals, talks about 'echelons' and 'echelon control'. This is used to describe the typical authority system of such an institution. For example '*any* member of the staff class has certain rights to discipline *any* member of the inmate class, thereby markedly increasing the probability of sanction' (Goffman, 1961: 42).

While there are clearly examples of the direct exercise of authority in educational institutions, very often the situation in universities is different. Often it is difficult to square the practical exercise of dominion by a worker in the academy with the formal description of his or her role from the point of view of the criteria identified by the institution's human resources department. Sometimes, the responsibilities far exceed the person's sanctioned authority to carry them out. The experience of being a 'programme director' or 'programme leader' for a degree course is a case in point.

Sometimes one is struggling to cover the teaching to which the university is committed, yet one has no control over staffing levels or staff budgets to recruit new colleagues to cover. One may find that professional and statutory bodies which accredit the degree programme withdraw their support as a result of chronic under-resourcing. At that point, one becomes answerable to one's host institution for why this has happened, even though it occurred as a result of factors well beyond one's control. This kind of complex interplay of power, responsibility and authority is characteristic of many educational institutions.

As well as a complex interplay of power pervading institutions and their frequently reorganized organizational frameworks, there are lines of influence that can be traced within subject areas and disciplines themselves. As we have already seen, for Foucault (1980), power relations are a general condition of social life and are involved in securing relations of domination at different levels in organized social activity. Within the university system, each discipline has its 'regime of truth' (1980: 131) which is manifested through forms of accepted discourse which provide a code of 'normalisation' for its practices (1980: 106). The nature of the discipline is visible in the boundaries and limits concerning what can be included or excluded, set by bearers of discourse (Foucault, 1982). In this view, says Arreman (2005), discourses and power are closely allied and allow what can be said, who can say it, and how it is expressed. In the UK, it is possible to see this in the debates over what constitutes a proper subject to study at university. This was brought into particularly sharp focus in 2003 with the discussion of so-called 'Mickey Mouse' degrees. The term was used by the then Minister for Higher Education Margaret Hodge. These, said Hodge, were degrees in which 'the content is perhaps not as rigorous as one would expect ... and may not have huge relevance to the labour market' (Brockes, 2003). In the same article, Brockes reports the Cambridge historian David Starkey who uttered the now famous aphorism 'There are Mickey Mouse students for whom Mickey Mouse degrees are quite appropriate' (*ibid.*). These kinds of discussions were reignited in April 2005 when soon-to-be Shadow Higher Education Minister Boris Johnson was reported as denouncing 'loony degrees in windsurfing from Bangor University' (Gimson, 2005). University of Wales, Bangor does not offer a degree in windsurfing, loony or otherwise. However, this exemplifies the casual dismissal of courses and institutions that are not perceived to be at the top of the hierarchy which is sometimes betrayed by people at policymaking level.

The point here is that there are struggles over what can be said and what can count as a legitimate education. In the UK this is exacerbated by a range of pressures that universities are under. On the one hand the UK has transformed itself into a service sector economy whose employment demands the university system is striving to meet. On the other hand, attempts to meet the needs of economic activity driven by leisure and tourism lay the institutions open to suggestions that they may be 'dumbing down' or offering 'Mickey Mouse' courses. A vocationalist ethos has propelled the colleges, institutes and art schools which eventually became polytechnics and then 'new universities' for many years. Often, the kinds of courses offered were guided by the needs of local industries, so that for example one might find courses in textiles being offered in cities with a reputation for garment manufacture. The more practical, applied disciplines, while not entirely excluded from the so called 'traditional universities' had apparently found a congenial home in the new, post-1992 institutions.

Yet, perhaps as a result of the power gradients we have just been talking about, the vocationalist ethos has always had an uphill struggle in the British Isles. Many commentators, for example Pring (1995) and Marks (1999) note the problems associated with vocationally orientated reforms of the education system. It seems that every well-intended move made to incorporate vocationalism into education, whether this was through 'technical' schools of the old tripartite era, youth training schemes, NVQs or modern apprenticeships, is hampered by a residual 'snobbery' within the system. The ideological divide between 'thinking' and 'making', says Marks (1999) is still pronounced. Vocationally oriented education is considered beneath those who are academically gifted and is often seen – even by the ministers of a government apparently committed to greater vocational relevance – merely the repository of those deemed either incapable or unworthy of what Bertrand Russell described as 'sterner studies'.

Thus, given the popularity of the game of golf in the UK, it is unsurprising that the Universities and Colleges Admissions Service (UCAS) lists 23 courses at UK institutions leading to degrees with an emphasis on golf technology, management, or course maintenance. Yet this level of vocationalism reaps derision from commentators in the press such as Midgely and Stimson (2006). This is despite the content of such degrees involving human resources management, materials science, the study of learning, teaching, coaching and motivation – topics which would scarcely cause amusement in a business studies or engineering degree.

Thus the notion of education is neatly sutured into broader notions of culture, intellectual life and the legitimacy of certain occupations over others. An economy increasingly reliant upon leisure and tourism exists with intellectual values drawn from earlier ages of manufacturing and commerce as well as ideas concerning the accomplishments of men of letters. Consequently, the vocationalism involved in engineering degrees is somehow more acceptable than that in golf management or surf science and technology. Vocationalism of course is itself nuanced in different ways in different social groups. Degrees in classics from Oxford and Cambridge are 'vocational' in the sense that they appear to be excellent preparations for careers in politics or the senior levels of the civil service.

The construction of knowledge and legitimacy is characterized by interruptions, breaks and discontinuities. We would not expect a unified theory of knowledge to be held across all institutions of learning and policymaking bodies. In the production, distribution and control of what can be said, discourse constructs reality and practice. Similarly, Bourdieu (1994) argues that continuous struggles over power are constitutive of social space, with knowledge and education being fields particularly affected by power relations. In contrast to Foucault's idea that power cannot be localized, Bourdieu relates power to the distribution of cultural, economic or symbolic power which is held in varying degrees by different actors. Using the notion of 'misrecognition', Bourdieu (1988) argues that there may be power structures which are not formally recognized, yet tend to be accepted and legitimized by individuals in subordinated positions. The economic and political climate of consumption-oriented economies in a neoliberal world order may help create the circumstances under which degrees focusing on, let us say, golf or surfing may be created. Yet at the same time journalists, and even politicians under whose administration these courses proliferate, may find much to sneer at by alluding to more primordial orders of intellectual stature. Power relations thereby have symbolic effects as the individuals involved do not question established practices or frameworks of understanding but rather see them as 'the order of things' (Bourdieu, 1992: 168). Bourdieu (1982), like Foucault, also emphasizes the role of language, and its links to power in the production and legitimization of discourses and educational activities.

When we look at something as pervasive and fundamental as language, Bourdieu (1991) maintains that linguistic utterances or expressions can be understood as the product of the relation between a 'linguistic market' and a 'linguistic habitus'. This means that when individuals use language in particular ways, they are deploying their accumulated linguistic resources. Moreover, they may also engage in 'recipient tailoring' so as to adapt their words to the demands of the social field or 'market' that is their audience. In this view, every linguistic interaction, however personal or insignificant it may seem, bears the imprint of the social structure that it both expresses and helps to reproduce. The idea of habitus may apply to both institutions and to individuals. Reay *et al.* (2001) discerned what they called an 'institutional habitus', such that schools and colleges have identifiable habituses involving practices which mutually shape and reshape the institutions in collaboration with their students, their communities and the wider socio-economic cultures of their catchment areas and cultures.

The cultural adjustments required of students from social groups who do not usually attend university have been of interest to many writers. Bamber and Tett (2001: 10), using Bourdieu's concept of habitus, stated that working-class students must 'critically examine and change some of the underlying assumptions on which their lives have been built' in order to succeed at university. Some writers have gone further and melodramatically described the change in roles, thinking and behaviour that students from disadvantaged backgrounds go through on commencing university as a kind of 'cultural suicide' (McLaren, 1989; Tierney, 1999), such that students from educationally disadvantaged backgrounds will need to make a 'clean break' from the communities and cultures in which they were raised in order to achieve academic success.

This is not to say that students assume the attitudes and values necessary to succeed in post-compulsory education unwillingly. Some embrace the experience almost with a sense of having been saved. The perceptions of the following interviewee in Baker are striking, as she described the experience of going to Cambridge after growing up in poverty and seeing her mother abandoned by successive partners:

> it's just really changed what I can do, who I can be, all aspects of my life ... before university my morals were very much that you grew up, had five different children by different rubbish men who then went off and left you on the dole with the kids and that's pretty much what I thought my grown-up life would be. (Baker, 2005: 151)

In the early part of her life this participant did not expect to go to university, yet through her experiences at school and via her own explorations of the educational and cultural capital that she encountered there, she formed the idea that university was an appropriate destination, and reported no difficulty in making the transitions once at college.

This illustrates how in McDonald's view (1999), young people in contemporary society need to act with a calculative attitude, and weigh risks and possibilities, as they negotiate networks of opportunity. They must become, he says, 'entrepreneurs of self' (McDonald, 1999: 121). This might well involve some degree of acceptance of middle-class competitive striving (Connell *et al.*, 1982). This participant is in a sense demonstrating this kind of agency, consciously choosing education as a resource for self-improvement and a means of escape from circumstances that appeared hostile. McDonald (1999) believed education to be of great importance to disadvantaged youth in opening up possibilities denied to their parents. At the same time, however, like many authors, he acknowledges that movement away from their families of origin both geographically and culturally is often involved in the path to university-level education.

Power, policy and decision making

The relationships between knowledge and power of course not only inform the kinds of lives that students and staff enjoy within the academy. There are larger scale relationships at stake between educational institutions, governments and commercial enterprises (Olgiati, 2006). Indeed, the post-World War 2 era in Europe and North America has seen a number of determined attempts to make this relationship closer and more tightly determined. For example, American historians of the process point to the optimism of certain official narratives, such as that of Vannevar Bush's report to US President Roosevelt in 1945 (Bush, 1945), in which science was described as an 'endless frontier' leading to a wealth of unambiguously positive outcomes. This kind of approach represented a relatively new way of thinking about the relationship between the state, commerce and the academy. The issue had been thought about in rather more idealistic terms prior to the 1939–45 conflict. Earlier in the twentieth century those who had thought about the issue at all tended towards the so-called 'manna approach' to science: that is, the idea that higher knowledge exists in a realm somewhat detached from other social systems so that its benefits fall upon them, as the manna's metaphorical image suggests (Olgiati, 2006). In this formulation it is as if the benefits of science itself, and university-level research and learning, are unproblematical, and are devoid of social costs. In this formulation the lines of influence are linear and relatively direct between discoveries and applications in government and commerce.

Vannevar Bush's (1945) notion of the endless frontier, ripe with the promise of technological and social benefits, was soon joined by the voices of many other pundits and politicians. The same kind of idea could be seen underlying the 'white heart of technology' speech delivered by UK premier Harold Wilson in 1963.

However, the picture in the present is much more complex. On the one hand it is believed by many policymakers and senior managers in institutions that the sharing of intellectual and physical resources by way of public–private partnerships can create productive opportunities in research. This is particularly attractive to governments who, while declaring support for publicly funded research, are seeking ways to boost the funds available. Thus policymakers are ever more committed to encouraging public–private partnerships as a way of securing research that is economically productive while at the same time limiting the burden upon the public purse. Equally there are concerns that people employed in colleges, institutes and universities are increasingly reliant on research funds from business and that their independence is thereby compromised. The relationship between the medical and biological sciences and the pharmaceutical industry is often a source of concern.

Let us begin our discussion here by thinking how we might conceptualize power as it applied in this context, where post-compulsory educational institutions are involved in research with external sponsors, and explore how knowledge and power might be allied. In his classic study, titled simply *Power*, first published in 1974, the political philosopher Steven Lukes (2005) identified three different kinds of power that may be deployed in political or social arenas.

The first – the one-dimensional view of power – focused on actions of decision makers in the political process. Power belonged to those whose will prevailed in any conflict of interest or policy. The key feature of this one-dimensional view is that to count as such, power must involve a visible conflict between actors with differing interests or preferences on a particular issue. Some would say that this was a 'classical' view of power and corresponds to the ways in which power has been thought of in many historical accounts – who won the battle or the ballot, for example.

Second, Lukes proposed a two-dimensional view of power which as well as this emphasis on conflict and decision making, adds the ability to control the agenda as a feature of power. Thus, power has to do with whether powerful interests are able to define what counts as an issue and what does not. In this kind of theorization of power, conflict and interests might be hidden as well as out in the open. In the light of this view, the one-dimensional view of power could be criticized as being overly concerned with the observable behaviour of participants. By contrast this 'two-dimensional' view attends to the latent or contextual issues in any conflict. Indeed, it does not even have to be formulated in terms of overt decision making, inasmuch as some management strategies may involve a deliberate withdrawal and non-decision making, leaving the minions to work around any difficulties.

Third, Lukes proposed a three-dimensional or what he saw as a 'radical' view of power. While this includes the one-dimensional and two-dimensional views of power mentioned earlier, and thus includes conflict and agenda setting, this extends the concept of power from the immediate political process to encompass the 'socially structured and culturally patterned behaviour of groups and practices of institutions' (Lukes, 1974: 22). Thus, where this variety of power is being exercised, people cannot complain because they do not have the language, the concepts or the means to make sense of their situation.

If we pursue the issue of the relationship between research in the health care disciplines and the role of the pharmaceutical and biotechnology industries, reports suggest that the influence of the pharmaceutical industry on academic medicine is substantial. Nearly 90 per cent of authors of papers in the *Journal of the American Medical Association* have received research funding from, or acted as a consultant for, a drug company (Healy and Thase, 2003). In Lukes' typology this reflects a one- and two-dimensional operation of power. However, the situation is more complex, in that there are allegations that the pharmaceutical industry has penetrated the very academic fabric of the health care disciplines. Concerns are being expressed that articles about drug trials in the medical literature are authored by the drug companies themselves, and academically based researchers and clinicians are merely invited to put their names to them. To busy teachers and researchers this gift of authorship may seem very attractive. They are in all probability struggling to meet teaching demands, demonstrate to their superiors that they are producing research of international significance, manage clinical caseloads and a myriad of administrative tasks. So a ready-made scientific paper which could be published with their name on it could prove irresistible.

The advertising placed in journals which are read by clinicians, the artefacts such as mugs, pens and notepads, the sponsorship, and overseas conferences that resemble holidays, are relatively 'transparent' and can be seen as bearing the interest of the companies whose names are emblazoned upon them. However the small-print footnote in a journal article indicating sponsorship of a study is not so conspicuous. Yet the influence may be substantial. Findings in studies of both antidepressants (Baker *et al.*, 2003) and antipsychotic drugs (Moncrieff, 2003) have been shown to be linked to the level of drug company sponsorship (Shooter, 2005). Even documents such as the prestigious Cochrane Reviews, often thought of as models of scientific rectitude and academic integrity and thoroughness, have evidence of drug company ghost authorship among them (Mowatt *et al.*, 2002).

Yet there is more to it even than this. Healy and Thase contend that the control of the pharmaceutical companies is even more pervasive and is driven primarily by their marketing departments:

the marketing department starts once a compound has been discovered. Marketing decides whether a new drug will be an antidepressant rather than an anxiolytic or a treatment for premature ejaculation. Marketing determines which journals with which lead authors clinical trials will appear in. Marketing recruits academics, including geneticists, neuroimaging specialists and social psychiatrists, to consultancy and speaker panels, and makes friends for the company. The marketing department supports educational events by putting on symposia, sponsoring speakers and bringing psychiatrists to international meetings. The work of the marketing departments is to create 'evidence' and establish consensus. (Healy and Thase, 2003: 388)

This then comes close to the situation characterized in Lukes' three-dimensional view of power. The warp and weft of the academic fabric is shot through with the influences of large companies and pecuniary interests. The knowledge reported with the gloss of impartiality is in effect something that has been purchased into being. The social structures, patterns of activity and forms of knowledge which are performable and thinkable are informed by the agendas and spending patterns of commercial groups. This is not to say that researchers or clinicians are invariably mindlessly duped by this kind of material. Indeed, these concerns are being expressed by people in influential professionals and academic positions such as Mike Shooter (2005), president of the Royal College of Psychiatrists, or Richard Smith (2005), former editor of the *British Medical Journal*. Yet these critical voices are often relatively muted when set against the thousands of scientific papers which represent the broad consensus of a discipline where the effectiveness and safety of a particular drug are concerned. Power then, is clearly at work.

The important feature of Lukes' definitions of power, and one which is germane to our consideration of the role of commercial interests in academic life, is that power is seen as a phenomenon that originates with collectivities. Now of course, some individuals may be more powerful than others, but groups and communities of interest are central to this view. Lukes' view of power was not restricted to overt conflicts between well-defined interest groups, but is also exercised to prevent needs or grievances finding political expression in the first place. At the time, in 1974, Lukes' views were aligned with progressive or liberatory politics, because incorporated within his definition of power is the possibility that any consensus might be 'artificial' and that material interests could exist beyond those that were visible in the particular social situation under scrutiny.

Dowding (2006) adds that within this view, the most insidious and important form of power is domination. Lukes' third dimension involves domination, but also involves the dominated acquiescing in their subordinate position. If we think within the confines of the knowledge that has been purchased into being and published accordingly, if we are not in a position to disrupt the manufactured consensus in a field, then clearly Lukes has a point which is relevant even today. According to Scott this kind of acquiescence may happen in both a 'thick' and a 'thin' sense (Scott, 1990). The 'thick' sense involves people actually subscribing to the values which disadvantage them, but in the 'thin' sense they have merely a grudging sense of resignation to them. In other words we may grudgingly accept that the kinds of knowledge we have in many fields of enquiry are those that governments or commercial interests find congenial, or we may, unless we think very carefully, begin to accept that this is merely how nature is. In the latter case we would be signed up to a commercial or governmental agenda in the 'thick' sense.

In this way, governmental and commercial interests may come to hold a dominant position in the realm of knowledge, wisdom or consciousness without us necessarily realizing their role. However, the kinds of knowledge that rely on this sort of sponsorship represent only a part of the total stock of human experience, albeit a very influential one in some spheres of activity. To fully grasp the notion of power we need to broaden our search for writers whose understanding of thinking, knowledge and ideas has incorporated notions of power, stake and interest. In many situations there is considerable competition between different voices and interest groups, and it is to these incompletely determined situations we now turn, via the work of Antonio Gramsci.

The idea of power in contemporary social science owes a considerable legacy to Antonio Gramsci. In the *Prison Notebooks* compiled in the 1930s, Gramsci (1971) introduced the notion of 'hegemony'. With this concept he sought to explain how the power of a ruling class was exercised not so much by coercion as by its intellectual and moral capacity to win the consent of the mass of the population. Thus, Gramsci was interested in the role of the mass media, the education system and the production of cultural artefacts, as it was these kinds of phenomena that held the fabric of society together and, as a consequence, enabled societies to avoid succumbing to unrest and revolution, even in the face of substantial inequality. To his credit, Gramsci saw this process of ideological leadership as a complex one, not as a matter simply of propaganda and manipulation. Hegemony involved more than crude ideological messages being directed at the populace. Rather, it was involved in the construction of a whole lived reality such that society's political, economic and social structures would be taken for granted by the mass of the people. In other words the dominant social order would be seen as the 'common sense' way of doing things.

Gramsci's view of power was notable because it was one of the earliest attempts to try to explore how power, and hegemony, was constructed through a process of negotiation between the dominant and the dominated. Hegemony could represent a smoothly negotiated consensus, but it could also yield crises and struggles, such as, within the education system, the turbulence we noted earlier over questions of 'dumbing down', or over what constitutes a proper subject of study and what the purpose of education might be. In a sense, these are struggles over the kinds of ideas that might become dominant and hence represent the kinds of jockeying for position of practices, belief systems and interests that Gramsci might have had in mind.

This kind of conflict and negotiation can be seen at all levels in the education system from matters of national policy to the means by which more local difficulties evolve and undergo moments of crisis. To follow the commercial examples above, let us consider another case where pecuniary interests and academic values appear to clash. At the time of writing, we can see a site of struggle emerging over the question of how much of a role commercial assistance to students can play in their educational success. Students from many countries of the world have been assailed by offers of help with their work in exchange for a fee. Services range from private tuition, 'proofreading' and essay writing. The Management School at the University of Bradford was reported to be offering students the services of an approved list of proofreaders. This, it was said, could offer 'opportunities to equalise a relationship in higher education that is weighted toward the home student . . . with good command of written English' (Baty, 2006).

As well as services for students apparently approved of by universities there are more controversial activities. Other services, especially those available over the internet, are less kindly thought of by university authorities. There are many websites offering coursework for sale. For example, ukessays.com was in the news in 2006 because it had earned its proprietor a turnover of £1.6 million in the previous year. In the three years since it has been running it has made its proprietor ex-barrister Barclay Littlewood a wealthy man (Taylor and Butt, 2006). A stable of writers supply the needs of the student and provide a custom written essay for around £500. One of the writers was reported as saying:

It took me a while to get my head round what Barclay was doing, I wanted to make sure it was all above board. I'm proud of what I do. If I've helped someone who's been sweating it out and point them in the right direction; that gives me a sense of satisfaction. (Taylor and Butt, 2006: 3)

Intriguingly, the firm boasts on its website that its own writers are held to a more stringent discipline than many students in universities who might presumably be handing their purchases in to meet coursework requirements. All the writers' work is checked for plagiarism against a large variety of other sources so that the work will be proof against plagiarism detectors used by educational institutions.

These manoeuvres on the part of commercial organizations and universities illustrate how the various interest groups or constituencies are competing for the upper hand in this particular battle. It may be that educational institutions return to an assessment strategy which places greater stress on examinations rather than coursework. Equally, it may be that the sums of money involved themselves become large enough to grant a kind of moral legitimacy to the activities concerned.

In any event, the commercial processes undertaken by students and outside suppliers of work continue to metamorphose in inventive ways and increasingly exercise universities and their staff. As well as commercial websites enabling the purchase of 'guaranteed' coursework, there is increasing evidence that some students are putting their work out to tender (University of Central England, 2006). Two researchers recently looked at outsourcing websites where computing solutions could be negotiated between purchasers and programmers and found that one in ten of all requests were from students trying to get their coursework completed for them. These invitations to supply computer programming as well as other computing assignments and essays for other subjects appeared to come from students at UK institutions (Clarke and Lancaster, 2006). As they said: 'What we've identified is a new type of cheating where students put their coursework out to tender and suppliers bid to complete the work.' As an acquaintance of the authors' said: 'I remember not so long ago I was always looking for ideas in students' work but now I'm just a plagiarism checker.'

These examples are intended to demonstrate how there is a complex interplay of powers and processes at work. Universities and colleges seek to preserve the notion that students should hand in their own work, yet themselves are nibbling away at the edges of this integrity in some cases. For example, English-speaking PhD students may even be paid by universities themselves to improve the work of overseas postgraduates.

At the same time graduates of the UK university system are – in best entrepreneurial spirit – organizing themselves through bodies such as ukessays.com to supply the work which those who are enrolled on courses need to produce in order to pass. Universities are 'target hardening' themselves, with a combination of electronic plagiarism detection measures and hostility towards companies supplying services to students, including attempts to stop them advertising on university notice boards. Companies, meanwhile, are offering students incentives to sell services on to their classmates, thus avoiding the problem of advertising altogether.

Now many of us who work in the education system tend to see this as a rather bad thing. We cling to the notion that students should be able to do impressive work on their own from original source material such as we recommend to them or find for themselves. We spend hours checking for plagiarism. We develop plagiarism policies, debate them and implement their enforcement. It is, perhaps as Gramsci would have it, commonsensical for us to do so. Yet clearly, when we take a step back, it is odd how some kinds of advantage which may be purchased are seen as less problematic.

The intrusion of economic forces into educational success is of course nothing new. As well as buying private education for their offspring, parents who can afford to do so are buying houses near 'good' – or at least popular – schools (Gibbons and Machin, 2006). So powerful is this tendency that at UK 2004 prices, the difference between the cost of an average dwelling outside a weak school, compared to one outside a top over-subscribed school, was around £61,000.

Thus, almost without our being aware, and certainly without much debate, lines have been drawn between the kinds of interventions and advantages which are legitimate and those which are not. In a sense, some advantages, such as those conferred by one's postcode area, are seen as irksome, whereas others merit a 'target hardening' approach and the involvement of many people in efforts to eliminate it.

In Gramsci's view, the consent of the population to the processes of government and their enlistment in activities that supported the existing social order was always provisional and therefore had constantly to be renegotiated and re-secured in economic and historical circumstances which were themselves always shifting. Especially important for Gramsci was the transition in early modern Europe from an aristocratic society, where the political class was kept aloof by an effective caste system, to a capitalist society, in which a bourgeois state actively sought to mobilize society as a whole in support of its aims and projects. Yet even in this new bourgeois state, with its motivations towards productivity, efficiency, education for work and the pursuit of profit, factions, interest groups and competing institutions and castes would emerge. Contests between Trades Unionists in education and the representatives in the institutions themselves in the Universities and Colleges Employers Association may develop over questions of pay and contractual demands, so even in the same institutions factions may develop with perceivedly different interests.

Hence, the theme of this chapter has not been to identify clear lines of domination from government to institutions to staff to students, but rather to highlight how there are a variety of opportunistic interest groups jockeying for position and for legitimacy both inside and outside post-compulsory educational institutions.

While power can be seen in a variety of shapes and forms in education systems, this does not preclude individuals acting creatively and even sometimes playfully to reconfigure the ebb and flow of power around them. There is a constant evolution of means by which advantage can be gained in the education system, a meticulous and frequently adjusted process of policing the boundaries between legitimate and illegitimate forms of advantage which may be purchased, and a multitude of ways in which power affects the lives of those who study or work in institutions. Thus, to develop an adequate notion of power, we must allow these subtleties to be placed centre stage. Bourdieu himself often evoked Althusser as an example of a theorist who had too mechanical a view of internalized domination, while Sartre represented the opposite extreme of a philosopher who proposed that we enjoy an excess of free will. Rather than being subject to a single unassailable dominant ideology, our account of the experience of post-compulsory education shows how important it is to animate the narrative with a view of power as a dispersed, emergent process, rather than something possessed by a single person or institution, or held at a particular place. The social space of education is inherently complex, and we have drawn on multiple theorists to give an underlying sense of the complexity of that social space and the competing interests which have emerged within it. It is among these that flesh-and-blood students and staff construct their identities and engage in practices that further their immediate and long-term interests.

Turning back to Bourdieu for a moment, it is our contention that his insistence on a strong notion of 'symbolic power' is a vital aid in grasping the pervasive nature of educational institutions' social impacts across a broader social field. In John Thompson's work (1995), which draws on Pierre Bourdieu and Michael Mann's work, Thompson valuably insists on the symbolic as an important dimension of power alongside the political and the economic aspects. In Thompson's definition 'symbolic power' is defined as the 'capacity to intervene in the course of events, to influence the actions of others and indeed to create events, by means of the production and transmission of symbolic forms' (1995: 17). This definition helpfully captures the power relations between a number of social institutions over symbolic production in education, involving the economy, industries both national and international, governments, and even religious institutions. Thompson then offers a bridging point over to another important conceptualization of power in relation to education which we have not hitherto addressed fully. The relationship between the economy and the means of production is important in many accounts of power and education. We have, of course, remarked upon notions of skill and employability, but we yet have to fully grasp the role that education plays in the economies of the twentieth and twenty-first centuries. It is to these questions we now turn.

Education and economic power

Prior to the development of radical approaches in American sociology in the 1960s and 1970s the dominant way of explaining differences in educational and occupational status of individuals in contemporary societies was through functionalism. This was signalled by Davis and Moore's generative statement that: 'Society must somehow distribute its members in social positions and induce them to perform the duties of these positions' (Davis and Moore, 1945: 242).

This differentiation was seen as an efficient functional necessity. Indeed, this is still a persuasive point of view and can be seen in treatises on leadership and technological change in the university, such as Bates (2003: 131–4) where, by analogy with the natural sciences, the notion of a 'healthy' institution is introduced. This is one which can be re-engineered so that it is 'fit for purpose', and felicitously 'organized to ensure that their goals and purposes are achieved in the most effective and economical manner'. This can be achieved by ensuring that the people who work there are fully signed up or 'bought in' to the agenda, developing a 'vision', overcoming barriers and deploying 'strategies' for change. In the middle years of the twentieth century, functionalist explanations of the development of social institutions such as schools and universities in the North American continent stressed their rational and functional nature.

In the UK at present too, some commentators such as Prideaux (2001; 2005) see these assumptions about rationality, function and implied fairness at work in UK public policy:

All rely upon a belief that a morally acceptable social generation of 'motivation' – through the provision of 'opportunity' – can sufficiently fuel and satisfy 'aspiration' so as to inspire a renewed social order based on feelings of 'obligation' alongside those of 'responsibility'. (Prideaux, 2001: 86)

Identifying the pathways between knowledge and power was boosted in 1976 by the publication of Samuel Bowles and Herbert Gintis's book *Schooling in Capitalist America*. Bowles and Gintis's analysis was informed by – but was not identical to – a Marxist position, in that the education system was seen to be tailored to the needs of corporate America. They note the stratified and hierarchical nature of occupations pursued by adults, the stratified system of schools and universities that vary in prestige and the stratified nature of societies as a whole and see these three elements as being connected. They argue that these stratifications in the education system and the occupational system are best seen as institutions which preserve the fundamental inequality rooted in the social system. Bowles and Gintis see inequality and the accompanying conflict surrounding this as inevitable in contemporary capitalist societies. In their view the 'ruling class', in order to manage this conflict, has to rule by force, on occasion, and by persuasion. Its policies tend to cause confusion and are intended to manage or contain conflict. Equally, not all the organs of the state work efficiently nor do they necessarily all follow the same agenda. Governments and businesses are sometimes taken unawares by social developments or technological innovations. While there is not believed to be a grand conspiracy, the resulting mosaic of conflicting policies and ideas is often one which is congenial to the established interests. There is a long history in many nations of struggle and resistance, so the relative position of different interest groups or occupational caucuses may be somewhat uneven.

In Bowles and Gintis's work, they challenge the notion that measures of intelligence, in the form of IQ tests, substantially predict educational or occupational success. The relationship, they say, is not strong. School qualifications are not tightly connected to subsequent occupational success either: there is no really strong evidence that people are employed because of their skill. Other factors may be involved but Bowles and Gintis are unwilling to see these as being to do with 'luck' or 'opportunity', but instead they say, these seem to be mediated by variables such as age, sex, ethnic group and 'personality', which is itself connected to social class. As we have argued earlier, the labour market often has more skill than it knows what to do with. Indeed, better-educated employees are not automatically of value to employers (Bowles *et al.*, 2005). In post-compulsory education teaching, the postgraduate staffer is often just as much use as the internationally reputed polymath. Usually more so, because the latter's teaching timetable might be inconveniently interrupted by his or her popularity as a conference speaker. In many other walks of life, even literacy itself is not related to productivity.

Despite these kinds of analyses, the UK's New Labour government has been at the forefront of a movement to promote education as a panacea for a variety of economic and social ills:

> to overcome economic and social disadvantage and to make equality of opportunity a reality, we must strive to eliminate, and never excuse, under-achievement in the most deprived parts of our country. Educational attainment encourages aspiration and self-belief in the next generation, and it is through family learning as well as scholarship through formal schooling that success will come. (DfEE, 1998: 3)

Power and the academy: taking stock and turning to Foucault

In the kinds of complex organizations within which education takes place the actions of power inform our thinking, consciousness and activities. We have in this chapter only undertaken a survey of a few issues and covered a small number of the many perspectives that might have been taken on power. However, to draw our consideration to a close, let us turn again to Michel Foucault, for it is with his work that the sheer pervasiveness of power in higher education is brought to light. This aspect, which has been termed the capillary nature of power, means that it is always present, yet that it is always resisted:

> The omnipresence of power: not because it has the privilege of consolidating everything under its invincible unity, but because it is produced from one moment to the next, at every point, or rather in every relation from one point to another. Power is everywhere; not because it embraces everything, but because it comes from everywhere. (Foucault, 1978b: 93)

> Where there is power, there is resistance, and yet, or rather consequently, this resistance is never in a position of exteriority in relation to power ... These points of resistance are present everywhere in the power network. (Foucault, 1978b: 95)

As we hope to have highlighted in this chapter, power is intimately associated with knowledge, so that:

The exercise of power perpetually creates knowledge and conversely, knowledge constantly induces effects of power ... Knowledge and power are integrated with one another, and there is no point in dreaming of a time when knowledge will cease to depend on power. (Foucault, 1980: 52).

Yet this exposure to power does not always mean that involvement in the education system is unremittingly unpleasant. As Paechter (2006) notes, individuals gain powerful pleasures from participation in communities of practice, even when this is in other ways disempowering. Turning once again to Foucault, he argues that:

Power is exercised only over free subjects, and only insofar as they are free. By this we mean individual or collective subjects who are faced with a field of possibilities in which several ways of behaving, several reactions and diverse comportments may be realised. (Foucault, 1982: 221)

The pleasures or senses of accomplishment which are achievable through the process of participation in education can be seen when we consider the growing popularity of some of the technologies of monitoring the learning that is taking place. This was a dream enshrined in teaching quality assurance in the UK higher education system in the early 1990s, but it is becoming more widespread with the popularity of devices to enhance participation in the knowledge-acquisition process. As Philips (2005) reports, in some US universities these technological aids are seen as essential components of teaching. Carl Weiman, University of Colorado physics professor and 2001 Nobel Laureate, is apparently a devotee of these devices. To monitor his students' learning, he asks the class questions and they record their answers on consoles. This, he says, enables him to pinpoint whether something has sailed over students' heads. Discovering how little they understand sometimes come as a shock, especially when it appears that only 10 per cent of students understand what he has just said to them. Yet this can assist in letting teachers know whether they need to go through material again. Indeed, having used the devices for several years he wouldn't want to be without them – it would be like 'flying blind', he says, 'I'd feel out of touch'. Philips (2005) reports that in the US in 2004, over a million such handsets were sold, with the total predicted to climb to over eight million by 2010.

The management of knowledge and power then is not left to chance. It enhances the sense of pleasure and accomplishment in teaching for some, perhaps many, people. The extent to which students are learning can be determined with ever greater precision. This however, begs the question of what exactly they are learning. In the case of these electronic devices the questions are posed in the form of multiple choice items and the students select one out of four or more alternatives. This of course is a far cry from formulating an argument or other more prosaic scholarly virtues, yet it is visible, immediate and hence peculiarly compelling.

This places the participants in this drama in a strange position. They are on the one hand engaged in a teaching and learning project and yet on the other hand both students and teachers in this enterprise are very exposed. Whether the students have gained knowledge or whether the teacher has been effective in conveying it, are all open to scrutiny. It is almost as if teaching and learning have become 'confessional' processes. This has arisen at a time when other aspects of the self and what the self contains have been subject to revision and redevelopment. The ability to teach, to learn and to accrue the cultural capital of education and to do so in a way that can be inspected and evaluated by others – these are all parts of a particular kind of consciousness that has developed in the early part of the twenty-first century.

Some important aspects of this process have been captured by the highly influential Anthony Giddens, whose work has managed to affect the thinking of the UK's New Labour government. As Prideaux (2001) points out, his philosophy owes a little to the US libertarian strand of politics as well as a heritage within the 'ethical socialist' framework. Giddens famously promoted a variant of politics he called the 'Third Way' that would go 'Beyond Left and Right' (Giddens, 1994) and would place an emphasis on schemes 'of positive welfare, oriented to manufactured rather than external risk [and which] would be directed to fostering the *autotelic self* ' (Giddens, 1994: 192). This autotelic self would be 'a person able to translate potential threats into rewarding challenges, someone ... able to turn entropy into a consistent flow of experience ... as [part of] the active challenge which generates self-actualization' (*ibid.*).

Challenges are transformed into opportunities by this autotelic self. Now we might say that, for example, losing your job at the age of 50 doubles your chances of heart attack and stroke over the next ten years (Gallo *et al.*, 2006). Instead, under the regime described by Giddens, this is an opportunity, perhaps for a re-entry to education, a chance to pursue cultural and artistic interests and to spend more time with one's family. Even the prospect of being unable to continue paying for one's house might be construed as a positive, challenging experience. For academic staff, the modern era may be characterized by dilemmas such as whether one will have a job teaching the same topics in the future as one does now or whether the contractual arrangements undergirding one's employment will be robust enough to survive the closure of one's department or indeed one's institution. The autotelic self's Pollyanna vision of the world seems curiously myopic where the operations of power are concerned.

Power, of course, may be even more difficult to pin down than we have so far indicated. Sometimes, significant social transformations take place without it being apparent how the operation is executed. Rather than being reliant exclusively upon the will of an interest group, we are sometimes swept up in social currents that, while they may benefit certain economic and government interests, seem outside the deliberate control of many stakeholders. Some of these currents may have important implications for how education will play a part in society in the future.

For example, many commentators agree that we now live in a 'society of consumers' in which social membership is increasingly grounded in the 'aesthetics of consumption' (Bauman, 1998: 23–5). This is beneficial to the manufacturers of consumer goods, and to governments seeking a docile populace and pleasing levels of 'economic growth' in the absence of manufacturing. Yet it is hard to pin down to the activity of a particular group. As Hayward characterizes the present situation in the UK:

> what is unique about the last few decades of the twentieth century is the way that the creation and expression of identity via the display and celebration of consumer goods have triumphed over and above other more traditional modes of self-expression. (Hayward, 2004: 144)

Social and status differences are generated and maintained not so much via the academic prestige attached to qualifications, as via 'lifestyle', which in turn is organized through patterns of consumption. Indeed, lifestyle and health and lifestyle management courses are beginning to appear in universities. Individuals can formulate and understand themselves, and most crucially, are formulated and understood by others, through their publicly visible consumption and lifestyle choices (Hayward and Yar, 2006).

> In a culture of consumption, the collective focus is on self-definition through the purchase of goods. Status differentials are based less on one's role in the productive sphere than on one's ability to consume. Social relations are mediated through objects ... As group affiliation at work is replaced by individual achievement, and the role of the family as a source of ascribed status is lessened, individuals attempt to differentiate themselves through their 'lifestyles', a term which largely connotes consumption patterns. (Anderson and Wadkin, 1992: 149–50)

This relationship between consumer goods, of which qualifications and credentials are a part, and the construction of self in late modernity, is of great importance. The ethos of consumerism now runs so deeply through selves and identities within contemporary societies that many people's dual self-identity and self-realization may nowadays be accomplished largely through material means. Thus, identity, as Christopher Lasch (1979) suggested, comprises a 'consumption-oriented narcissism'. Over a quarter of a century after Lasch's generative work, his message is even more pertinent. As Hayward and Yar put it:

> In the school playground, the pub or restaurant, the nightclub and on the street corner, products and material possessions are now the primary indices of identity for virtually all strata of society, establishing status but, more importantly, imbuing individuals with a (narcissistic) sense of who they are. (Hayward and Yar, 2006: 18)

This zeitgeist of narcissistic consumption has gone hand in hand with a fascination with celebrity, where the imbrication of consumption with identity is most highly developed. The UK's Learning and Skills Council (LSC) (2006) announced that according to its research, a significant proportion of fame hungry teenagers were planning to ditch education and 'live in dreamland'. According to its survey, more than one in 10 (11 per cent) young people would drop out of education or training to be on TV. Over one in six (16 per cent) believed that they would actually become famous. By comparison, counsels the LSC gravely, the odds of being picked for a Big Brother style reality TV show and being successful afterwards are around one in 30 million, and thus considerably worse even than those of wining the UK's National Lottery Jackpot. Despite these apparently unfavourable odds against them, 9 per cent of young people questioned said that they thought fame was a great way to earn money without skills or qualifications. An additional 11 per cent were 'waiting to be discovered'.

In this context then, post-compulsory education itself takes on the aspect of a form of consumption such that it becomes a kind of trophy to enhance one's position among others, yet at the same time the hard work involved in obtaining qualifications looks dispiriting compared to the instant enhancements promised by celebrity, or the rapid gains in social status to be obtained by associating oneself with fashionable brands. Education takes its place among the shared consumption practices which furnish a basis upon which class and hierarchical boundaries are drawn between 'us' and 'them', defining those who are included and those who are excluded from group social membership (Southerton, 2002).

While social, political and economic changes have been responsible for material impoverishment and emiseration, crime and social disorder (Currie, 1997; Taylor, 2000), education may, as we have suggested here, represent a further means by which power finds its way into the lives of citizens. The consuming, identity forming autotelic selves of advanced liberalism might be adding qualifications and knowledge to their portfolio of transferable skills. In doing so however, they are further subjecting themselves to the very powers which detraditionalized them and substituted patterns of consumption for social bonds. Thinking about education and power then, has never been more urgent.

References

Anderson, L. and Wadkins, M. (1992), 'The new breed in Japan: consumer culture', *Canadian Journal of Administrative Studies*, 9(2), 146–53.

Arreman, I. E. (2005), 'Research as power and knowledge: struggles over research in teacher education', *Journal of Education for Teaching*, 31(3), 215–35.

Baker, C., Johnson, M. T. and Crimson, M. L. (2003), 'Quantitative analysis of sponsorship bias in economic studies of antidepressants', *British Journal of Psychiatry*, 183(6), 498–506.

Baker, S. (2005), *'Like A Fish In Water': Aspects Of The Contemporary United Kingdom Higher Education System As Intended And As Constructed*. PhD Thesis, University of Wales, Bangor.

Bamber, J. and Tett, L. (2001), 'Ensuring integrative learning experiences for non-traditional students in higher education', *Widening Participation and Lifelong Learning*, 3(1), 8–16.

Bates, T. (2003), *Managing Technological Change: Strategies for Academic Leaders*. San Francisco: Jossey Bass.

Baty, P. (2006), 'Fluency can be all yours ... for a small fee', *The Times Higher Education Supplement*, April 7 2006. www.thes.co.uk/search/story.aspx?story_id=2029111. Accessed 29/08/06.

Bauman, Z. (1998), *Work, Consumerism and the New Poor*. Buckingham: Open University Press.

Bourdieu, P. (1982), *Leçon sur la Leçon*. Paris: Editions Minuit.

Bourdieu, P. (1988), *Homo Academicus* (trans. P. Collier). Stanford, CA: Stanford University Press.

Bourdieu, P. (1991), *Language and Symbolic Power* (ed.) J. Thompson (trans. G. Raymond and M. Adamson). Cambridge, MA: Harvard University Press.

Bourdieu, P. (1992), 'The purpose of reflexive sociology', in P. Bourdieu and P. Wacquant (eds), *An Invitation to Reflexive Sociology*. Cambridge: Polity, pp. 61–215.

Bourdieu, P. (1994), *Raisons Pratiques. Sur la Theorie de L'action*. Paris: Seuil.

Bowles, S. and Gintis, H. (1976), *Schooling in Capitalist America: Educational Reform and the Contradictions of Economic Life*. New York: Basic Books.

Bowles, S., Gintis, H. and Groves, M. O. (2005), *Unequal Chances: Family Background and Economic Success*. Princeton, NJ: Princeton University Press.

Brockes, E. (2003), 'Taking the Mick', *The Guardian*, January 15 2003.

Bush, V. (1945), *Science – The Endless Frontier: A Report to the President on a Program for Post-War Scientific Research*, July 1945. Washington, DC: National Science Foundation.

Clarke, R. and Lancaster, T. (2006), *Eliminating the Successor to Plagiarism? Identifying the Usage of Contract Cheating Sites*. JISC Plagiarism Advisory Service's 2nd International Plagiarism Conference, Newcastle Upon Tyne, UK.

Connell, R., Ashenden, D., Kessler, S. and Dowsett, G. (1982), *Making the Difference: Schools, Families and Social Division*. London: George Allen and Unwin.

Currie, E. (1997), 'Market, crime and community: toward a mid-range theory of post-industrial violence', *Theoretical Criminology*, 1(2), 147–72.

Davis, K. and Moore, W. E. (1945), 'Some principles of stratification', *American Sociological Review*, 10(2), 242–9.

DfEE (1998), *The Learning Age: A Renaissance for a New Britain*. London: Department for Education and Employment.

Dowding, K. (2006), 'Three-dimensional power: a discussion of Steven Lukes' *Power: A Radical View*', *Political Studies Review*, 4, 136–45.

Feyerabend, P. (1987), *Farewell to Reason*. London: Verso.

Foucault, M. (1978a), *Discipline and Punish: The Birth of the Prison* (trans. A. Sheridan). New York: Pantheon.

Foucault, M. (1978b), *The History of Sexuality, Volume One*. London: Penguin.

Foucault, M. (1980), *Power/knowledge: Selected Interviews and Other Writings 1972–1977*. Hemel Hempstead, Herts: Harvester Press.

Foucault, M. (1982), 'The subject and power', in H. Dreyfus and P. Rabinow (eds), *Michel Foucault: Beyond Structuralism and Hermeneutics*. Brighton: Harvester Press, pp. 208–26.

Freire, P. (1974), *Pedagogy of the Oppressed*. Harmondsworth: Penguin.

Gallo, W. T., Teng, H. M., Falba, T. A., Kasl, S. V., Krumholz, H. V. and Bradley, E. H. (2006), 'The impact of late-career job loss on myocardial infarction and stroke: a 10-year follow-up using the Health and Retirement Survey', *Occupational and Environmental Medicine*, June 2006; doi:10.1136/oem.2006.026823.

Garcia, J. M. R. (2001), 'Scientia potestas est – Knowledge is power: Francis Bacon to Michel Foucault', *Neohelicon*, 28(1), 109–22.

Gibbons, S. and Machin, S. (2006), 'Paying for primary schools: admission constraints, school popularity or congestion?', *The Economic Journal*, 116(510), C77–C92.

Giddens, A. (1994), *Beyond Left and Right*. Cambridge: Polity Press.

Gimson, A. (2005), 'Boris and Stanley – the double act that is laughing all the way to Westminster', *The Daily Telegraph*, April 23 2005.

Goffman, E. (1961), *Asylums*. New York: Doubleday.

Gramsci, A. (1971), *Selections From the Prison Notebooks* (trans. G. Nowell Smith). London: Lawrence and Wishart.

Hayward, K. (2004), *City Limits: Crime, Consumer Culture and the Urban Experience*. London: Glass House Press.

Hayward, K. and Yar, M. (2006), 'The "chav" phenomenon: consumption, media and the construction of a new underclass', *Crime, Media, Culture*, 2(1), 9–28.

Healy, D. and Thase, M. E. (2003), 'Is academic psychiatry for sale?', *British Journal of Psychiatry*, 182(5), 388–90.

Lasch, C. (1979), *The Culture of Narcissism: American Life in the Age of Diminishing Expectations*. New York: W.W. Norton and Co.

Learning and Skills Council (2006), *Kids Seeking Reality TV Fame Instead of Exam Passes*. Learning and Skills Council. www.lsc.gov.uk/norfolk/Corporate/News/realityfame. htm. Accessed 20/10/06.

Liston, D. P. (1988), *Capitalist Schools*. New York and London: Routledge.

Lovibond, S. (1994), 'The end of morality?', in K. Lennon and M. Whitford (eds), *Knowing the Difference: Feminist Perspectives in Epistemology*. London: Routledge, pp. 123–52.

Lukes, S. (1974), *Power: A Radical View*. Basingstoke: Macmillan.

Lukes, S. (2005), *Power: A Radical View* (Second edn). Basingstoke: Palgrave Macmillan.

Marks, A. (1999), 'Really useful knowledge: the new vocationalism in higher education and its consequences for mature students', *British Journal of Educational Studies*, 47(2), 157–69.

McDonald, K. (1999), *Struggles for Subjectivity: Identity, Action and Youth Experience*. Cambridge: Cambridge University Press.

McLaren, P. (1989), *Life in Schools: An Introduction to Critical Pedagogy in the Foundations of Education*. New York: Longman.

Midgely, C. and Stimson, E. (2006), 'Useless? To a degree', *The Times*, March 16 2006.

Moncrieff, J. (2003), 'Clozapine v. conventional antipsychotic drugs for treatment resistant schizophrenia, a re-examination', *British Journal of Psychiatry*, 183, 161–6.

Mowatt, G., Shirran, L. and Grimshaw, J. M. (2002), 'Prevalence of honorary and ghost authorship in Cochrane reviews', *Journal of the American Medical Association*, 287(21), 2769–71.

Nietzsche, F. (1886/1973), *Beyond Good and Evil* (trans. R. J. Hollingdale). Harmondsworth: Penguin.

Nietzsche, F. (1888/1968), *Twilight of the Idols/The Anti-Christ* (trans. R. J. Hollingdale). Harmondsworth: Penguin.

Olgiati, V. (2006), 'Shifting heuristics in the sociological approach to professional trustworthiness', *Current Sociology*, 54(4), 533–47.

Paechter, C. (2006), 'Power, knowledge and embodiment in communities of sex/gender practice', *Women's Studies International Forum*, 29(1), 13–26.

Philips, S. (2005), 'Lectures that really do click', *The Times Higher Education Supplement*, October 21 2005.

Prideaux, S. (2001), 'New Labour, old functionalism: the underlying contradictions of welfare reform in the US and the UK', *Social Policy and Administration*, 35(1), 85–115.

Prideaux, S. (2005), 'John Macmurray and the "forgotten" lessons on capitalism and community', *Policy and Politics*, 76(4), 540–9.

Pring, R. A. (1995), *Closing The Gap: Liberal Education and Vocational Preparation*, London: Hodder and Stoughton.

Reay, D., David, M. and Ball, S. (2001), 'Making a difference?: institutional habituses and higher education choice', *Sociological Research Online*, 5(4). www.socresonline.org.uk/5/4/reay.html. Accessed 15.10.02.

Scott, J. C. (1990), *Domination and the Arts of Resistance: Hidden Transcripts*. New Haven, CN: Yale University Press.

Shooter, M. (2005), 'Dancing with the devil? A personal view of psychiatry's relationships with the pharmaceutical industry', *Psychiatric Bulletin*, 29, 81–3.

Smith, R. (2005), 'Medical journals are an extension of the marketing arm of pharmaceutical companies', *Public Library of Science: Medicine*, 2(5), e138.

Southerton, D. (2002), 'Boundaries of "us" and "them": class, mobility and identification in a new town', *Sociology*, 36(1), 171–93.

Taylor, I. (2000), *Crime in Context: A Critical Criminology of Market Societies*. Cambridge: Polity.

Taylor, M. and Butt, R. (2006), 'Q: How do you make £1.6m a year and drive a Ferrari? A: Sell essays for £400', *The Guardian*, July 29 2006.

Thompson, J. (1995), *The Media and Modernity: A Social Theory of the Media*. Cambridge: Polity Press.

Tierney, W. G. (1999), 'Models of minority college-going and retention: cultural integrity versus cultural suicide', *Journal of Negro Education*, 68(1), 80–91.

University of Central England (2006), *Cyber Cheats Buying Coursework Online*. www.uce.ac.uk/web2/releases06/4097.html. Accessed 29/08/06.

Young, I. M. (1987), 'Impartiality and the civil public: some implications of feminist critiques of moral and political theory', in S. Benhabib and D. Cornell (eds), *Feminism as Critique*. Cambridge: Polity Press, pp. 57–73.

Chapter 4

Education Systems and their Changing Roles: The University and Human Wellbeing

Introduction: wellbeing and widening participation

As universities in developed nations change to accommodate larger proportions of their host societies' populations, they are having to address a new range of problems and are taking on subtly different societal roles. We are witnessing a phenomenon which has been called the 'rectangularization of the progression curve' such that an increasing proportion of people are qualified to progress onto the next stage in education and more and more of them do so (Gorard, 2005). As more students are expected to progress from school to higher education, it is inevitable that different roles will need to be undertaken by universities. Moreover, as the roles of other institutions in contemporary society change this will have implications for the experiences we have in the higher education system. Changes in health care, family structure, the arts, industry and government service itself will afford new experiences, opportunities and problems in education.

University education has long been associated with improving human wellbeing. Baker (2005) found that people who passed through university in the 1960s and 1970s perceived university to have contributed to their wellbeing in terms of providing self-fulfilment through a liberal education. For this generation, such self-fulfilment was achieved by academic work or student activities and was only available to a small proportion of the population, those people usually – but not exclusively – coming from the more privileged groups in society. People who had passed through university as students during the 1980s and 1990s also looked back on it as a way of improving wellbeing, but usually had a much more instrumental perspective which involved using education to gain desirable employment and an improved 'lifestyle' (Baker, 2005). University is presented to the public by policymakers as a way of improving one's employment prospects, for example by the claim that it is a 'good time to be a graduate', by UK Higher

Education Minister Kim Howells (Taylor, 2004). At present though, the sort of wellbeing that universities are supposed to confer is rather different than was imagined in previous generations. It is growing apparent that, in many individual cases, higher education is now about providing social care and support for groups of people that are often no longer adequately assisted by the UK's welfare state. In another way, it is about universities either directly or indirectly playing a major role in bringing about social justice and undertaking social care.

In May 2004, the UK press reported a speech by Professor Anthony Smith, President of Magdalen College, Oxford, warning that the UK's higher education system must not become 'a branch of social welfare' (Smithers, 2004). The fact that Smith was speaking in the future tense – 'become' – masked the extent to which the UK's post-compulsory education system had already begun to undertake welfare work. Smith's comment was made in the context of a growing debate as to whether universities and colleges should take applicants' social backgrounds into consideration when offering places. There has yet to be a similar level of debate about the work that universities and colleges are being encouraged to undertake in order to support vulnerable students while they are undertaking their studies; nor has there been very much discussion of the way that this kind of work is increasingly seen by policymakers as a means of addressing the social inclusion agenda which has pervaded the social policy landscape of the early twenty-first century.

This chapter will explore how universities and colleges are now intimately bound up with social inclusion and indeed social care, by looking at some of the efforts being made to address students' problems, and help students in difficulty who are entering post-compulsory education for the first time. There are growing efforts to provide information to students and staff about such cohorts and their needs (Konur, 2002; Taylor, 2005). Yet we know far less of the experiences of staff and students as the inclusion of students with vulnerabilities, difficulties and disabilities unfolds. In the UK there is a good deal of interest from the point of view of the legislative framework, including the UK Disability Discrimination Act (DDA) 1995 and the Special Educational Needs and Disability Act (SENDA) 2001, but what is missing from much of the discussion is a sense of how the legislation and the institutions themselves have an impact on the lived experience of students and staff.

The recent policy alignment between learning and wellbeing was most explicitly stated in the Green Paper, 'The Learning Age', a key document in setting out New Labour's ideas for the role it sees education playing in Britain in the twenty-first century:

For individuals, learning will help everyone to acquire the new skills and qualifications needed for employment and advancement. Learning will increase our earning power. In addition, it will help older people to stay healthy and active, strengthen families and the wider community, and encourage independence. Opportunities to learn will lead us to greater appreciation of art, music, poetry and literature, and develop our potential as rounded human beings. (DfEE, 1998: 3)

In addition, education was seen as the remedy for a variety of other social and individual ills: 'learning will be the key to a strong economy and an inclusive society. It will offer a way out of dependency and low expectation towards self-reliance and self-confidence' (DfEE, 1998: 3).

This signalled new territories with which education was charged with colonising, and new tasks for educators and the institutions within which they work. Policies such as this play an important role in helping to construct the kinds of people who inhabit the landscape of what Rose (1999) has called 'advanced liberalism'. As we have suggested previously, a complex tapestry of forces involving the social sciences, medicine, criminology, educational studies and New Labour policymakers, have combined to create a situation where new forms of sociality and personhood can emerge. In line with scholars such as Rose, we suggest that the matrix of policies, initiatives, legal frameworks, research and information, calls into being new phenomena which can become socially effective agents in their own right.

Hence as we have argued, the changing climates in higher education have created novel forms of consciousness, obligation and responsibility for universities, their staff and students. The business of addressing human vulnerability and disability has shifted from what Foucault (1975) called 'the clinic' into other sites and moral surfaces. These have included prisons (Davies, 2004a) and, most importantly for our present purpose, the education system. These discourses of obligation, constructions of dysfunction and imperatives of inclusion have played a very significant role in making up our educational world in the twenty-first century, and the persons, phenomena and entities that inhabit it.

We live in a culture where the private conduct and distress of the individual is a matter for political intervention. Not merely the sicknesses of human beings, but also their personalities, intellectual capacities, passions, their 'employability' and the forces that mobilize them – their 'identities' themselves – now appear at least potentially to be explicable in terms germane to the policymaker and educationalist, and increasingly in terms of their potential to benefit from inclusion in the education system. The learning age is relentlessly inclusive, and, says Ecclestone (2004), increasingly therapeutic as well as educational.

There is a curious tension here. Education is charged with the role of keeping people healthy and strengthening families, as well as building independence and confidence and combating exclusion. Yet there are a growing number of reports to the contrary. The contemporary university graduate is debt ridden and is often unable to secure employment of a kind which allows any prospect of independence and self-reliance. Educators in the 1960s and 1970s, in the spirit of radical pedagogy and a heady infusion of Paulo Freire, might have seen emotions as a key to making sense of the social world in political terms, such that inequality and oppression might be challenged. Yet, in the present, any ambitions of student and teacher towards social reform must be domesticated. Instead, education takes on a therapeutic cast, such that the more anodyne processes of developing 'self-esteem' and 'emotional intelligence' have come to supervene (Ecclestone *et al.*, 2005; Ecclestone and Hayes, 2007). The result is that young people and adults are becoming anxious, cautious, passive and debt-ridden individuals rather than aspiring, optimistic and resilient learners.

The government's commitment to social justice is of course reflected among the personal ideals of many academics. Some academics, often working in the field of research on higher education or education policy themselves such as Diane Reay (1995) or Marion Bowl (2000: 33) explicity state their commitment to social justice. It should be noted that many of these scholars have been highly critical of government policies for widening access, believing them to be of limited effectiveness (Thomas, 2001).

By the time Professor Smith had made his comments in May 2004, the UK's post-compulsory education system had already become intimately involved in the practice of social welfare, catering to some of the most economically fragile and psychosocially vulnerable citizens in the UK. It had become an under-resourced branch of the social welfare system, expected to cater for some of the most deprived groups in society whose welfare has been systematically neglected by generations of policymakers.

To explore the way in which universities are now involved in the maintenance of human wellbeing in a way in which they have not been previously, we will explore the position of students with mental health or neurological problems in universities. Until the present day, these students were not usually found in universities. Of course, students have always developed mental health problems, but previously these students often withdrew from university. Students with problems such as ADHD (attention deficit hyperactivity disorder) or those on the autistic spectrum were seldom able to attend universities. The higher education system is now beginning to admit these students.

Students and their wellbeing: political *sturm und drang*?

There are a number of bodies, reports and articles which are raising concerns about the psychological wellbeing of students in higher education (Rana *et al.*, 1999; Roberts *et al.*, 1999; Stewart-Brown *et al.*, 2000; Stanley and Manthorpe, 2001; Royal College of Psychiatrists, 2003; Andrews and Wilding, 2004). While adolescence and early adulthood has been characterized as a period of *sturm und drang* for over a century, the present set of concerns goes back a decade, and can perhaps be dated from warnings initially raised about mental health problems in UK university students by Phippen (1995), who found that 85 (64 per cent) of the 152 counselling services surveyed reported an increase in the proportion of 'seriously disturbed' students seen. This report was instrumental in shifting attention and resources to the needs of this group. At the same time another key element in the present-day picture appeared, in the form of the Disability Discrimination Act 1995. This defined disability as a physical or mental impairment and required universities to ensure that their admission procedures avoid discrimination, but also to develop reasonable provision for disabled people. This is allied to a growing raft of evidence that the mental health of young people in the UK as a whole is getting progressively worse (Collishaw *et al.*, 2004). Thus, people entering the education system are likely to be more volatile and vulnerable than they were before.

New Labour policy on higher education and social inclusion currently suggests that people with mental health problems may benefit from education and should be encouraged to participate in this to combat social exclusion, because education can 'build self confidence and social networks' (Social Exclusion Unit, 2004: 28). Yet this contrasts with evidence of exactly the opposite taking place in the post-compulsory education sector. The substantial and increasing presence of mental health problems has been documented by scholars and professional bodies (Royal College of Psychiatrists, 2003). Whether this is because more students are developing mental health problems during post-compulsory education, or whether more students with pre-existing mental health problems are staying in the education system, is unclear. The phenomenon is reflected in many institutions' policies and services. Whereas universities have for some time typically provided counselling services for students, many now employ other mental health professionals and have structures in place to support students with mental health difficulties such as sheltered accommodation and make allowances where deadlines and examinations are concerned. Many have detailed policies relating to students with mental health problems (for example De Montfort University, 2004; University of Nottingham, 2004; University of Wales, Bangor, 2004). Some institutions have dedicated mental health support workers as part of the university team, such as Nottingham Trent University. Government policy encourages the belief that the 'socially excluded' and 'mentally ill' could and should benefit from education.

Government policy: New Labour, new responsibilities

The field of policy and practice in mental health care has helped to legitimate some profound changes in government approaches to welfare since the early 1990s. What is thinkable and unthinkable, valuable or worthless, is the product of the 'field' of policy in Bourdieu's sense. This affects in turn the structures within which ideas and policies arise and the principles of thinking which govern and legitimate their operations. This legitimation establishes an orthodoxy or doxa (Bourdieu, 1977: 164–71) where it is entirely reasonable to suppose that education has benefits for the individual and for the nation, that education enhances mental health and indeed, that education may circumvent the need for mental health care at all. In this way policymakers have presided over shifts in the topography of the field and 'the determinations they impose upon the occupants, agents or institutions' (Bourdieu, 1992: 72–3).

Many more people have been encouraged by the UK's New Labour administration to engage in post-compulsory education. The policy of widening participation has resulted in diverse social and cultural groups entering universities who have not traditionally done so (DfEE, 2000). Widening participation and the advent of mass higher education has had a profound effect on the higher education system, and the mental health care system has also undergone a revolution over the same relatively short period of time. Although many would argue that the provision of mental health services is far from adequate (Commission for Health Improvement, 2003), policymakers now seem to be seeing mental health care very differently. Policies of moving people with mental health problems out of institutions and into 'the community' have existed for many years, yet even as late as 1991 the Department of Health did not consider that education was appropriate for people needing 'care' (Austin, 1999: 225). By 1997 however, the climate had changed considerably and the opening shots in the New Labour 'joined up' agenda for health and social care had begun to fuse also with the expectations of the education system: 'Specialist mental health services ... need to work closely with the agencies responsible for housing, income support, education, employment, training and leisure ...' (Department of Health, quoted in Wertheimer, 1997: 151).

The field thus underwent a shift, such that a remit which had once been confined to health care providers and had not included educational institutions in 1991, had by 1997 expanded so that education was explicitly made a part of the matrix of care available to people with mental health problems.

This, like any good Bourdieusian field, is cross-referenced and cross-alluded, so the various components in the matrix sustain one another. The spirit of the Blair government's Education White Paper dovetails neatly with New Labour documents concerning mental health policy. The National Service Framework for Mental Health (DoH, 1999) talks of reducing the discrimination and social exclusion that is perceived to be associated with mental health problems. The Department of Health campaign 'Mind Out for Mental Health' ran between the 4 January 2002 and the end of July 2003 and was aimed at tackling the stigma and discrimination faced by people suffering from mental health problems and promoting their social inclusion. Campaign material contained a number of references to the necessity of enabling people with mental health problems to access education.

The document 'Mental Health and Social Exclusion' (Social Exclusion Unit, 2004), also deals with education for people suffering from mental health problems, both in terms of FE and HE. It is stated that 'participation in learning can have a positive effect on mental health' (2004: 80), detailing 'acquiring new skills, feeling more empowered and having a greater sense of purpose, being viewed more positively by others, establishing new friendships, access to better jobs, better housing and easier access to leisure pursuits' (2004: 80). It maintains that 'a lack of qualifications can cause and reinforce social exclusion for people with mental health problems' (2004: 80), that we need to 'promote access to adult learning, further and higher education' (2004: 105) and that educational institutions need to raise awareness, and to develop good practice and effective support for students. The logic then is irrefutable. To hesitate on this helter-skelter is to mark oneself as a reactionary, an elitist or the harbinger of the very kind of stigma or exclusion these policies seek to obviate.

The Social Exclusion Unit further counsels that:

Further and higher education institutions will review and make appropriate adjustments to their systems for raising awareness among all staff about issues for students with mental health problems, to ensure that no student is disadvantaged in their access to learning and services. (Social Exclusion Unit, 2004: 106)

The Universities UK (2000) guidelines on student mental health makes recommendations on developing policies and procedures across individual institutions and recommends raising awareness of relevant legal and 'duty of care' issues, as well as facilitating access to support and guidance services, the provision of training and development opportunities, and the greater use of liaison between internal and external agencies. Staff in universities are increasingly being made responsible for ensuring that the changes are implemented, not only in terms of institutional frameworks, but also on themselves, as they are reconfigured into hyper-aware inter- and intra-institutional communicators, securing the safety and wellbeing of students. The follow-up document about suicide prevention (Universities UK, 2002) is even more explicit about the duty of care to universities, and their responsibility to ensure that they are health-promoting institutions rather than ones which erode the coping resources of students, and the desirability of welfare and counselling services working with statutory mental health services is promoted (2002: 18). Tutors and academic staff monitoring student attendance and studying the appearance and demeanour of students to detect any changes is recommended as good practice (2002: 17).

Thus, universities and their staff are seen as key players in fighting the social exclusion that people with mental health problems face, and in keeping them on their courses and indeed in keeping them alive. New forms of scrutiny are unfolded, where universities are checked against their statutory and moral responsibilities and staff encouraged towards a role which involves scrutiny not only of students' academic capabilities, but also what they think, say, do and even look like.

University staff are called upon to monitor and transform the personal and subjective capacities of the students. They are, in the tradition of New Labour political discourse identified by Fairclough (2000), individualized and made responsible. What is virtually absent is any consideration of structural, economic or political forces that might conspire to make people vulnerable or distressed, or reduce their material powers or educational potential. These are reduced to the binary of social inclusion versus exclusion, and oppression is reduced to its anodyne counterpart, 'stigma'. To anyone accustomed to looking at societies in terms of their being structured by means of economics, politics, power and social stratification, this might appear to be an extraordinary omission. To such a critic it might appear that universities and their staff will have an uphill struggle – not necessarily because 'mental illness' itself in intractable, but because of the sheer weight of forces ranged against those unfortunate enough to have acquired such a label. The point of mentioning this is not to suggest any simple superiority of one view over another, but to highlight how the picture of policy is artfully constructed to align itself 'naturally' with what we had always hoped to believe about 'human nature'. In a Bourdieusian sense, it has been legitimated (Bourdieu, 1977).

Post-compulsory education and students with mental health problems

Our interest in this field was initially alerted by a conversation that one of us (SB) had in 2004 with an acquaintance who had longstanding mental health problems. This client told SB that she was thinking of going to the university and could SB answer some questions. SB expected to be asked questions about courses or 'would I be clever enough' as these were the most usual. Instead, our acquaintance had not yet considered the kinds of courses available and what they entailed, but was most crucially concerned about whether it was true that there were counsellors at the university. On hearing that there were, she disclosed that the main reason for her interest in going to university was that her social worker had told her that she needed counselling and would never get a counsellor on the NHS in this area, but that if she went to the university she would be able to get a counsellor. With the passage of two years between this conversation and the time of writing in 2006, the pattern seems to have intensified. We are hearing even more accounts from people who are clients of the UK's mental health services and who are claiming welfare benefits. The consistent theme of these narratives is that people feel coerced into applying for further and higher education courses. For example, one woman told us that some people had been informed that they would be denied mental health care if they did not agree to return to work or education.

The degree to which educational institutions are now undertaking welfare work was further illustrated by an extraordinary situation which became known to us in 2005. An article appeared in a local paper regarding the plight of a young man with serious mental health problems and his mother. She was a mature student undertaking an access course at a higher education institution. The article explained that no respite care for the seriously ill man was available and so he was sleeping in his mother's car in the college car park during the day. The mother had become sufficiently angry with the health and social services that she'd given the story to the press. She subsequently told us that the lecturers at the college had been 'absolutely fantastic', a good deal more helpful in addressing her and her son's problems than the 'useless' mental health services. She mentioned that the college was trying to find a suitable course and support for her son as well. Education then, is a source of succour to sufferers and their carers too.

Although the Royal College of Psychiatrists (2003) found that 'major' psychiatric disorders are under-represented in the student population, students were found to have increased symptoms of mental ill health compared with age-matched controls. The report maintained that a number of factors combine in creating an environment in which students with pre-existing mental health problems may be at greater risk of illness, and even those who do not have psychiatric problems on entry to higher education may become more vulnerable to them. It is noted that 'Students from less privileged backgrounds are more likely to suffer mental ill health' (Royal College of Psychiatrists, 2003: 24) and that it is 'likely that the increased intake of students from less privileged and more disrupted families and communities . . . will be associated with an increase in the prevalence of mental disorder' (2003: 25). Again, there is inconsistency as to whether higher education helps or hinders people with mental health problems. The Report states that 'in certain cases, entry to higher education is an important part of a patient's recovery from psychiatric illness' (2003: 11) and that 'positive aspects of student experience are powerful factors in promoting the self-esteem, resilience and sound mental health that protects against psychiatric disorder' (2003: 12). Yet the Report also talks of the 'well-known stresses of university life' (2003: 24), such as pressure for academic achievement, time management, financial constraints, social relationships, loneliness and homesickness, and notes that these increase the likelihood of breakdown in students with pre-existing mental health problems.

Mounting evidence is beginning to suggest a far greater degree of hardship and personal distress among students than was previously suspected. It is difficult to reconcile this with the picture of personal advancement, enhanced 'self-esteem' and social inclusion accomplished through education painted in 'The Learning Age' (DfEE, 1998). There is evidence that the stress of university life is increasing. Garner (2004) reported in *The Independent* that research carried out at the University of London had found high levels of stress among students, leading to anxiety and depression, which was attributed substantially to students' financial difficulties.

As the difficulties of student life increase, the legislative framework supporting the access of students with pre-existing mental health problems to post-compulsory education has been interpreted and implemented with growing zeal. In the late 1990s then, the full implications of disability discrimination legislation were increasingly appreciated. Wright (1998: 5) referred to 'the changes in the legal, funding and educational frameworks [which] create a new agenda for institutions of changed responsibilities and expectations' in the context of the 1995 Disability Discrimination Act. Rana *et al.* (1999: 4) note that the Disability Discrimination Act 'is already perceived as increasing the numbers of disabled students entering higher education, including students with mental health problems, and this augurs major changes for many universities'.

Neville Harris (2004a), Professor of Law at Manchester University, argued in *The Times* that universities owe students with mental health problems a legal duty of care in terms of pastoral care and welfare, claiming that under-performance of pastoral duties by a university could give rise to contractual liability and that students threatened with exclusion from their course when their needs prove too difficult for the university to manage, may have an enforceable right. This is believed by Harris (2004b) to be part of broader concerns of citizenship and inclusion. Despite the possibly substantial ramifications of the use of litigation by students, the full implications of the Disability Discrimination Act and European Human Rights legislation have yet to be completely brought to bear on the universities.

Thus, growing awareness of the implications of disability legislation is propelling a change in the climate in the post-compulsory education system. The implications of making 'reasonable adjustments' for students with physical disabilities have been appreciated for some time. In recent years however, the ambit of the legislation has been understood to reach out to cover learning difficulties such as dyslexia and dyscalculia, and by extension emotional and behavioural difficulties too. Inasmuch as these problems can be thought of as disabilities, then the obligation to consider reasonable adjustments in the running of institutions and the delivery of teaching to accommodate students' needs is mandated. This then contributes to the welfare promoting functions of educational institutions, and this in turn has implications for how their members feel, think and act to address the changes in their remit.

Post-compulsory education as part of the welfare system?

The strands in further and higher education policy that might be called 'welfarist' or 'therapeutic' have been incorporated into policy and practice at a variety of levels. In the late 1990s and early twenty-first century the Higher Education Funding Council for England (HEFCE) funded a number of projects at different institutions to develop and promote what was seen to be good practice in dealing with mental health problems. This included initiatives at Nottingham Trent, Leicester, Lancaster, Teeside and Hull. The initiatives involved a number of activities including surveys and focus group exercises to determine the principal threats to wellbeing, the development and provision of information in leaflet, booklet and/or electronic form, as well as training programmes. A great many schemes sought to 'raise awareness' either in terms of the identification of problems on the part of students, or of universities' legal obligations.

In terms of our focus on mental health issues, there are signs that universities are not simply admitting increasing numbers of students with mental health problems, but are responding to their needs with commitments of time and resources. Universities have for many years provided health care facilities for their students and in recent years many have expanded such facilities to include counselling services. However, now a number of universities have extended their provision to cater specifically for students with mental health problems. Nottingham Trent University, Loughborough University, South Nottingham College and Loughborough College have joined together to create a particularly well-developed system of support for such students, concerned with the development of initiatives to ease the transition between different stages in their educational careers. For example, workers at Nottingham Trent University support students with mental health difficulties through their studies. Other institutions also provide support in conjunction with the statutory services. Some universities are now employing professionals such as community mental health nurses. Similar trends can be seen in further education colleges, so as to enable students supported in this way to move on to university.

However, although many universities are making valiant efforts to respond to the needs of students with mental health problems and there are some examples of meticulous and dedicated practice, an increasingly austere resource base is blighting the potential rehabilitative and therapeutic effects. Although individual institutions may want to support students with mental health problems, finances are now very strained indeed and academic staff, who often bear the day to day workload of supporting students with difficulties, are now faced with a vastly increased workload (Stanley and Manthorpe, 2001). For example, even if an institution has the resources to run training sessions for staff in working with students experiencing mental health difficulties, many staff may find these learning opportunities conflict with their teaching timetable, or their programme management and quality assurance duties. Furthermore, models of training used to educate mental health professionals are not commonly used to educate university staff on such courses. Consequently, it has been suggested to us that the awareness raising often employed on courses is not adequate to create an environment for experiential learning. Through the 1990s and the first five years of the twenty-first century, the reality was often a mental health booklet or policy document provided on the universities' intranet for any member of staff motivated to read it.

The task of caring for students with physical or mental health difficulties is a complex and demanding one, especially where students have intensive support needs or specific learning styles which require specialized instruction. Universities are under-prepared and under-resourced for the task of dealing with ever larger numbers of students with special needs. The whole drift of the advice given makes a number of assumptions about the enigma of distress or learning difficulties. In particular, it often seems to be assumed that these diverse experiences and problems can be addressed through an awareness-raised, leaflet-rich, protocol-driven, good practice-enhanced regime. This much is often taken to be commonsensical, but, like generic models of good practice in teaching itself, a moment's reflection suggests that these are merely assumptions which might well prove to be rather fragile in practice or in the face of critical scrutiny (Grenfell and James, 2004).

Allied to the issue of students suffering from mental health problems is the issue of 'neurodiversity', an expression now used when discussing students with a variety of educational and mental health problems, some of which are believed to be constitutional in origin. On the Brain.HE website (www.brainhe.com) the term embraces problems such as anxiety disorders, depression, Asperger's syndrome and autism, attention deficit hyperactivity disorder, dyslexia, dyscalculia, dyspraxia and Tourette's syndrome. BRAIN.HE is a HEFCE funded initiative that aims to be the provider of the 'best resources for achievement and intervention re neurodiversity in higher education'. It provides a support network and information for higher education students and tutors.

The BRAIN.HE website has a wealth of information for students and staff. The website acknowledges that there are now students entering universities with conditions such as ADHD or those found within the autistic spectrum who did not previously apply to enter universities in any substantial numbers and that anecdotally the numbers of such students in universities is rising. BRAIN.HE draws parallels with the situation in which dyslexic students found themselves in previous decades and reminds institutions of their responsibilities under the Special Educational Needs and Disability Act (SENDA) 2001.

This initiative forms part of a broader concern with human potentials in the education system. For example popular books such as *The Price of Privilege* (Levine, 2006) catalogue the allegedly 'epidemic levels' of depression and anxiety disorders among the offspring of affluent families who have traditionally provided the major part of the student body. Equally, more sober publications have sounded alarms. The British Medical Association (2003; 2006) has raised concerns about the level of binge drinking, drug use, obesity and poor nutrition among the UK's youth, as well as the apparently increasing presence of mental health problems such as depression, anxiety, anorexia, bulimia, hyperactivity, excessive anger, self-harm and suicide attempts. Equally, there has recently been a slew of publications relating to autism and Asperger's syndrome, where the potential achievements of sufferers have been highlighted, especially in the educational arena (Nazeer, 2006; Tammet, 2006; Williams, 2006). Ordinary childhood too is believed to be changing beyond all recognition and some commentators suggest that it has become 'toxic' (Palmer, 2006). Indeed, in September 2006 a group of over 100 'experts' wrote to national newspapers condemning what they saw to be 'a sinister cocktail of junk food, marketing, over-competitive schooling and electronic entertainment [that] is poisoning childhood' (Fenton, 2006).

The implication of all this is that universities are educating and caring for what is seen to be a particularly vulnerable section of the population. As well as the malaise which is believed to be affecting childhood and young adulthood, there is a growing insistence upon universities addressing responsibilities towards individuals with the kinds of difficulties highlighted in BRAIN.HE. Now this may be seen as an intensification of vulnerability culture (Furedi, 2003) such that trauma, fragility and fear is foregrounded in public life. Nevertheless, it is an important part of the contemporary cultural landscape, and one within which the personal and organizational technologies of initiatives such as BRAIN.HE seem naturally placed to intervene.

University staff are enjoined to be particularly vigilant lest the needs of vulnerable students are insufficiently addressed during their sojourn in the academy. For example, among the information for staff that the BRAIN.HE website supplies, is an extensive list of difficulties that autistic spectrum students may well encounter and an account of their very high – or as they say 'strong' – support needs. Under 'useful strategies', strategies which are described as assistive to such students are strategies that could be extraordinarily difficult to implement in today's university sector. For example, even using the student's name regularly could be difficult in large lectures or seminars, considering the high number of students now moving through our university system. Recommendations to avoid the cancellation or rescheduling of meetings or to avoid the interruption of meetings by phone calls or visitors could be difficult to follow. A passing acquaintance of how university departments work and how pressured staff now are would suggest that this is hard to achieve. There is advice to 'beware of jokes', lest a student should misunderstand them – this may be good advice in a sensitive situation, but how would this be maintained among other students? Of course, many students enjoy it when lecturers joke and as long as cruel or personal 'jokes' are avoided, it could be argued that the atmosphere would be diminished if they were disallowed. There is information that states that some autistic spectrum students will need additional support to develop 'social skills in context' which might include advice with money, shopping, hairstyles, clothes and hygiene. Implemented sensitively, this is undoubtedly good advice directed at those responsible for assisting in the social care of people in the autistic spectrum and other students with interpersonal difficulties. However, in situations where this kind of support is needed, one wonders who, in today's climate in which some universities are desperately short of funding and most students are desperately short of money, will provide the funding for such support.

The BRAIN.HE website mentions the role of peer supporters, but although some students perform well in caring roles and a number are keen to become involved in such work, difficulties are encountered when a continuous, high level of support is needed, as this is hard to sustain when it is demanded of peer supporters or volunteer befrienders. Students working in such schemes also suffer stresses and pressures of their own and some organizations dependent upon student volunteering have told us that the voluntary effort is often 'patchy'. Initial enthusiasm may decline, input from volunteer students diminishes during exam periods, and the success of projects dependent upon voluntary student help varies from year to year depending on the enthusiasm and commitment of that year's cohort of students. For example, we know of one project supporting people with mental health problems dependent upon student volunteers that virtually collapsed when a particularly enthusiastic group of volunteers graduated and left the area. We also know of a project that used student volunteers to support distressed or suicidal people that ran into problems when the students were unable to cope with the level of distress that their 'clients' were experiencing. It is worth noting that under UK legislation, such volunteers would nowadays have to undergo checks with the Criminal Records Bureau, a process not known for its speed, value for money or even accuracy. It is also suggested by BRAIN.HE that the students in difficulty who are being supported in this way may need an academic mentor to mediate between them and the staff and also to explain academic 'etiquette'. Again, this requirement may be difficult to fulfil in an under-resourced, overstretched institution. This may not be the end of the institutions' problems however. When discussing the possible problems of students with ADHD, the BRAIN.HE website states that the 'student should be encouraged to take ownership of dealing with aspects of ADHD which bring him into conflict with others'. It is also mentioned that autistic spectrum and ADHD students may abuse alcohol or drugs as a reaction to their condition.

One is left with a picture of students with very high support needs, who may have multiple problems that could bring them into conflict with the law or other students and staff. Even if staff were to be educated and trained as to the best way of working with these students, there is no information about how other students will cope. We have been told of situations where other students were frankly quite frightened of students with problems of this nature, which in some cases has led to bullying. We have spoken to a lecturer who told us that students were so disturbed by a schizophrenic student's habit of talking back to his voices that some ugly scenes of intimidation occurred. A professor of English literature told of an episode where a psychotic student became extremely aggressive in a lecture, threatening him and terrifying some women students. From our own experience, a few years ago, a young man who was attempting to come up with topics for a final year dissertation persistently created topics such as 'DOES MALE VIOLENT (RAPE) RESULT FROM FEMALES PSYCHOLOGICAL SEXUAL SEDUCTION TECHNIQUES?' (capitalisation reproduced as in his original) and 'FEMALES CONTRIBUTIONS TO SEXUAL ABUSE AGAINST THEM AS A RESULT OF THEIR OWN PSYCHOLOGICAL TACTICS' (again, his original emphasis). His tendency to see women as actively responsible for their victimization was pervasive and consistent and he was eventually steered towards a less contentious project. These of course are merely anecdotes and do not necessarily reflect the broader pattern of engagement between students with difficulties and the institutions which are providing them with an education. However, they highlight the fact that the pattern of difficulties is not always consistent or predictable and they are not necessarily expressed in sufficiently forgiving circumstances to allow them to be accommodated easily.

Teaching and learning with students in difficulty: deepening the rift between students and staff

While we have at present no overall figures concerning the prevalence, we are encountering more and more firsthand accounts from colleagues of their difficulties. These difficulties do more than merely confront staff with puzzles and dilemmas. They have far more problematic consequences. They tend to drive a wedge between staff, no matter how well-intentioned, and the students they are trying to serve.

Let us try to explain this by reference to the experience of one of our informants. Working as a media studies lecturer in the further education sector, he had a strong record of support for humanitarian causes in his early adulthood and would presumably have had the potential to be an enthusiastic exponent of the new welfarist spirit in post-compulsory education. His experience highlights how the implementation of a caring role for institutions and their staff can become divisive. Having worked in a teaching and learning environment in classes with a high proportion of students with special needs and with challenging behaviour, he had become somewhat disillusioned about the potential to provide education to this constituency of students. As he said in despair 'there are students in FE who should be in care'. He talked eloquently of the difficulties encountered when he had several students with so-called ADHD (attention deficit hyperactivity disorder) in one class of 20 difficult students, without being informed of their diagnosis: 'five of the students had ADHD and they didn't even tell me – they were a nightmare and someone said "oh didn't you know they've got ADHD they're always like that" ... I got on with all the students individually, but with twenty disturbed students in the class, you just couldn't do it.' He mentioned that some students were so aggressive that they had 'minders' or 'social workers' (presumably care assistants or support workers) in the classroom with them. While this could provide a solution for students needing additional help with learning, in practice it seemed that no one had quite known what to do. 'They have social workers with them to stop them attacking the other students ... [but] the minders just sit on their arses while you control the students.' This despair was compounded by a sense of what the institution was doing with the resources that accompanied the students and which were intended to help support and educate them:

> the disturbed students come with money – one of our students was alleged to come with ten thousand pounds – because they're insane and dangerous the money is supposed to be for minders and security but it's not spent on that, the poor bloody teachers are left to deal with them ... there's all these layers and layers of management but they don't help dealing with these students ... social inclusion means there's nutters in the classroom.

Now, the foregoing comments seemed odd for someone of our informant's impeccable progressive credentials, and his previous involvement with work helping disadvantaged groups. As a student himself, he was actively involved in a variety of radical or humanitarian causes and campaigns for social justice. This then raises the question of how his apparently reactionary response to this variant of social inclusion has come about. Perhaps it originates in his frustration at having to pursue an academic curriculum with students whose personal difficulties meant they had little to gain from it. The students' problems in social interaction and in achieving cooperative dialogue with others often meant that it was difficult for them to participate productively in the recommended group work exercises. Our informant had simply been placed in an impossible, frustrating situation. The avenues for discussing the difficulties frankly or engaging in teamwork with colleagues had been effectively closed off. In his words: 'I wouldn't dare complain . . .'

While this is just one example, it suggests that a dynamic is at work which intensifies rather than reduces the gap between the students and those who teach them. We are hearing a great many stories from staff and students of situations where students, many of whom have unhappy prior experiences of education, are exposed to learning experiences and syllabi which were never intended for them. Equally, staff are presented with challenging situations for which their training provides few clues as to how to proceed. Sometimes they may not even be forewarned of their students' problems. An acquaintance teaching in a further education college was presented with the task of teaching a class of particularly boisterous young adults, whose horseplay sometimes bordered on frank aggression. It was only later that she discovered that her students included a number of young offenders, some of whom were sex offenders, and their presence in the college was part of a scheme to divert them from custodial sentences.

The response of many staff, who under other circumstances might have had the potential to be caring and dedicated, is to try to escape from the education system altogether and thus avoid these kinds of experiences. Our informant who had attempted to teach media studies to the challenging youngsters eventually left the further education sector, saying that he would never take on such a stressful job again. His mother had been a further education lecturer 20 years previously and couldn't understand why he had done so, as she thought it was a good career and he had a young family to support:

FE's just been wrecked, they've wrecked it . . . I think it did used to be a good job but not anymore . . . my mum was a teacher − she has no idea, she couldn't understand why I wouldn't go on, she thought it was a career . . . I'd never go back, I'd never touch it again . . . just wasn't worth it, I spent nearly as much on petrol as what I earned and the stress . . .

This summed up what a number of further education lecturers have told us, even those who are teaching 'HE in FE'. We also came across the case of a young woman who was a student in a further education college who was believed to have unspecified neurological or mental health difficulties. Her behaviour towards male students was so sexually aggressive and predatory that other students refused to remain in the class with her. Outside the college, this young woman's difficulties were sufficient to warrant her being in residential care. When the college told the care providers that the student was no longer welcome at the college, the care providers threatened legal action under the Disability Discrimination Act. The college had no stomach for an extended legal battle and the young woman was subsequently readmitted, but was taught alone in an isolated classroom where it was staff rather than other students who bore the brunt of her egregious tendencies.

This sequence of events highlights the dilemma that staff in higher and further education face. Mental health care staff in the UK National Health Service have developed considerable discretion in whom they will and will not treat. Clients who are disruptive, or who are deemed to be aggressive or to be suffering from so called 'personality disorders' are often excluded from treatment. Schools teaching 5–16 year olds can exclude pupils. Yet post-compulsory education establishments seem to be relatively powerless players in the mosaic of health and social care. Consequently they are apt to accommodate students for whom other agencies have succeeded in avoiding responsibility. Other staff in further and higher education remarked upon a fear of litigation. Lecturers' and managers' understanding of whether the relevant legislation affords them any rights or resources is relatively under-developed compared to the sense of threat if they demur from the inclusive orthodoxy.

One of our interviewees remarked that traditionally, further education was for the educational 'no hopers' or 'second chancers', some of whom always eventually succeeded. She felt that this had led institutions to be extremely inclusive and accepting towards a great many students whose chances of success were limited despite extensive support systems.

We should emphasize here that in preparing to write this book we listened to many tales of students with severe difficulties, struggling to make progress in further and higher education. At the same time, their difficulties were sometimes having a knock-on effect for staff and other students. Furthermore, even in describing those difficulties, there was a sense of shame on the part of those who related their accounts. We were repeatedly asked not to quote people and to ensure that no institution could ever be identified – some people explicitly spoke of their fears for their jobs if they were known to be speaking to researchers about the near chaotic situations that prevail in their institutions.

The general pattern of the narratives related to us suggests that the situation and the pressures faced by staff are far worse in further education than in universities. But we hazard that the situation will soon be similar for universities. Students with serious difficulties are now being 'prepared' for university and are certainly being encouraged to apply. Staff are being told, in a myriad of different ways, that supporting very needy or challenging students is now part of their job. Although a small minority of staff we have spoken to are frankly resentful of and hostile to such students, the usual reaction was strongly sympathetic, and lecturers wanted to do the best for all students, including those with difficulties.

The wedge that has been driven between students with difficulties and staff seems to have originated with the sense that there is more and more to do, and that there is little or no allowance in the calculation of class sizes or working hours to compensate for the additional needs of students. Indeed, finding out about students' needs after having experienced difficulties teaching the students, rather than being prepared for the experience beforehand, can be discouraging. There is also a sense that the additional monies colleges get to provide services for students with special needs are not necessarily apparent in the classroom. Thus, many people feel that they simply don't have the time or resources to give students with special needs the support that they require. This contributes to the sense of resentment we identified earlier.

At the same time, one of the further education lecturers we spoke to observed that in the past, the prevailing conditions of service and Local Education Authority employment allowed lecturers time and space for extensive tutoring and counselling. Now lecturers are under contradictory pressures, encouraged to recruit more and more 'high maintenance' students, but with less time to support them. Moreover, staff feel themselves to be under pressure to ensure that these students 'succeed'.

One would therefore question the worthy ideals that are perpetuated in government policy documents and echoed by various pressure groups. The benefits agency and welfare state are clearly not prepared to help these students – the burden is being pushed very firmly onto educational institutions, including universities, which may in turn themselves be unable to cope. It is the individual staff members who end up under enormous pressure, attempting to assist seriously distressed people. If they are unable to support needy students further, these very staff are then accused of being elitist and unsympathetic.

There are also suggestions of a rift between staff who work at the front line teaching or managing student accommodation as 'residence tutors' or 'hall wardens' and the staff employed in disability or learning support roles. Those who work full time in disability or learning support are believed not to understand the pressures. The feeling was expressed to us that the support staff lead a comparatively 'leisurely life', producing documents, organizing responses or strategies, or dispensing advice, and it is the academic staff who are expected to support the students, as well as conduct research, teach and carry out administrative duties. Staff who work as residence tutors or hall wardens in student accommodation in some cases are taking on a great deal of pastoral work, particularly those in universities in areas where mental health services were poor. One warden regularly had suicidal students sleeping on her couch. She knew that it was against university rules but: 'I'm not going to see them die. There's no one else to look after them – the hospital doesn't want to know and their family's hundreds of miles away.'

Supporting students: care on the cheap?

We have concentrated in this chapter on certain sorts of wellbeing for which universities are now made responsible. In this discussion we have concentrated largely on students with mental health and social difficulties. Partly, this reflects the priority attached to these issues in public debate and the mass media. There has not been the same amount of publicity relating to the inclusion of physically disabled students compared to the amount there has been concerning people with mental health problems, social problems or neurological problems in the education system. We are not sure why this is – whether it is because issues relating to the physically disabled are deemed less worthy of coverage because they are less emotive or controversial, or whether it is because physically disabled people have been present in universities for quite some time, so the topic is not so contentious.

The extent of the university sector's preparedness to accommodate a proportion of students with difficulties related to mental health, neurodiversity and social and behavioural problems in the early years of the twenty-first century has been documented by Stanley and Manthorpe (2001; 2002). The impression is that of educational establishments struggling to accommodate the needs of vulnerable students. The ethos of self-reliance and independence on which institutions have hitherto relied is counterproductive when students in difficulty are reluctant to seek help or the help that might be available is inaccessible. Indeed, in some cases, for example, where courses lead to qualifications in the health care professions, students may be highly motivated to evade 'help' entirely, lest it affect their career prospects (Chew-Graham *et al.*, 2003).

Post-compulsory education staff have themselves felt ill-equipped and under-prepared for the caring role into which the presence of distressed and vulnerable students places them. There was also concern that universities and society as a whole were avoiding the issue of providing appropriate care for students by means of an expansion in the pastoral role of staff, over and above the traditional role of academic guidance. As one respondent in Stanley and Manthorpe's study put it: 'I find I have to do considerable "counselling" myself and I think that the university should not put so much pastoral care onto academic staff on the cheap' (Stanley and Manthorpe, 2001: 47). Academic staff also highlighted a lack of time to deal with students' distress adequately, a finding which echoes that of other surveys (Wassall, 1999). A crucial difficulty is that there is little effective liaison between academic staff and other health care agencies such as GPs, community mental health teams and staff in hospitals, who, even if they could be located, were often not forthcoming, perhaps due to the pressures within their own organizations or concerns over confidentiality. Stanley and Manthorpe (2001) report that contact with university counselling services was often easier to initiate, yet there were nevertheless concerns about the difficulty in ascertaining the progress a student might be making, as a result of the need to maintain confidentiality.

Hence, the picture painted in these investigations of the preparedness of universities to accommodate students with difficulties is that there is some considerable way to go before the services are established to an appropriate level. In many institutions the pathways to a 'joined-up' service such that academic and care services can operate seamlessly and provide care for vulnerable people are fragmented.

Given the difficulties we have identified, it might be wondered whether there is a financial or political incentive behind the growing trend towards the containment of distress, psychosocial difficulties and 'mental health problems' in educational institutions. Perhaps one part of the answer can be found when we scrutinize funding arrangements for students. Education looks cheap yet functional, especially as funding arrangements have increasingly been reconfigured so they do not appear to burden the public purse. Successive governments, including New Labour, have been successful in substantially reducing financial support for students. Full-time students in HE now have to contribute varying amounts to their tuition fees, which in the academic year 2006–7 are being charged at £3,000 per year for full-time courses. In an effort to combat hardship in a small number of cases, the government has introduced a system of grants to offset the new higher rate of fees. The non-repayable means-tested grant of up to £2,700 can be paid in full to students with a household income of less than £17,500. Partial sums are available to students with household incomes over this value, up to £37,425 over which students are not eligible to receive the higher education grant. The only other means of support available to most students, at the time of writing, no matter how impoverished, is the repayable student loan. However, along with implementing 'top-up' fees, many universities have now developed scholarships for some disadvantaged students. These are frequently for 'outstanding' students.

To be eligible for other state support, students have to demonstrate special circumstances, for example, by having dependants or disabilities. Some students with mental health problems are technically eligible for Income Support, Incapacity Benefit and Disability Living Allowance. Anecdotal evidence from disability advisers suggests such claims from students are rarely successful, because regulations state that claimants must be 'incapable of work' or 'substantially incapacitated'. Students who are able to demonstrate that they have a disability may be eligible for the Disabled Students' Allowance from their Local Education Authority. However, anecdotal evidence from some university disability advisers suggests that their experience with people seeking to obtain the Disabled Students' Allowance for mental health problems is that this is often very difficult. Thus, in the case of students with mental heath problems, the financial situation is more austere than if they were unemployed or supported through incapacity or sickness benefit.

Although some 'flagship' schemes which have been set up with extra funding in some universities are supplying some students with assistance such as support workers, most institutions are not able to provide such help. Neither is there any indication that the funding which is currently being employed to sustain people on incapacity and sickness benefits will be redeployed to support initiatives within the education system. Yet very often this seems to consist of exhortations to teaching staff to do more, by adapting their teaching, providing more pastoral support and extending new interventions into the personal lives of students. To policymakers keen to disguise the consequences of systemic failure, the care and support available via the education system is therefore more cost-effective and politically expedient than if it were administered via the usual pathway of health and social welfare agencies.

These policy developments intersect in complex ways with other recent popular and political anxieties about the 'cost' of sickness and disability themselves. The growing numbers of people claiming long-term incapacity benefit in the UK have yielded increasing concern in popular and political circles, and after announcing a 'war on welfare' in late 2004, moves have now begun to cut the bill for incapacity benefits, estimated to exceed £7 billion a year (Wintour, 2005). It has been suggested in a number of spirited features in the *Daily Mail* that 'bogus' claimants have been tempted to give up work because of 'generous' sickness benefits, and journalists charged that many of these people are feigning illness (Reid, 2004; Wilson, 2005).

To a government faced with the need to address this self-defined political problem, education – with its much vaunted power to increase people's employability and decrease social exclusion – might be especially attractive. While the process of persuading people with health or social problems onto courses in educational establishments is largely done through low-level individualized intervention by their key workers, the overall outcome of such a policy is to lessen the number of potential claimants of sickness and disability benefits per se and transfer them into another segment of the economy where they are as yet invisible to journalists and place a less obvious burden on the public purse.

There is also little to assess the 'success' of students experiencing, for example, mental health problems who enter post-compulsory education. Consequently it is hard to assess whether the therapeutic and reformist ambitions of policymakers are sustained by any evidence in this regard. In many cases there is no formal research to follow up and assess the student's outcome, and in other areas follow-up is widely believed to be inadequate. However, some statutory services perceive a mental health worker as having been 'successful' if one of the clients they have worked with enters education, and at a local level this is believed to be driving the migration of existing clients into the education system. Despite a widespread belief that this is beneficial, there is instead, as we have seen, growing evidence of the fragility of student mental health. Thus New Labour's policy of encouraging people with mental health problems to enter education is encouraging them into a situation which is demonstrably likely to yield deterioration in a person's mental health rather than improvement. Despite a policy advocating the inclusion of service users' voices in the formulation of strategy and service planning, as in the National Service Framework (DoH, 1999), there has been no discussion in public fora about the desirability of this policy. Hence, parties such as the universities, the statutory services and most importantly, people experiencing mental health problems themselves, have not had an opportunity to comment on the problems or success ahead. It is as though this policy has been smuggled in by the government with no open debate and very little media coverage.

From a policymaker's point of view, education might well be a particularly yielding and forgiving environment in which to place difficult or

challenging individuals with complex multiple problems. There is an interesting paradox here. As the NHS increasingly operates a 'zero tolerance'
policy (that to our knowledge no university or HE/FE college operates),
clients that the mental health services have refused to treat are now apt to be
found within the education system. Our acquaintance who found herself
teaching a class of young offenders told us of the daily abuse and threats
that she received from students and of the lack of support from the institution's management. By contrast, her partner is a clinical psychologist
employed by an NHS Trust that has become well known locally for refusing
to treat patients who are verbally abusive or threatening to staff – he has the
luxury of refusing difficult customers if he wishes. The trend then is for existing legislation to be interpreted in a way that is increasingly supportive of
students with difficulties and their carers in accessing post-compulsory education. This contrasts with hospitals, GPs and psychiatrists, who are currently exercising their options to refuse to treat patients who are perceived
to be too difficult or costly or who would put the institution at odds with the
'challenging new targets' which are imposed (Carvel, 2002; Carr-Brown,
2003; Davies, 2004b).

Conclusion: policies, consciousness, legitimation

However social policies are deployed, whether through widespread reform
or individual action, a number of theoretically significant features should
be noted. The tendency to corral people with mental health and related
difficulties within the education system is a policy which is of relatively
recent origin but one which appears to have a long and commonsensical
pedigree which offers it a degree of legitimation. It is thus unapologetically
identified with progress, reform, equality, modernity and with the aboli-
tion of stigma and with the gain of apparently desirable personal qualities. It fits neatly with currently modish political discourse to the effect
that individuals themselves can be recapitalized – made more employable,
have their self-esteem raised, their social networks strengthened and their
employability enhanced.

This phenomenon demonstrates how the field in which the various
actors play out the drama of mental health and illness in relation to post-
compulsory education has made new phenomena visible and what was
once private distress and personal conduct is now a matter of policy, legislation, as well as socially, morally and legally mandated obligation, and
changes in the mindset and inferential framework of college and university
staff are being encouraged. This again is done in such a way as to appear

commonsensical. After all, who could possibly disagree with helping to prevent suicide, or facilitating people with disabilities to enter universities? Yet these changes have populated the educational landscape with new phenomena: 'What was fundamentally invisible is suddenly offered to the brightness of the gaze, in a movement of appearance so simple, so immediate that it seems to be the natural consequence of a more highly developed experience' (Foucault, 1975: 195).

This process of legitimation is concerned with making it look as if we have just learned to see things clearly after years of being bound by prejudices: 'free at last of theories and chimeras, the newly enlightened professional can "approach the object of ... experience with the purity of an unprejudiced gaze"' (Foucault, 1975: 195). As Rose puts it: 'the personal and subjective capacities of citizens have become incorporated into the scope and aspirations of public powers' (Rose, 1989: 1).

This new policy landscape, this psychologization and individualization of the ways in which professionals, policymakers, service users and students themselves are encouraged to think about the situation, means that Rose's words – originally written to describe the role of psychology in helping to create the forms of modern life – are equally applicable now to the university system. As Rose says:

> we need to trace out the ways in which psychological modes of explanation, claims to truth, and systems of authority have participated in the elaboration of moral codes that stress an ideal of responsible autonomy, in shaping these codes in a certain 'therapeutic' direction, and in allaying them with programs for regulating individuals consonant with the political rationalities of advanced liberal democracies. (Rose, 1996: 119)

References

Andrews, B. and Wilding J. M. (2004), 'The relation of depression and anxiety to life-stress and achievement in students', *British Journal of Psychology*, 95(4), 509–21.

Austin, T. (1999), 'The role of education in the lives of people with mental health difficulties', in C. Newnes, G. Holmes and C. Dunn (eds), *This is Madness: A Critical Look at Psychiatry and the Future of the Mental Health Services*. Ross-On-Wye: PCCS Books, pp. 207–31.

Baker, S. (2005), *Like a Fish in Water: Aspects of the Contemporary UK Higher Education System As Intended and As Constructed*. PhD Thesis, University of Wales.

Bourdieu, P. (1977), *Outline of a Theory of Practice*. Cambridge: Cambridge University Press.

Bourdieu, P. (1992), 'The purpose of reflexive sociology', in P. Bourdieu and P. Wacquant (eds) *An invitation to reflexive sociology*, Cambridge: Polity, pp. 61–215.

Bowl, M. (2000), 'Listening to the voices of non-traditional students', *Widening Participation and Lifelong Learning*, 2(1), 32–40.

British Medical Association (2003), *Adolescent Health*. London: British Medical Association Board of Science and Education.

British Medical Association (2006), *Child and Adolescent Mental Health – A Guide for Healthcare Professionals*. London: British Medical Association Board of Science and Education.

Carr-Brown, J. (2003), 'Hospital turns away patients to meet targets', *The Sunday Times*, October 5 2003.

Carvel, J. (2002), 'Mental care denied to refugees: NHS psychologists refuse to treat "traumatised" asylum seekers', *Guardian*, June 4 2002.

Chew-Graham, C. A., Rogers, A. and Yassin, N. (2003), ' "I wouldn't want it on my CV or their records": medical students' experiences of help-seeking for mental health problems', *Medical Education*, 37(10), 873–80.

Collishaw, S., Maughan, B., Goodman, R. and Pickles, A. (2004), 'Time trends in adolescent mental health', *Journal of Child Psychology and Psychiatry*, 45(8), 1350–62.

Commission for Health Improvement (2003), *Mental Health Services Still Have a Long Way To Go*, News Release, December 18 2003.

Davies, N. (2004a), 'Scandal of society's misfits dumped in jail', *Guardian*, December 6 2004.

Davies, N. (2004b), 'Trapped in a cycle of self-harm and desperation for want of a psychiatric bed', *Guardian*, December 7 2004.

De Montfort University (2004), *What Sort of Support is Available?* www.dmu.ac.uk/Images/2.15728.pdf. Accessed 05/01/05.

DfEE (1998), *The Learning Age: A Renaissance for a New Britain*. London: The Stationery Office.

DfEE (2000), *The Excellence Challenge. The Government's Proposals for Widening the Participation of Young People in Higher Education*. London: HMSO.

Department of Health (1999), *National Service Framework for Mental Health*. London: Department of Health.

Ecclestone, K. (2004), 'Learning or therapy? The demoralisation of education', *British Journal of Educational Studies*, 52(2), 112–37.

Ecclestone, K. and Hayes, D. (2007), *The Dangerous Rise of Therapeutic Education: How Teaching is Becoming Therapy*. Abingdon: Routledge.

Ecclestone, K., Hayes, D. and Furedi, F. (2005), 'Knowing me, knowing you: the rise of therapeutic professionalism in the education of adults', *Studies in the Education of Adults*, 37(2), 182–200.

Fairclough, N. (2000), *New Labour, New Languages?* London: Routledge.

Fenton, B. (2006), 'Junk culture "is poisoning our children". Experts blame fast food, computer games and competitive schooling for rise in depression', *Daily Telegraph*, September 12 2006.

Foucault, M. (1975), *The Birth of the Clinic: An Archaeology of Medical Perception* (trans. A. M. Sheridan Smith). New York: Vintage Books.

Furedi, F. (2003), *Therapy Culture: Cultivating Vulnerability in an Uncertain Age*. London: Routledge.

Garner, R. (2004), 'Student depression is linked to debt woes', *Independent*, April 17 2004.

Gorard, S. (2005), 'Where shall we widen it? Higher education and the age participation rate in Wales', *Higher Education Quarterly*, 59(1), 3–18.

Grenfell, M. and James, D. (2004), 'Change in the field – Changing the field: Bourdieu and the methodological practice of educational research', *British Journal of Sociology of Education*, 25(4), 507–22.

Harris, N. (2004a), 'Features; Public agenda', *The Times*, June 1 2004.

Harris, N. (2004b), 'Students, mental health and citizenship', *Legal Studies*, 24(3), 349–85.

Konur, O. (2002), 'Assessment of disabled students in higher education: current public policy issues', *Assessment & Evaluation in Higher Education*, 27(2), 131–52.

Levine, M. (2006), *The Price of Privilege: How Parental Pressure and Material Advantage are Creating a Generation of Disconnected and Unhappy Kids*. New York: Harper Collins.

Nazeer, K. (2006), *Send in the Idiots, or How We Grew to Understand the World*. London: Bloomsbury.

Palmer, S. (2006), *Toxic Childhood: How the Modern World is Damaging our Children and What We Can Do About it*. London: Orion.

Phippen, M. (1995), 'The 1993/4 survey of counselling services in further and higher education', *Newsletter, Association for Student Counselling*, November, 25–36.

Rana, R., Smith, E. and Walkling, J. (1999), *Degrees of Disturbance: The New Agenda, the Impact of Increasing Levels of Psychological Disturbance Amongst Students in Higher Education*. Rugby: Association for University and College Counselling Services.

Reay, D. (1995), 'Using habitus to look at 'race' and class in primary school classrooms', in M. Griffiths and B. Troyna (eds), *Anti-racism, Culture and Social Justice in Education*. Stoke-on-Trent: Trentham Books, pp. 115–32.

Reid, S. (2004), 'Sick note Britain', *Daily Mail*, September 25 2004.

Roberts, R., Golding, J., Towell, T. and Weinreb, I. (1999), 'The effects of economic circumstances on British students' mental and physical health', *Journal of American College Health*, 48(3), 103–9.

Rose, N. (1989), *Governing the Soul: The Shaping of the Private Self*. London: Routledge.

Rose, N. (1996), *Inventing Ourselves*. Cambridge: Cambridge University Press.

Rose, N. (1999), *Powers of Freedom: Reframing Political Thought*. Cambridge: Cambridge University Press.

Royal College of Psychiatrists Council Report CR112 (2003), *The Mental Health of Students in Higher Education*. London: Royal College of Psychiatrists.

Smithers, R. (2004), 'Oxford attack on admission reforms', *Guardian*, May 13 2004.

Social Exclusion Unit (2004), *Mental Health and Social Exclusion*. London: Office of the Deputy Prime Minister.

Stanley, N. and Manthorpe, J. (2001), 'Responding to students' mental health needs: impermeable systems and diverse users', *Journal of Mental Health*, 10(1), 41–52.

Stanley, N. and Manthorpe, J. (eds) (2002), *Students' Mental Health: Problems and Responses*. London: Jessica Kingsley Publishers.

Stewart-Brown, S., Evans, J., Patterson, J., Peterson, S., Doll, H., Balding, J. and Regis, D. (2000), 'The health of students in institutes of higher education: an important and neglected public health problem?', *Journal of Public Health Medicine*, 22(4), 492–9.

Tammet, D. (2006), *Born on a Blue Day: A Memoir of Asperger's and an Extraordinary Mind*. London: Hodder and Stoughton.

Taylor, M. (2004), 'Students round on minister over graduate claims', *Guardian*, December 14 2004.

Taylor, M. (2005a), 'The development of the special educational needs coordinator role in a higher education setting', *Support for Learning*, 20(1), 22–7.

Thomas, L. (2001), 'Power, assumptions and prescriptions: a critique of widening participation policy-making', *Higher Education Policy*, 14(4), 361–76.

Universities UK (formerly CVCP) (2000), *Guidelines on Student Mental Health Policies and Procedures for Higher Education*. London: Universities UK.

Universities UK (formerly CVCP) (2002), *Reducing the Risk of Student Suicide: Issues and Responses for Higher Education Institutions*. London: Universities UK.

University of Nottingham (2004), *Mental Health Difficulties: Information for Staff*. www.nottingham.ac.uk/counselling/Mentalhealth-infostaff.doc. Accessed 05/1/05.

University of Wales, Bangor (2004), *The Mental Health Guide for Students*. Bangor: University of Wales.

Wassall, H. J. (1999), *Experience of Academic Staff Supervising Students with Mental Health Problems: A Report for the University of Aberdeen Counselling Service*. Aberdeen: University of Aberdeen Counselling Service.

Wertheimer, A. (1997), *Images of Possibilty: Creating Learning Opportunities for People with Mental Health Difficulties*. Leicester: NIACE.

Williams, D. (2006), *The Jumbled Jigsaw: An Insider's Approach to the Treatment of Autistic Spectrum 'Fruit Salads'*. London: Jessica Kingsley Publishers.

Wilson, G. (2005), 'The cut-price cure for sicknote Britain', *Daily Mail*, January 27 2005.

Wintour, P. (2005), 'Plans to overhaul incapacity benefit', *Guardian*, January 27 2005.

Wright, M. (1998), *Paper for Staff and Student Affairs Committee Re: Proposed Working Party to Consider Mental Health Related Issues Within the University*. Hatfield, Hertfordshire: University of Hertfordshire.

Chapter 5

Education as Shaping, Growing and Cultivating

Introduction: agendas for change

As we have seen, one of the peculiar triumphs of post-compulsory education is that it encompasses so much variety. The bewildering cornucopia of activities that institutions and their students engage in makes it sometimes difficult to identify common themes in this diversity. The teaching and learning process may encompass specific skills related to a discipline, generic competencies, techniques, theoretical content as well as particular custom and practice relating to crafts as diverse as podiatry and beauty therapy, horticulture and leisure management. It may, in more classically informed definitions of the activity, also impart something less tangible but more profound: the creation of knowledge, good judgement and wisdom.

How, then, is contemporary higher education shaping the citizens of tomorrow? And to what extent are they shaping the universities of today? Can it be that as Bompard (2006) reports at Bologna University, staff who do not achieve high student satisfaction ratings do not get their contracts renewed?

Education is often said to have as one of its fundamental goals the imparting of culture from generation to generation. This notion is premised on the idea that human functioning is always situated in a context. It involves the shared symbols of a community, 'its traditions and tool-kit', passed on from generation to generation and constituting the larger culture (Bruner, 1996: 43). Governments in developed and developing nations have been mesmerized by the advantages which might accrue from having a higher proportion of graduates in the population – that crime may be lower, mortality and morbidity may be improved and family stability enhanced – by encouraging more people to enter university. These notions derive from the work of a variety of educational researchers and theorists over the last half century (Bowen, 1977; Havighurst *et al.*, 1967) who argued for the value of the non-monetary and social benefits of education.

Education therefore came to be seen as a sort of social engineering, as being about shaping the culture of the nation, its communities, families and individuals in a way which is potentially governable by policymakers. It is clearly not merely about imparting skills and knowledge but can be used as a means of addressing a variety of other social policy issues. This urging can be seen in more recent policy documents too, for example the *All Our Futures* report from the UK's National Advisory Committee on Creative and Cultural Education (1999).

The relationship between education and culture is not only subject to great expectations, it is changing too. Higher and further education have not merely expanded, but have introduced wholly new subjects and approaches into the academy and are inculcating different disciplinary cultures and kinds of ethos. Students may participate in programmes not only in the traditional subject areas but also in complementary and alternative therapies, lifestyle studies and landscape gardening. So a greater variety of activities are subject to the cultural reconfiguration of making them into academic disciplines and in turn having their effect on both the rising generation and on learners returning to education.

The methods of shaping cultures, academic experiences and students themselves are changing too. Whereas once students might have been advised via tutors and college careers services, there are innovations in the approaches used here. Of course, careers services and appointments services are still in existence, but we are increasingly discovering other approaches flourishing. In a college in Yorkshire we have come across student advisers who are just as likely to use horoscopes and clairvoyance to counsel students as conventional techniques of pastoral or careers guidance. The education system is opening up to these kinds of approaches in a similar way to that in which health care has undergone these very transitions. As we shall suggest later, this epistemological diversification is allied to the liberalization of markets in education and the casualization and outsourcing of teaching and student services.

Education then is shifting its epistemological fabric, shaping the kinds of cultures which are accepted as knowledge, and the sorts of personal orientations to the world and its problems which are encouraged, as well as the orientation to the inner world of problems faced by the learner and the teacher. As we have seen in the previous chapter, there are many initiatives to promote welfare on the part of students. This has resulted in different role orientations on the part of academic staff, and new kinds of functions for the education sector as a whole in aiding national and international policy objectives. In this chapter therefore we will concentrate on two tendencies which we hope will illuminate some hitherto under-appreciated tendencies in post-compulsory education. We will pursue the theme of welfarization of education which we have alluded to already, and following on from this we will explore the curious parallels between education and a Disney theme park – the so called Disneyfication thesis.

We will begin by expanding on some of the themes identified in the previous chapter concerned with welfare and higher education as this is one most conspicuous area where higher education is itself urged to change, and where changing the lives of students with problems is most conspicuously foregrounded as a virtue.

This is not intended to be read as an indictment of welfare services for students or as an argument for an exclusionary approach to higher education. Our commitment to offering higher educational experience as widely as possible is reflected in our collectively having 20 years' experience in doing just that. However, the 'inclusionist' or 'welfarist' agenda in higher education is curiously diligent or assiduous in some areas, demanding ever greater reform, yet other areas of hardship are curiously unexamined.

The process at work here is not simply a matter of providing a university education and attending appropriately as necessary to students' needs – the Bourdieusian field has shifted considerably. The picture, as we shall suggest, is becoming increasingly clear – this is university education as social care.

Welfare in the academy: changing cultures and changing care delivery

The hegemony of the welfarist orientation in the post-compulsory education system has a variety of ramifications and implications. Some of the extra requirements for students with special needs in the classroom can arguably represent improvements for students as a whole. There is after all, only a small step between students who have difficulty writing using audio recordings of lectures and the class as a whole being available as a podcast. Yet sometimes the support needs of students are so great that academic staff and the institutions they work for are actually being asked to fulfil a very different remit than in the past.

This role change is highlighted by some of the information on teaching on the BRAIN.HE website mentioned in the last chapter. This forms part of the process by which the activities involved in teaching and learning are being shifted and reconfigured to accommodate the needs of a greater variety of students. If, for example, we take the problems associated with dyscalculia, BRAIN.HE draws upon a characterization of the syndrome by Jan Robertson, who identifies extreme dyscalculia as 'difficulty ordering and comparing numbers under 10, judging time and direction' (BRAIN.HE, 2006). This description suggests that such a student would have serious difficulties with many university courses, even with support. Indeed, Robertson herself describes the intensive process of working with a student with dyscalculia (Robertson, 2004). Despite the substantial investment of time and resources involved in helping students with problems of this severity, it is stressed by many experts in the field that under the Special Educational Needs and Disability Act (SENDA), passed in the UK in 2001, reasonable adjustments must be made and discrimination is outlawed. The tips given for helping a dyscalculic student suggest that much time, creativity and ingenuity is needed. Through web-based advice and case studies, it is suggested that a gradual approach with many explanations is indicated. With a small class or teaching one to one, perhaps where the teacher has a speciality interest this might be achievable. Yet in many higher education settings there may be practical, financial and organizational difficulties involved in achieving this level of intensive support.

This then is an issue at the heart of contemporary higher education. As class sizes increase, so too, paradoxically, do the numbers of students needing specialized and individualized assistance to gain the best from their educational experience. This trend is intensified by the fact that courses are deemed viable only if they attract larger numbers of students. Yet more individualized support is also required as students are recruited for whom the 'one size fits all' learning experience and the anonymity of the large class are themselves problematic.

This welfarist ethos has pervaded technological aspects of education too – in April 2006 CETIS (the Centre for Educational Technology Interoperability Standards) held 'Forging the Future', their DDIG (Dyscalculia and Dyslexia Interest Group) conference. With the financial support available to students with certificates vouching for their disability, more companies are marketing technological equipment geared to non-physically disabled, as well as disabled students (www.techdis.ac.uk/).

It is clear that academic staff themselves are supportive of the inclusion of students with disabilities in the educational experience. The majority of academic staff that we have interviewed were sympathetic to the idea of social inclusion in education, yet some retained a suspicion that the agenda is being exploited or manipulated by individuals and systems. As one commented: 'there's a lot of people making careers for themselves'.

To illustrate the relationship between the manifest position of inclusion and welfare support for students and the shortcomings in practice, let us consider the story of a student we interviewed for this book in more detail. She was from a cohort which previously did not enter university. She had however, become a mature student in a highly starred social science department in a traditional university, who had been allowed to enter university with few formal qualifications. She had mental health problems and also disclosed that she was a frequent drug user. When we interviewed her she was halfway through the second year of her degree, deeply in debt and struggling seriously with academic work. Given her department's reputation for imposing difficult and rigorous assessments on students, we were mystified as to how she had managed to stay on the course so long. After seeking reassurance that the interview was confidential, she explained that every essay that she had ever submitted had been plagiarised from the internet. She coped with exams by, in her words, 'playing the mental health card' and gaining concessions on behalf of her health problems. She was now at a point in the course where these strategies were no longer able to sustain her, as second-year assessments demanded greater ingenuity and could not be satisfied with ready-made products from the internet. She withdrew from the course some weeks later, her difficulties probably somewhat greater than they were before she came to university.

The position of this student seemed to reflect much of what we have been told by academic staff. There are now excellent support systems that undoubtedly enable many to succeed who would not otherwise have done so. However, there are concerns that these support systems can result in students being excused or absolved from the normal academic procedures. The student then either succeeds in a way that undermines the validity of the exercise or drops out further down the line. As a member of staff remarked: 'the system often operates unconsciously', although some students may possibly 'knowingly manipulate it'. As in our example above, when the student ends up withdrawing anyway, one has to ask the question, was this education or social care? And in either case, could this be counted as a success?

An internet search will reveal enormous quantities of material regarding disability support for students. There is much cross-referencing with material from disability organizations. There is far less material relating to the financial help that may be available to students (DfES, 2005) and as we have seen, some students receive scant financial help at all, despite all the initiatives regarding 'embedding' and 'raising awareness' of disability issues.

Staff involved with students with, for example, dyslexia, tell of a 'shopping list' of equipment that is often requested, including computers and software as well as a catalogue of handheld devices, additional time in examinations and consideration for coursework deadline extensions. Reports from educational psychologists seldom seem to contain much analysis of the cognitive difficulties experienced by students, or strategies of remediation, but instead are oriented to a range of consumer products as a means of ameliorating presumed impairments. Yet some students suffering serious difficulties – who are in the very groups the government wishes to include in higher education – still receive scant help. A PhD student with a severe and enduring mental illness who actually had a research interest in such issues and 'knew the ropes' was unable to gain any assistance at all other than her PhD scholarship. At one point she lived in a house condemned as unfit for human habitation and was going without meals due to lack of money and debts left over from several years of living on incapacity benefit. However, she was unable to gain assistance from the student hardship fund. She was told that so many students were now experiencing so much hardship that she simply couldn't be considered as she actually had a scholarship, so was 'fortunate'. Her PhD supervisor regularly lent her money to assist her in completing her studies.

Much of the welfare work that universities are now undertaking has arisen from the government's explicitly stated aim that universities should play a role in social justice. The White Paper 'The Future of Higher Education' (DfES, 2003) talks of the role universities and colleges have to play in embracing 'social inclusion' (2003: 20), states that education is 'the best and most reliable route out of poverty and disadvantage' (2003: 68) and states that education must attract and retain 'vulnerable students' (2003: 71). The controversial Higher Education Act (2004) and government widening participation policies have also brought increased numbers of vulnerable students needing various kinds of support into the system. The student profile today, particularly in the post-1992 sector, is thus very different to that of 20 years ago, and promoting the wellbeing of such students is now clearly a remit.

A strategic, managerial approach to promoting equality in the higher education sector was furthered through the establishment of the UK's Equality Challenge Unit in 2000 to promote diversity issues among staff in higher education. In 2006 its remit was extended to include students. As part of this new agenda, its 2006 conference held a workshop entitled 'Curriculum Equality', exploring disability projects (www.ecu.ac.uk/conference2006/workshop4. htm). One aim of the conference was 'embedding disability into the learning and teaching agenda' and it featured disability awareness for academic and other staff. One project, led by Dr Val Chapman, involved extending the existing framework and resource of HEFCE projects to benefit traditionally disadvantaged groups other than just disabled students, under the aegis of 'inclusive teaching'. Dr Chapman sees barriers and challenges in accessing the curriculum for students from a wide range of traditionally disadvantaged groups – based on age, ethnicity, religion, low socio-economic status, or their status as carers. There is further cross-linkage to the work of BRAIN.HE, and additional initiatives are interconnected in a matrix of inclusion, opportunity and wider access promotion. For example, the AchieveAbility project – a successor to the UK Government's 'Aimhigher' national project – aims to improve access and continuation rates in higher education for students with specific learning difficulties and aims to 'raise awareness of opportunities and support' and boasts ministerial endorsement from Bill Rammell, Minister for Higher Education and Lifelong Learning who was a keynote speaker at its 2006 conference. Intersecting with these initiatives are commitments on the part of the UK's Higher Education Academy to embed disability awareness and practice in the professional standards framework. The UK's national coordination team on widening participation, Action on Access, also signals its responsibility for working to promote inclusive approaches to disability within higher education in the context of its work within widening participation partnerships and institutions.

Therefore there appears to be a formidable array of support from bodies benefiting from statutory endorsement. The UK press regularly highlights stories of students with disabilities and educational institutions responding successfully to challenges, from the elite such as Cambridge (Buxton, 2005) to post-1992 institutions (*The Sunday Times*, 2006).

This is a position with which, on the face of it, it is difficult to disagree. Clearly the inclusion of students who are determined, talented, but held back by disadvantage or disability is a vision which all liberal minded people should applaud. This seductive prospect, complete with its focused, determined initiatives and proud success stories prompts us to reflect upon just how it is that universities are changing, but also on how the notion of disability is being remodelled to interface more effectively with the institutional and legislative surfaces of education.

Within the discourse of inclusion and disability, the students' disabilities are treated in a somewhat homogenous fashion. Characteristics such as dyslexia and dyscalculia are treated in ways which are curiously reminiscent of mobility impairments or blindness. Moreover, the many initiatives that have been commenced to tackle these kinds of access issues are apt to treat disability as something that can be normalized through the inclusion of disabled students and through adjustment on the part of the institutions and their staff. In that sense then, they draw upon what has been called the social model of disability, where a person's impairment becomes a disability as a result of discriminatory practices and disabling environments. At the same time, these notions of disability are strangely complacent about the nature of the impairments and leave the basis of these largely unchallenged. It is as if the dyslexia, dyscalculia or other more esoteric syndromes are irretrievably hard-wired. While sufferers from head injuries or

strokes may regain their lost faculties, the dyslexic will forever labour with
the vicissitudes of his or her condition. As Meekosha (1998: 175) says, the
kind of social model of disability in these projects leaves 'the impaired body
as untouched, unchallenged: a taken-for-granted fixed corporeality'. After
all, the UK's premier website concerning these issues is called 'BRAIN.HE'
and the talk is of 'neurodiversity'. This seems to imply a grounding in
an irrevocable neurological condition. Yet as a number of authors have
argued, this is not the only way to see disabilities (Edwards and Imrie,
2003). Elizabeth Grosz (1994: 19) suggests that the body should be seen as
a 'site of contestation' or reactive to social processes. She argues for a
rethinking of the relationship between the biological and societal by suggesting that 'the openness of organic processes to cultural intervention,
transformation or even production, must be explored' (Grosz, 1994: 23).
Edwards and Imrie see disability as a form of practice, in the sense of
the term used by Bourdieu (1990), which revolves around the habitus, or the
ways in which the body develops habitual ways of relating to broader socio-
political environments and relations. For Bourdieu (1990: 23), 'the habitus,
as society written into the body, into the biological individual' bridges
the biological and social aspects of being human. In this view, the biological
differences between people are not some sort of scientifically verifiable pre-
cursor to their social being, but are instead themselves produced through
practice and collective work. Bordo (1993: 165) notes that the body 'is a
powerful symbolic form, a surface on which the central rules, hierarchies,
and even metaphysical commitments of a culture are inscribed and thus
reinforced through the concrete language of the body'.

   The construction of common categories across the sector including people
from disadvantaged backgrounds, those with physical disabilities and those
with specific learning difficulties is intimately related to the kinds of legislation, policy and widening access interventions to which they are subject.
As Stone (1984: 90) says, disability originated in the eyes of the state as an
'administrative category out of a collection of separate conditions understood to be legitimate reasons for not working'. Thus, in the world of work,
disabled people are a kind of 'other' which defines who, and what, a normal
worker is. The same could be said of students with disabilities, inasmuch as a
variety of disparate needs have been administratively grouped together
against an implied norm of bodily and mental integrity. While life with
aids, benefits and academic concessions may well be easier for these students, it also implies that they cannot add to their own value in the way
that other students can, except with these sorts of subsidies. This is the kind
of practice which Oliver (1990: 12) describes as the 'de-valuation of the

disabled body' which isolates disabled people, and brings their corporeal differences to the fore.

As Bourdieu (1990: 69) argues, 'symbolic power works partly through the control of other people's bodies' and the judgements of policymakers, disability specialists and widening-access professionals affect 'the recognition we have of our own body practices, and the body practices of others as "right" and proper, or in need of control and correction' (Shilling, 1993: 145).

The welfarist movement in higher education then is actively involved in the making of a certain kind of disabled student, whose very existence as an enfranchised member of the educational community depends on their needs being relentlessly assessed, their participation subject to manifold bureaucratically sanctioned concessions and their consumption of technological aids. All these might make their passage through the degree course easier, yet at the same time these practices define them through their disability and consolidate its hold upon their identity. In a sense then, the student who enters with difficulties reading, writing or adding up will not necessarily leave the institution as an educationally competent graduate with their disabilities remedied. Rather, they are just as likely to have had their alignment with the educational system reconfigured as that of the 'student with a disability' replete with 'special needs'. The institutional adaptations to these needs, ironically, force these 'disabilities' deeper into the putative core of their being. Universities, in this sense, are shaping their students' futures.

'Mickey mouse' degrees: vocationalism in the service economy

As we saw in Chapter 3, there has been a good deal of discussion in the UK concerning 'Mickey Mouse degrees'. Such a term is nearly always applied to subjects relatively new to academic study. Frequent suspects have been surf science, popular music and golf management studies. Media studies has also often been a target for such derision and was specifically mentioned by Maragaret Hodge when she was Higher Education Minister (Nordling, 2005). Courses derided as 'Mickey Mouse' are proliferating and there have been allegations that universities are turning hobbies into subjects for study in higher education (Harris and Clark, 2004). A brief UCAS course search of less traditional subjects for 2006 entry revealed, for example, 64 courses on complementary medicine, including reflexology and Chinese medicine, as well as more mainstream counselling courses. Virtually all these courses were offered in post-1992 universities. Coventry, Leeds Metropolitan and Wolverhampton Universities offer courses on lifestyle management, leading to honours degrees. The University of Derby offers 16 courses involving healing arts that can be taken alongside other subjects, but interestingly these are not biomedical subjects. Guilford College of FE and HE offers two courses in garden design. Sixteen institutions offer courses in golf management studies, including the University of Birmingham, a Russell Group institution.

There are paradoxes when such accusations have been made. Some 'Mickey Mouse' subjects are highly vocational, such as golf management studies (Arnot, 2004) or have a relatively high rate of graduate employment, such as media studies (Curtis, 2005). Journalism has faced 'Mickey Mouse' allegations, but is heavily oversubscribed, so has high entrance requirements. The defenders of Mickey Mouse subjects employ three dominant lines of argument – these subjects are a reflection of what students want and/or the new careers market (Matheson, 2004); they are a result of widened participation and universities having to take less academic students (Blair, 2004; Blair *et al.*, 2004) or, they are cynically constructed by universities who want bums on seats and know that 'journalism' in a course title will tempt applicants (Cole, 2005). Universities are clearly defensive about Mickey Mouse courses – interviews in the media often involve academics teaching on such courses stressing how much hard science is involved. The University of Birmingham includes materials science in its golf management course and pointed out in a press interview that the materials and metallurgy department has a 5-star research rating (Arnot, 2004). The University of Plymouth's surf science and technology degree course includes oceanography, the advanced composites used in the manufacture of surfboards and marine meteorology (Gordon, 2004). The content of courses with the same title can vary considerably. Lifestyle management at Leeds Metropolitan has an emphasis on the skills and knowledge needed to assist 'corporate clients' and 'busy professionals' to 'co-ordinate their life outside work', for example, 'organising events and parties, arranging property relocation, co-ordinating travel and holiday plans and providing concierge services' (prospectus.leedsmet.ac.uk/main/detail.htm?&p=32&course.id=3091&attendance=1). However, the lifestyle management course at Coventry University (promoted in the University online information as a 'star course') has an emphasis on health and wellbeing disciplines, such as psychological and behavioural factors and communication skills. Research skills are also emphasised and science and laboratories are mentioned (www.coventry.ac.uk/courses/undergraduate-full-time-a-z/a/450).

The use of the term 'Mickey Mouse' for a university course (or institution), although used loosely by anyone intending to be disparaging, is interesting in the light of scholars who have written about 'Disneyfication' or 'Disneyization' (Schickel, 1986; Warren, 1994; Bryman, 1999) of society or aspects of it. There is a body of literature highly critical of the style of, and values and messages imparted by, Walt Disney films (Sayers, 1965; Schickel, 1986) and more recent work has critically explored the whole of the burgeoning Disney Corporation (Wright, 2006). Holbrook (2001) wrote about the role played by the Disney Corporation in the commercialism of popular culture. Bryman (1999) proposed that a process of Disneyization is taking place in society. Bryman defines Disneyization as 'the process by which the principles of the Disney theme parks are coming to dominate more and more sectors of American society as well as the rest of the world' (Bryman, 1999: 26). Hebdige (2003) also gives an account of what he terms the Disneyfication of many aspects of society. Giroux (1995) described the Disneyfication of children's culture and saw it as a means by which patterns of authority were established and reproduced, in a way far more effective than anything children experienced at school. There are important parallels with post-compulsory education. The quest for authority over an increasingly diverse student population and a quest for measurable and auditable standards of quality has led, we would suggest, to a similar process in higher education. The Disneyization of post-compulsory education has proceeded apace, but perhaps not quite in the way in which those who label courses and institutions as 'Mickey Mouse' believe. The process of growth, cultivation and shaping in education has resulted, like Disney's work on many traditional stories, in a curious denaturing of the academic content and an authoritarian focus on the processes of learning and engagement of students.

The extent to which the path taken by the Disney entertainment enterprise has been followed by the education system deserves further exploration. If we use Holbrook's (2001: 141) idea of Mickey Mouse, 'think opiate of the people, bread and circuses, ticket to oblivion, underbelly of marketing theory', there are many concepts which can be fruitfully applied to understand the progression of post-compulsory education towards these market imperatives. Holbrook speaks of the pervasive breakdown in the cultural hierarchy – the effacement of boundaries between art and entertainment, the blurring of distinctions between high culture and popular culture, the widely observed promiscuous cross-fertilization in which highbrow art has climbed into bed with lowbrow pursuits, the division between class and mass breaking down, the boundary between elite and vulgar breaking down and the refined world of serious culture embracing the dirty detritus of everyday life. Holbrook states that the 'trashing of taste' reigns triumphant (2001: 156). He has elucidated what he calls the 'Ricky principle' – the 'fun-dumb-mental' law of cultural behaviour that holds

that any aspect of culture ... that once began as something authentic –
something guided by artistic integrity, something informed by a true
creative gift, something aspiring to shared standards of excellence – will
under relentless pressure toward commercialisation, inevitably devolve
in the direction of a dumbed down, cheapened, easily accessible, vul-
garised, formulaic, commodified version ... (Holbrook, 2001: 156)

Theme park consumers – students in the Disneyfied university

This tendency towards reconfiguring the educational enterprise along
Disney lines can be seen with progressively greater clarity in further and
higher education. As students are now consumers (Johnson and Deem,
2003; Modell, 2005), education has increasingly become entertainment
and is frequently marketed as such (Addis, 2005). Popular culture has
infused higher education curricula, and many courses demonstrate a combination of highbrow and lowbrow – the much derided courses in surfing
technology and golf management spring to mind – where 'soft' areas of
study are complemented with 'hard' science. This makes courses that are
geared towards labour markets in a leisure economy, but it also sugar-coats
the pill of what Bertrand Russell called 'sterner studies'. Nevertheless, the
UK's body for higher education institutions, Universities UK (2006) gave
a warm endorsement of these new hybrid courses and points out that as
the sports industry is a major player in the UK economy to the tune of
£9.8 billion annually, so degrees in sports-related subjects may not be so
frivolous. The justification, of course, is that it is of economic benefit, which
in this logic trumps more archaic questions of value and meaning. Indeed,
policymakers are currently hopeful that there will soon be a whole new generation of these highly specific, vocationally oriented degrees, in some cases
awarded by further education colleges (Meikle, 2006).

In part this reflects the ethos of widening participation. The teenagers
who are presently disaffected by education may be tempted by a new generation of vocational diplomas (Henry, 2006). Much of the debate surrounding the 'quality' of today's universities and their students is underlaid
by the fear that the universities are indeed embracing the dirty detritus of
everyday life, or perhaps even everyday people – indeed the 'unwashed'
(Tysome, 2002). To those schooled in the ways of the elite universities in
previous generations, the 'trashing of taste' must seem evident. No matter
what one's views regarding recent further and higher education policy,
it is clear that as it has become more accessible, the post-compulsory
education system has also become more commercialized and commodified

(Parker, 2003). Moreover, as we have noted, the ethics of the liberalized marketplace are making significant inroads into the educational sphere with the foregrounding of corporate entertainment values at its core (Saltman, 2002).

The motifs of entertainment have for a long time been part of educational experiences. Humour, engaging anecdotes and spectacle, have been at the heart of memorable and inspiring pedagogy since the days of classical civilizations. Yet there is something new here that deserves our attention. The new vocationalism of degrees oriented to leisure and consumption – the surf science, cosmetic science and golf management programmes – belies a step-change in the ethos of post-compulsory education. The 'Mickey Mouse' slurs cannot be easily dismissed by pointing to the economic significance of the leisure industry. The fusion of leisure, entertainment and neoliberal corporate ideologies, and their progressive capture of the educational agenda is not just accidental. It also has profound implications for what the education system will be doing to its members – the students and teachers – in the foreseeable future.

Fortunately, this fusion of corporate neoliberal ideas and educational practice has already been subject to a great deal of scrutiny on behalf of this group of scholars who have delved deeply into the meanings of Mickey Mouse and the corporations which have made him one of the most recognizable and enduring icons of the twentieth century. As we shall see, the analysis of Disney products, services and organizational cultures has a great deal to offer the observer of education. The recent turbulence about Mickey Mouse courses and their likely effects conceals a much more substantial process of Disneyfication or Disneyization of public life and education in particular.

Henri Giroux (1999) has been at the forefront of discussions of Disney's pedagogical influence. Again the analysis can be applied to the changes in the present day higher education system in many Western countries. Giroux quotes a Disney 'imagineer': 'we carefully program out all the negative, unwanted elements and program in positive elements' (Giroux, 1999: 150). This recollects the many higher education courses where the 'difficult' bits have had to be removed, as some of the students are no longer able to cope, or are unwilling to engage with them. A colleague who has taught statistics and research methods over a period of ten years told us of how his folder of notes for his first-year course had grown thinner every year, like Orwell's Newspeak Dictionary, as more problematic concepts and techniques were progressively eliminated. Fun elements have been introduced into syllabi, and marks moderated upwards with consequent allegations of 'deplorable dumbing down' (Baty, 2005).

The elimination of more challenging and difficult academic content, or its containment lest it impact negatively on the 'student experience', is not the whole of Disneyfication however. The education involved in a Disneyfied syllabus is conceptually distinct too. Giroux describes Disney's planned school in its proposed community, 'Celebration', as a carefully orchestrated plan to indoctrinate students into company-approved corporate group-think, emphasizing the acquisition of skills over critical, ethical thinking. Giroux believes that this sort of education produces students and workers trained to adapt to the world rather than shape it (Giroux, 1999: 72). Giroux notes that 'in the name of "edutainment" ... Disney educates and entertains in order to create corporate identities and to define citizens primarily as consumers and spectators' (1999: 43–4). In the Disneyfied higher education curriculum, 'learners', as they are now styled, are prepared for lives in the leisure economy.

Disneyfication in education and the proletarianization of leisure

Once upon a time, when Thorstein Veblen wrote *The Theory of the Leisure Class*, people who engaged in leisure tended to belong to elite groups and leisure was allied to other symbolic insignia of wealth such as conspicuous consumption (Veblen, 1899). On the other hand, the late twentieth century and twenty-first century have seen the proletarianization of leisure. Those in work in the traditionally professionalized roles work longer and harder and after their longer commuting time has eaten into the hours available for leisure, more of their evenings and weekends are spent in work-related activity. Those who are marginally employed in casualized positions or who are not in work have greater leisure time in which to consume. In this context, education itself is a kind of leisure or entertainment product to be consumed by those who have no pressing business elsewhere. Those who have been 'let go' from previous employments, those who have grown up in workless states or wander through post-industrial landscapes are assiduously urged to add value to themselves through entering or re-entering the education system. We have already argued that education is an important aspect of social policy and of New Labour's welfare agenda. Once we grasp the implications of the Disneyization thesis however, other aspects fall into place more readily.

Giroux believes that one of Disney's prime functions is to indoctrinate, and its agenda involves promoting 'a corporate culture that subordinates political, public and historical discourse and culture to the pleasures of consumption, escapist entertainment and corporate profits'

(Giroux, 1999: 79). Holbrook (2001) maintains that Disneyspeak educates children hegemonically into unthinking obeisance towards what he calls WIMP culture – Western-white, Individualistic-imperialistic, Materialistic-militaristic, Paternalistic-protestant-ethic and profit orientated. Even 'diversity issues', dissent and challenge can be assimilated to this agenda. Welcoming gestures towards other cultures, inclusion of variant perspectives and appreciations of neurodiversity are readily incorporated to the model. The diversity, as Heath and Potter (2004) remind us, is all part of a competition for distinction. Rebellion and dissent have been driving consumer culture for the past two generations. In a postmodern age where the death of the author has been advertised, the question of who one is and what demographic diversity boxes one ticks has never been more important. Yet the diversity achieved is curiously neutered.

Warren's early writings on Disneyfication (Warren, 1994) identified features such as a social order controlled by an all-powerful organization; a breach between production and consumption achieved 'through the visual removal of all hint of production and the blanketing of consumption with layers of fantasy so that residents are blinkered from seeing the actual labour processes that condition and define their lives' (1994: 92). Only the resident's capacity to consume is viewed as significant or important. The 'blinkering' of the labour process is evident in post-compulsory education – students are often shielded from scholarship, as some courses are almost wholly reliant on handouts, ready-made notes and bitesized chunks of salient information that will fit on a Powerpoint presentation (whose pages are nostalgically called 'slides') or which can be downloaded as a podcast. Academic stars who are valuable in terms of their likely contribution to success in the Research Assessment Exercise or its metrics-based successors are often carefully protected from student contact. Furedi (2004) has documented that it is now sometimes possible to complete a degree course without ever having read a book.

The retreat from demanding tasks has been formally sanctioned by widening-access specialists. Bamber and Tett (2001: 8–16) maintained that students had difficulties with tasks such as essay writing, library work and using academic language – the traditions and requirements of good scholarship. Yet the thrust of their paper was not to question why students had such problems with these skills, or how such techniques could be taught to those who found them difficult – it was that this sort of activity should be avoided. Indeed, these are things which place a drain on the resources of the institution and are said in the words of an internal policy document at one of our institutions to 'impact negatively on the student experience'.

While the complex or challenging aspects of knowledge may be receding from higher education's pedagogioc agenda, there are other tendencies which have gained a place at high table. If we talk about the significance of an individual's capacity to consume, a huge change has been documented in academia in recent years. The notion that students are indeed 'customers' or 'consumers' is supported at high levels within funding organizations. Sir Howard Newby, the then head of the Higher Education Funding Council for England is reported to have said that 'Students are consumers in other spheres of their life, which universities are going to have to match', and that 'there is a need for universities and colleges to be much more client-facing and focused' (Lipsett, 2005). There is encouragement from other quarters too. Universities should be more like supermarkets and offer students satisfaction or their money back, according to Sir Geoffrey Holland, former vice-chancellor of the University of Exeter (*Times Higher Education Supplement*, 2003). There is increasing evidence that in the global higher education marketplace, more students now see themselves as consumers buying a degree. Newson (2004) describes situations such as that of a professor of English at a Virginia liberal arts college who recounts how he and his colleagues are delivering 'lite entertainment' to bored students, rather than developing their critical capacities, cultural literacy or love of learning. He describes how his own teaching practice has been disciplined by the consumerist demands of his students to deliver an easily accessible and serene learning experience.

Once they have paid their fees and entered into serious debt, a degree is expected, irrespective of the quality of their work. This also erodes the status of academics. We were undergraduates on maintenance grants 20 years ago and can clearly remember lecturers whose halting, outdated and soporific teaching discredited the university, and who had an appalling attitude to the undergraduates. Both of us were among groups of students who tried to complain about very bad academics and who were told firmly by senior staff that we were only undergraduates and that these people were lecturers. Thus nothing would be done. We would never defend a situation in which students were unable to raise a grievance or in which a grievance was simply immediately dismissed. Yet the kinds of complaints now being made have changed. A colleague teaching statistics was faced with the problems of providing a test as part of the assessment for his module. As this took place in the middle of a semester there were no examination rooms available. To ensure that the results reflected the students' own work, he therefore produced several different versions of the test, whose questions broadly addressed the same principles but whose arithmetic used different numbers. These were mixed up so that adjacent students would not be likely to have the same questions. Upon discovering that their neighbours' questions were different, some students were aggrieved and mounted a complaint against him.

In similar vein, Newson (2004: 232) describes the example of a black woman teaching in a North American University who was judged by her students to be incompetent and not a serious scholar when she challenged the notion of a 'right' answer and exhorted them, in best critical pedagogic fashion, to question the established canons of knowledge. As Newson adds, it is ironic that critical teachers, who were among the first to advocate that the learner should be at the centre of pedagogic strategies, now find themselves confronted by students who demand, as consumers, that they are provided with the 'right' knowledge to secure future employment. Certainly, this demand for epistemological security and certainty seems more palatable than theoretical perspectives and critical skills to enable them to critique the prevailing social order.

Once students have been established as consumers and once the epistemological flattening of knowledge has occurred, the stage is set for further incursions of business culture. The 'dumbing down' of the public sphere, the arrival of 'post-intellectual' (Wood, 1996) and post-literate culture among which students and other browsers can pick-and-mix may appear democratic. Yet it is a form of knowledge which yields remarkably few opportunities to critically evaluate social and cultural trends, and which is amenable to further reshaping in the light of changes in corporate ethos.

In describing the broader implications of this process, Hebdige (2003) characterizes Disney's activities as a kind of retooling of knowledge, art and culture. In a relatively small way, Disney set the scene for changes in the present-day higher education system. At the start of the new millennium the Disney Magic Kingdom included two 'edutainment' universities, one affiliated with Disneyland, one with Disney World. Hebdige maintains that Disney involves a 'mania for nothing less than absolute control' (2003: 151) and observes that the consumers of Disney storylines are positioned 'as innocent by-standers at the carnival of signs rather than as knowledgeable customers' (2003: 153). Similarly, one could say that the present day customers of post-compulsory education are being positioned as consumers or spectators in the learning process, where the knowledge is dispensed to them in pre-digested chunks where they do not have the experience of having to wrest it from primary source materials or indeed from nature itself. The problematic, difficult messy bits of disciplines have begun to be left out of some of today's pre-packaged, bitesized, easy to follow, sanitized higher education courses. Hebdige remembers that Baudrillard (1983) identified Disneyland as 'the elephant's graveyard of the real – the place where all the big old mythologies of the West: history, politics, transcendence, etc., come lumbering in to die' (Hebdige, 2003: 155). Perhaps the same could be said of universities, where as well as manufacturing truth, they are inventing also its simulacra, in Powerpoint or podcast form. In our own institutions, the simulacra have an ascendant power which scruffy reality is powerless to match; the artists' impressions of new buildings yet to be constructed that appear on stands at open days, the characters resembling Lego people that appear in TV advertisements for the institution, and the endless play of virtualization in quality reports, newspaper league tables and student survey results. The battles are increasingly played out with these simulacra, rather than flesh and blood people with phenomenally authentic experiences.

Hebdige coins the neologism 'dis-gnosis', meaning the opposite of knowledge, or positively lacking in knowledge. He uses this term to refer to

> culturally valorized mentalities and institutional modes of sanction that bestow a positive value on and reserve practical and professional benefits for a disposition towards awkward knowledge that resists its acquisition, that suppresses its articulation, that does not just idealize child-like states and the myriad associated simulacra that support ad infinitum the intricate machinery of no-and-never-knowing but which actively reward states of arrested development, denial, disavowal and unacknowledgement. (Hebdige, 2003: 151)

Wright (2006) drew on Elias's theory of the civilizing process to show how Walt Disney World theme parks construct social control over visitors, yet still allows the assumption that they are free, choice-making, experience-seeking individuals. The guests are presented to themselves as responsible and self-regulating persons, allowing Walt Disney World to maintain civilized non-coercive discourse. Wright argues that Walt Disney World do this by symbolic representations of civilized and uncivilized nature, the visitors to the parks being invited to identify themselves with the former and thus conform to civil norms.

This Disney experience has curious parallels with the higher education environment that students find themselves in. The promise of a personalized learning experience turns out instead to be a mass experience. There is a view of learners who are important as consumers, whose feedback is sought at every turn and whose responses to the national student survey are apt to get university managers and academic staff desperately formulating plans to increase the ratings. Yet at the same time the experience that they get at university treats them in a curiously infantilized way. Their attendance at classes is monitored, sometimes with systems akin to electronic tagging. Their creativity in responding to challenges presented by assignments and assessments is trammelled by means of elaborate guidance as to how to write essays, practical reports or examination answers. The finished products they produce are often guided by supporting materials which advise them what to put in each paragraph. In the same way, theme parks and entertainments are dependent on consumers, but also guide them, surround them with regulations and direct their attention to the features which they should attend to. Their work output is micromanaged to the extent that the programme of assignments across the year is planned in advance, the ways in which they are allowed to contact and address members of staff are laid down for them, and the learning experiences are split up into digestible chunks that will not over-tax them. This could be seen as a kind of 'Taylorization' of learning or proletarianization of pedagogy where the tasks have been minutely subdivided.

As with theme parks, where the employees in animal costumes not only entertain but help organize and direct the visitors, the customers in the new higher education theme park are rendered docile but at the same time given the message that their preferences are sovereign. In this sense, then, the theme park analogy is apt. In Henry Giroux's work, this process of Disneyfication is seen to start early and has already gained hegemony in the school system and in the media experiences of childhood. In what Giroux (1995) calls the the Disneyfication of children's culture, he claims that the identities of children and youth are shaped politically and pedagogically in the visual culture of videogames, television, film, shopping malls and amusement parks. This popular culture forms the basis for forms of learning for children. Giroux argues that what Disney films do is to exceed the boundaries of entertainment itself. Instead they are 'teaching machines' which inspire as much cultural authority and legitimacy for teaching roles, values and ideals as schools, religious sites and families do. Disney combines the ideology of enchantment and an aura of innocence in narrating stories, helping children understand who they are and what society is about. Giroux maintains that the postmodern media-scape usurps traditional sites of learning and prioritizes the pleasure of image over the intellectual demands of critical inquiry and also reduces the demands of human agency to the ethos of facile consumerism. Cartoon characters become prototypes for marketing and merchandising blitz.

In Giroux's view, Disney is a cultural institution that protects its status as a purveyor of American innocence and moral virtue, defining itself as a vehicle for education and civic responsibility, sponsoring 'Teacher of the Year' awards, providing scholarships and educational programmes.

Disney's reach into everyday life means that the boundaries between education, entertainment and commercialization collapse and it educates children in virtues of active consumerism, presenting itself as pleasure although people have to buy that pleasure. To expand on the previous quote from the Disney 'imagineer':

> what we create in post-compulsory education is a sort of Disney realism, a kind of utopia, where there are such things as right answers, there is a correct way to address work assignments and virtue can be gained through answering neat lists of questions. As staff, we carefully program out all the negative, unwanted elements and program in the positive elements. (Giroux, 1999: 150)

Thus, like Giroux's account of Disney, we produce a sanitized, edited, nostalgic view of knowledge, of the kind that students, their parents and commercial organizations can live with. It is a process of what Hebdige (2003) calls 'disenstrangement', where knowledge and nature are rendered tidy, familiar and the notion of risk has been subtracted from knowledge.

Giroux thus argues convincingly that Disneyization is shaping the people who will enter our universities. Although he demands that this process is contested and analysed and that young people are provided with the skills to understand what is happening, at present they are not. Instead, the higher education system is having to undergo a process of Disneyization itself to meet their needs and demands.

From theme park experience to service economy careers

Giroux predicts that in a few years, the only choice for the majority of graduates will be a steady job at a mall outlet or food chain. There is evidence from the UK (Taylor, 2005) that the majority of graduates do not now work in what were considered 'graduate jobs' 20 years ago.

In line with the theses propounded by Giddens and Beck (Beck *et al.*, 1995), young adults in developed nations presently live in a world where there are comparatively few certainties. Detraditionalization, a disembedding process that strips away cultural roles and occupational memories, is contributing to a sense of instability and transitoriness among 18- to 25-year-olds. Sometimes it seems that they live in a world with few steadfast psychological, economic or intellectual markers. The modernist world of certainty and order has given way to a postmodern culture with hybridized forms of cultural performance and identity, combined with a reduction in recognizable political agency (Kluzig *et al.*, 2005).

From this vantage point, scholars such as Kluzig *et al.* (2005) have pointed to the way in which identities merge and shift rather than become uniform and static. Youth inhabits shifting cultural and social spheres marked by plurality of languages and cultures. Communities are disbanded and reconfigured as time and space mutate into multiple and overlapping cyberspace networks. New electronic technologies have altered the pedagogical context for the production of subjectivity, but also how people 'take in information and entertainment'. This blurring of identity is not univocal however. At the same time as identity slips from our grasp it is insistently thrust upon us. As the cliché has it, we are what we consume. Yet we are also often hard at work developing ourselves, investing in ourselves and training ourselves, as if our identity were something which we could pull up by its bootstraps (Miller, 1993; Dunn, 1998). Indeed, this idea of investing in oneself through education in the hope of promised gains in 'employability' is at the very heart of widening-access ideology. Gaining respect and value through a stable and diligently pursued occupational identity is more difficult than ever to achieve, yet employability is the touchstone of the new ethos in higher education.

Giroux (2001) observes: 'Corporate advertisers are attempting to theorise a pedagogy of consumption as part of a new way of appropriating postmodern differences among youth in different sites and locations.' The period of relative poverty while being a student offers no respite from being targeted by advertisers. The websites of Student Unions offer advertising space to businesspeople seeking to communicate to students where space in diaries, magazines, websites and direct-to-consumer SMS text messaging are all made available. When students arrive at institutions in late September or early October the paths are awash with discarded leaflets and promotional flyers advertising bars, nightclubs and musical events and the drinks which will be available at these venues. As the Bishop of Aimens was alleged to observe in the 1600s and conservative writer Thomas Sowell has latterly repeated, the poor are a goldmine.

Giroux (2001) describes what he calls the 'assault by corporate America on public education' and an aim for education to be a 'global business'. In the UK a similar range of opportunities for business can be seen opening up in the higher education system. The assault by corporate business on the UK higher education system can be seen by the change in Student Union activities. Not so long ago, Student Unions were renowned as sites where embryonic political activity (no matter how inept or extreme) took place. A generation ago, Student Unions regularly declared solidarity with Sinn Fein and during the 1980s it seemed that most Student Unions had part of the building named after Nelson Mandela. Student Unions are now principally concerned with a very commercial type of entertainment, frequently manifested by business deals with big corporations that supply the Student Unions with, for example, cut-price alcohol. In 2005, the Student Union at University of Wales, Bangor was sufficiently delighted to have struck up an affiliation with McDonald's that it announced it on the university's intranet. Businesses are making inroads into education as never before. Student centres are the home to a variety of franchised businesses from coffee shops to estate agents. Educational and laboratory supplies, teaching materials, teaching services, and as we have seen, students' work itself are all providing opportunity for entrepreneurs and investors. The culture of student social life too is engineered. 'Lads mags' and media enterprises with titles like 'Totty TV' make commercially lucrative inroads into student social life, and Student Union presidents vigorously deny that these are in any way exploitative of women (Tysome, 2006).

But the alignment between educational and business cultures goes deeper still. Chairs, buildings and other facilities are being endowed by rich corporate benefactors, and a brand-name mentality has begun to emerge in higher education. The UK's vice-chancellors are increasingly relishing the title 'CEO' and fund-raising is considered more important than intellect in considering candidates for professorial positions. There have been suggestions that professors should be renamed 'academic entrepreneurs'.

The alignment between UK higher education and the kinds of management strategy adopted by large corporations has been pre-figured in Giroux's writings on what has been taking place in the American education system since the mid-1990s. Giroux (1994) argued that the system in America deskilled teachers and reduced them to depoliticized clerks. In the UK, similar changes can be seen in the staffing of higher education institutions. There is a good deal of concern that university staff are losing power, autonomy and status. While they and their offerings are audited for quality – as if a degree were something that could be delivered as a standardized product – there are no comparable audits to ensure that academic freedom is protected (Alderman, 2006).

This process of proletarianization of university staff, where they are no longer professionalized (Wilson, 1991; Dearlove, 1997), has proceeded apace since it was first noticed over a decade ago. Through 2006 the UK's higher education establishments were involved in a dispute over pay, where many academic staff were campaigning for a programme of increases. Consistent with the proletarianization thesis, in the language used in the debate and related news coverage vice-chancellors were referred to as 'the employers' and lecturers were the 'employees' – ultimately very powerless ones at that. Demonstrations and pickets were organized, if anything adding to the sense that the academics were impotent – powerful people do not need to demonstrate with placards. Along with the loss of power, autonomy and status of academics, demographic changes are occurring within their population that are common to present day professions undergoing such a loss of prestige, particularly in the post-1992 sector. With the decline in wages relative to other occupations which were once comparable and the casualization of the academic labour force (45 per cent of UK academic staff are believed to be on fixed-term or hourly-paid contracts), academia is a less attractive occupation for those seeking security (Baty, 2006).

At the lower points on the pay scale for higher education academics, the number of women is fast approaching the number of men. There is thus a feminization of the relatively low paid end of the pay framework (Sanders, 2005). Among the higher paid grades of staff, the proportion of men is much higher. There are growing numbers of women and people from less advantaged socio-economic backgrounds. As with careers in medicine, accountancy and the law, increasing numbers of middle-class men who might previously have been enthusiastic applicants are seeking fortunes elsewhere. Indeed, lower pay and short-term contracts in the early career period mean that middle-class men have increasingly decided that careers in universities are no longer desirable employment. A university senior manager summed up for us the future for academia when he observed that 'people with firsts don't do PhDs any more. When school teachers are paid more than academics people are not going to become academics.' In some institutions, considerable numbers of people without doctorates have been appointed to senior posts and the best salaries and even the most handsomely appointed offices are often reserved for non-academic managers, while academic staff are packed three or four to a room.

Conclusion: towards a heretical pedagogy

This then is the picture of growing, shaping and learning which we can see expanding apace in the post-compulsory education system. The recasting of education as a kind of social welfare for the student body and the reframing of education as a sort of theme park entertainment where staff are clerks and students are consumers has wrought profound changes upon the educational ideas and practices that can be seen going on in universities. A few decades ago Richard Hoggart and Raymond Williams, in a way which now seems quaint, introduced a sense of how teaching, learning, textual studies and knowledge were political issues, and which could enable us to foreground and unpick considerations of power and social agency. Williams showed a desire to make learning part of the process of social change itself, such that pedagogy becomes an act of cultural production. In the right hands, teaching can show us how knowledge and social identities are produced in different sites. Reading, watching television, surfing the internet or visiting a theme park are all ways of being and which encourage specific feelings, attitudes and ways of interacting with the world. The point is to give people an awareness of how this happens, and how they are made up by the organizational and political contexts within which they consume. Williams's notion of permanent education suggests that pedagogy could provide the discourse for understanding how power and knowledge mutually inform each other in the production, reception and transformation of social identities, forms of ethical address and 'desired versions of a future human community' (1989: 12). Giroux argues that before too long, education will not enable pupils for social mobility and that rethinking is needed – we need to re-examine the mission of schools and the changing conditions of youth.

In the view of cultural theorists like Williams and Hoggart, intellectual work is incomplete unless it assumes responsibility for effects in larger public culture while addressing the profound and inhumane problems of the societies that we live in. Williams's formulation of what education should be about is instructive:

> I wish, first, that we should recognize that education is ordinary: that it is, before everything else, the process of giving to the ordinary members of society its full common meanings, and the skills that will enable them to amend these meanings, in the light of their personal and common experience. If we start from that, we can get rid of the remaining restrictions, and make the necessary changes. (Williams, 1989: 14)

Thus, from the point of view of cultural studies, which Williams and Hoggart are credited with founding, questions as to how knowledge is produced in universities and how it is consequential in extending and deepening the possibilities for democratic public life are raised. In this ideal, education should be founded in the ordinary. But that is not merely to reproduce the banal and commonplace, or to reify the dis-gnosis of those who do not want to know. Political education, central to critical pedagogy, means decentring power from pedagogical sites so that the dynamics of institutional and cultural inequalities that marginalize certain groups and privilege others can be addressed. Politicizing education is a form of pedagogical terrorism. At its best it can enable students and teachers to transcend the constraints of the clinic or the theme park and begin to unpick the processes and forces which have given shape to their experience and to their education itself. It is this that will enable them to gain a genuinely critical understanding of what they are embarked upon and give them the tools to, as Williams put it, 'amend meaning'. The other insight was given by Richard Hoggart in interview in the late-1990s, where he was still, after 40 years, very much caught up in debates about social change, what it meant for education, and what is at stake more generally:

> what I'm going around arguing, until people start saying 'Oh he's at it again', is this: if you train people only to the level which is required by all these [government] initiatives, all you do is produce a society which is capable of being *conned*. People are not encouraged to be critical, they're not given a *critical literacy*. They're given a literacy which is just enough to fill in the football pools and the lottery coupon and read the *Sun* and so on, and that's not good enough in a democracy – in a commercial democracy above all ... People look a bit awry, as though you're expecting too much of most people, which you're not. (quoted in Gibson and Hartley, 1998: 13)

What is fast disappearing from the post-compulsory education system is a way of retaining this critical awareness. Students are allegedly equipped with skills but, as Hoggart, Giroux and others fear, maybe they are being equipped for little more than subaltern roles in the service economy. We need instead to think of new ways to engage students and transcend the limitations under which they are presently labouring. If we embrace and explore the processes of welfarization and Disneyfication rather than simply reproducing them, we can achieve a critical pedagogy which engages with culture as part of the movement towards a shared conception of justice and radicalization of social order through a genuinely heretical pedagogy.

References

Addis, M. (2005), 'New technologies and cultural consumption – edutainment is born!', *European Journal of Marketing*, 39(7/8), 729–36.

Alderman, G. (2006), 'Too timid to make a stand for freedom', *The Times Higher Education Supplement*, November 17 2006.

Arnot, C. (2004), 'Par for the course', *Guardian*, May 25 2004.

Bamber, J. and Tett, L. (2001), 'Ensuring integrative learning experiences for non-traditional students in higher education', *Widening Participation and Lifelong Learning*, 3(1), 8–16.

Baty, P. (2005), 'Inquiry into "deplorable dumbing down" move', *The Times Higher Educational Supplement*, June 3 2005.

Baty, P. (2006), 'Part-timers merit equality', *The Times Higher Education Supplement*, June 2 2006.

Beck, U., Giddens, A. and Lash, S. (1995), *Reflexive Modernization: Politics, Tradition and Aesthetics in the Modern Social Order*. Cambridge: Polity Press.

Blair, A. (2004), 'Scrap university target say teachers', *The Times*, July 29 2004.

Blair, A., Coulombeau, S. and Brown, O. (2004), 'Students not as clever as they used to be', *The Times*, August 10 2004.

Bompard, P. (2006), 'Student ratings prompt sackings', *The Times Higher Education Supplement*, December 15 2006.

Bordo, S. (1993), *Unbearable Weight: Feminism, Western Culture, and the Body*. Berkeley, CA: University of California Press.

Bourdieu, P. (1990), *The Logic of Practice*. Cambridge: Polity.

Bowen, (1977), *Investment in Learning: The Individual and Social Value of American Higher Education*. New York: Jossey Bass.

BRAIN.HE (2006), *Dyscalculia*. www.brainhe.com/staff/types/dyscalculiatext.html. Accessed 16/12/06.

Bruner, J. (1996), *The Culture of Education*. Cambridge, MA: Harvard University Press.

Bryman, A. (1999), 'The Disneyization of society', *The Sociological Review*, 47(1), 25–42.

Buxton, A. (2005), 'Extra access puts everyone in credit', *Daily Telegraph*, May 7 2005.

Cole, P. (2005), 'Media: journalism courses: why some are a con: everyone wants to be in the media it seems, and some universities', *Independent on Sunday*, August 28 2005.

Curtis, P. (2005), 'Mouse trap', *Guardian*, June 28 2005.

Dearlove, J. (1997), 'The academic labour process: from collegiality and professionalism to managerialism and proletarianisation?', *Higher Education Review*, 30(1), 56–75.

DfES (2003), *The Future of Higher Education*. London: HMSO.

DfES (2005), *Bridging the Gap: A Guide to the Disabled Students' Allowances in Higher Education*. London: Department for Education and Skills.

Dunn, R. G. (1998), *Identity Crises: A Social Critique of Postmodernity*. Minneapolis, MN: University of Minnesota Press.

Edwards, C. and Imrie, R. (2003), 'Disability and bodies as bearers of value', *Sociology*, 37(2), 239–56

Furedi, F. (2004), *Where Have All the Intellectuals Gone?* London, New York: Continuum.

Gibson, M. and Hartley, J. (1998), 'Forty years of cultural studies: an interview with Richard Hoggart', *International Journal of Cultural Studies*, 1(1), 11–23.

Giroux, H. A. (1994), 'Teachers, public life, and curriculum reform', *Peabody Journal of Education*, 69(3), 35–47.

Giroux, H. A. (1995), 'Animating youth: the Disnification of children's culture', *Socialist Review*, 24(3), 23–55.

Giroux, H. A. (1999), *The Mouse That Roared: Disney and the End of Innocence*. Lanham, MD: Rowman and Littlefield.

Giroux, H. (2001), Vocationalizing higher education: schooling and the politics of corporate culture, in H. A. Giroux and K. Myrsiades (eds), *Beyond the Corporate University: Culture and Pedagogy in the New Millennium*. Lanham, MD: Rowman and Littlefield, pp. 29–44.

Gordon, B. (2004), 'Pop studies? Tough call Mickey Mouse courses, such as a BA in popular music, can be rigorous, relevant and lucrative', *Daily Telegraph*, July 10 2004.

Grosz, E. (1994), *Volatile Bodies: Towards a Corporeal Feminism*, Bloomington, IN: Indiana University Press.

Harris, S. and Clark, L. (2004), 'Universities in a Grade A muddle', *Daily Mail*, August 20 2004.

Havighurst, R. J., Neugarten, B. L. and Faulk, J. M. (1967), *Society and Education* (Third edn). Boston, MA: Allyn and Bacon.

Heath, J. and Potter, A. (2004), *The Rebel Sell: Why the Culture Can't be Jammed*. New York: Harper Collins.

Hebdige, D. (2003), 'Dis-gnosis: Disney and the re-tooling of knowledge, art, culture, life, etc.', *Cultural Studies*, 17(2), 150–67.

Henry, J. (2006), 'Fairy story of the three Es. Education, education, education promised Tony Blair 10 years ago', *Sunday Telegraph*, December 10 2006.

Higher Education Act (2004), London: The Stationery Office.

Holbrook, M. B. (2001), 'Times square, Disneyphobia, hegemickey, the Ricky principle, and the downside of the entertainment economy. It's fun-dumb-mental', *Marketing Theory*, 1(2), 139–63.

Johnson, R. N. and Deem, R. (2003), 'Talking of students: tensions and contradictions for the manager–academic and the university in contemporary higher education', *Higher Education*, 46(3), 289–314.

Kluzig, A., Blossfeld, H. -P., Klijzing, E., Kurz, K. and Mills, M. (2005), *Globalization, Uncertainty and Youth in Society: The Losers in a Globalizing World*. London: Routledge.

Lipsett, A. (2005), ' "Customer" students to call tune', *The Times Higher Education Supplement*, November 11 2005.

Matheson, C. (2004), 'Worthwhile degrees', *Independent*, July 28 2004.

Meekosha, H. (1998), 'Body battles: blind spots in feminist theory', in T. Shakespeare (ed.), *The Disability Reader: Social Science Perspectives*. London: Cassell, pp. 163–80.

Meikle, J. (2006), 'From surfing to brewing beer: "Mickey Mouse" courses have come of age', *Guardian*, November 28 2006.

Miller, T. (1993), *The Well-Tempered Self: Citizenship, Culture, and the Postmodern Subject*. Boston, MA: Johns Hopkins University Press.

Modell, S. (2005), 'Students as consumers? An institutional field-level analysis of the construction of performance measurement practices', *Accounting, Auditing & Accountability Journal*, 18(4), 537–63.

National Advisory Committee on Creative and Cultural Education (1999), *All Our Futures: Creativity, Culture and the Arts*. London: Department for Education and Skills.

Newson, J. (2004), 'Disrupting the "student as consumer" model: the new emancipatory project', *International Relations*, 18(2), 227–39.

Nordling, L. (2005), 'Warden in wonderland', *Guardian*, June 14 2005.

Oliver, M. (1990), *The Politics of Disablement*. London: Macmillan.

Parker, J. (2003), 'Reconceptualising the curriculum: from commodification to transformation', *Teaching in Higher Education*, 8(4), 529–44.

Robertson, J. (2004), *Dyslexia, Dyscalculia and Engineering: A Case Study*. Paper presented at the Dyslexia and Dyscalculia Interest Group event, Loughborough, March 2004.

Saltman, K. J. (2002), 'Junk king education', *Cultural Studies*, 16(2), 233–58.

Sanders, C. (2005), 'Gender pay gap "has got wider" ', *The Times Higher Education Supplement*, March 4 2005.

Sayers, F. C. (1965), 'Walt Disney accused', *Horn Book*, December, 602–11.

Schickel, R. (1986), *Intimate Strangers: The Culture of Celebrity*. New York: Fromm International Publishing Corporation.

Shilling, C. (1993), *The Body and Social Theory*. London: Sage.

Stone, D. (1984), *The Disabled State*. London: Macmillan.

Sunday Times (2006), *Sunday Times University Guide 2006*. London: The Sunday Times.

Taylor, M. (2005), 'Research reveals harsh reality of life after college: one in three university students find themselves in non-graduate jobs as well as being saddled with debt after finishing their courses', *Guardian*, January 3 2005.

Times Higher Education Supplement (2003), 'Former VC advocates a superstore approach', *The Times Higher Education Supplement*, February 21 2003.

Tysome, T. (2002), ' "Unwashed" must brush up on their social skills', *The Times Higher Education Supplement*, May 17 2002.

Tysome, T. (2006), 'Campus bid to ban racy "totty" contests', *The Times Higher Education Supplement*, December 22 2006.

Universities UK (2006), *Higher Level Learning: Universities and Employers Working Together*. London: Universities UK.

Veblen, T. (1899), *The Theory of the Leisure Class*. New York: Macmillan.

Warren, S. (1994), 'Disneyfication of the metropolis: popular resistance in Seattle', *Journal of Urban Affairs*, 16(2), 89–107.

Williams, R. (1989), *Resources of Hope: Culture, Democracy, Socialism*. London: Verso.

Wilson, T. (1991), 'The proletarianization of academic labour', *Industrial Relations Journal*, 22(4), 250–62.

Wood, D. N. (1996), *Post-Intellectualism and the Decline of Democracy: The Failure of Reason and Responsibility in the Twentieth Century*. New York: Praeger.

Wright, C. (2006), 'Natural and social order at Walt Disney World: the functions and contradictions of civilising nature', *The Sociological Review*, 54(2), 303–17.

Chapter 6

Higher Education Under Advanced Liberalism

Introduction: taking stock

In this chapter, we will take stock of what we have learned so far and revisit the notions of 'advanced liberalism' and 'neoliberalism' and see what they can offer as a means of making sense of what post-compulsory education is accomplishing in developed nations and particularly in the UK.

We have linked the changes ongoing in further and higher education to the notion that, under contemporary conditions, personal identity becomes a kind of project of self-production – a reflexive endeavour undertaken by relatively autonomous individuals (Giddens, 1991; Bauman, 1994; Beck *et al.*, 1994). As we have seen, the sociological story to which this notion cleaves is that once upon a time, prior to the current era of change, the self, its roles and responsibilities were provided or imposed within the constraints of kinship and community, braced further by the fixed cosmology of a closed theological worldview or derived from formalized or normatively structured interactions in a largely ceremonial public sphere. In such times, the university might have been a finishing school for gentlemen, in preparation for a determined set of public or professional roles in the upper or middle classes.

Today, by contrast, traditional supports to identity have been stripped away through political, economic and cultural change and the self 'bowls alone'. Autonomous individuals confront and develop themselves under conditions of risk, amidst deregulated, liberalized social arrangements and freed from the constraints of tradition. People can, according to this account of contemporary social life under advanced liberalism, assume sole responsibility for the production and maintenance of their own identities (Lash and Friedman, 1992; Hall and Du Gay, 1996; Heelas *et al.*, 1996). Like the self in existential philosophy, freedom is something to which citizens are condemned. In these circumstances the management of personal autonomy requires considerable technical prowess in adding to the self, through education, training, embracing change and adding cultural capital to oneself.

In addition, there has been a related thrust from what has come to be called governmentality studies. Rather than the process of government itself, as we have seen, scholars in this tradition take their cue from the later work of Foucault and attend to the way in which people self-regulate, self-engineer and conduct their personae – the conduct of conduct, if you will (Bennett, 1998; Rose, 1998; 1999; Foucault, 1991; Cruickshank, 1999; Dean, 1999; Bratich *et al.*, 2003). Under the conditions created in the present neoliberal climate, these scholars have sought to conceptualize the relationship between the state and the market, whose equilibrium is carefully nurtured, and whose trajectory is believed to form the basis of much contemporary social change traversing many realms of contemporary social and personal life, including the education system. Part of this change is the oft remarked withering of the state's role in social welfare, regulation and justice and instead, the burgeoning of its role in smoothing the path for entrepreneurs and investors to play hitherto unanticipated roles in the creation of what were once public goods. Under these circumstances, uniquely new modes of freedom and identity proliferate.

Looking at education in this way requires a reversal of much previous thinking on the subject. A good deal of scholarship on education has looked at the learner in terms of the presumed machinery under the skull. Students on teacher training courses learn about Piaget and Vygotsky; success or failure in the education system is correlated with cognitive and attitudinal variables ranging from IQ scores to self-esteem, to more complex theories of reasoned action that rely upon the learners' expectations of success. Equally, a good deal of sociological thinking has attempted to relate the role played by pupils in the education system to their parents' social class and the cultural, emotional and linguistic capital that they carry to the school from their family and community. Both these ways of thinking about education, and the learner's progression within it, retain a sort of anthropological metaphysics. There is something measurable or tangible about the learner that informs their response to education.

Governmentality theories, of the kind to which we have related the events and processes described in this book, link the new subjective freedoms of late modernity not with declining moral authorities, existential anxieties, or crises of masculinity, but with the specific techniques of governance and political programmes aimed at the 'conduct of conduct'. In our case, these might be concerned with the acquisition of literacy, mathematical skills, employabilities, or with widening access/increasing the proportion of the population who proceed to university. These are new political rationalities which localize the autonomy of the subject within programmes and practices which attempt to encourage their growth and development in a particular direction, through the technologies of governmentality (Gordon, 1991).

The particular focus of much of the work on governmentality we have mentioned has foregrounded the changing relationship between individuals and their occupational and political worlds, as well as their changing relationship to themselves with the unfolding of new disciplines dealing with psychology, psychoanalysis and psychiatry. In the latter decades of the last century to the present day, we have seen particular changes concerned with risk and how it is organized. Physical risks are subject to increasing attempts at regulation, but responsibility for the economic and cultural risks of modern life has been progressively transferred from state welfare organizations to other agencies. In particular these risks have fallen upon the shoulders of the 'self-responsible' individuals themselves.

Thus, as we have seen, these individuals are called upon to propel the economies of developed nations through their duties to consume, to cultivate the flexibility, mobility and adaptability – indeed, the 'skills' – demanded in an increasingly risky world. Moreover they have to consolidate these qualities around a durable sense of self (Heelas and Morris, 1992). To sum up the task facing the individual, one has to make oneself flexible, productive, and ensure that one is a highly mobile enterprise, whose outputs are competitive and whose labour is readily transferable through the constant process of self-development, through acquiring experience, knowledge and skills of the kind the market will need next. Under 'advanced liberalism', freedom is thus a personal accomplishment of the individual, who has correctly anticipated the needs of a globalized labour market.

Governmentality and post-compulsory education

The highly particular kind of freedom which neoliberal governance makes available is part of a broader strategy on the part of the state in many developed nations. As Rose sums up the philosophy: 'to govern better, the state must govern less, to optimize the economy one must govern through the entrepreneurship of autonomous actors – individuals and families, firms and corporations' (Rose, 1999: 139).

While governmentality theorists have had a great deal to say about the inroads that market practices and ideologies have made into the governance of everyday life, they have yet to say very much about the specific processes that individuals have to go through to achieve this flexibility, this repository of pluripotent skills and experience that the deregulated labour market depends upon. Moreover, this process, through which individuals adapt themselves to the demands of the market, creates new opportunities for entrepreneurs, from essay writers to the purveyors of fully accredited degrees themselves. These fuse together with the opportunities for advertisers, creators of spectacle and providers of entertainment that make the process of acquiring higher learning itself a lucrative suite of opportunities for investment. Consequently they are yet another arena for licentious self-invention, marketized rebellion and enlistment of the learner in educational consumption. In the literature on governmentality, education is often relegated to the margins, conveniently integrated into other pedagogical and didactic rationalities for the governance of individuals. Little attention has so far been paid to the unique methods of seduction typical of post-compulsory education that enlist learners, teachers and educational administrators in pedagogic consumer cultures.

That then, is what we have tried to supply, through our documentation of processes whereby the institutions, ideologies and practices have changed and are demanding new forms of consciousness, new agendas of concern and new forms of consciousness.

These changes in the warp and weft of education have not been programmed in deliberately by an evil cadre of policymakers or industrialists. Most theorists concerned with how this situation has come about stress the role of accident and serendipity:

> The various tactics enacted by the British Conservative government under Margaret Thatcher in the 1980s were not realizations of any philosophy ... They were, rather, contingent lash-ups of thought and action, in which various problems of governing were resolved through drawing up instruments and procedures that happened to be available, in which new ways of governing were invented in a rather *ad hoc* way, as practical attempts to *think about* and act upon specific problems in particular locales, and various other existing techniques and practices were dressed up in new clothes. But, in the course of this process, a certain rationality, call it neoliberalism, came to provide a way of linking up these various tactics, integrating them in thought so that they appeared to partake in a coherent logic ... in order to govern one needs some 'intellectual technology' for trying to work out what on earth one should do next. (Rose, 1999: 27–8)

The governmentality approach, then, has shown how we can make links between the embedded rationalities of work, occupational identity and institutional life and how, within this matrix, individuals are directed towards defined collective purposes, which are in turn connected with ongoing projects of self-control and personal development.

A further key feature is that the collective processes we have identified under this new liberal regime are global. At least, they have inspired the governments of many nations, and this global spirit is apparent in the educational field too. As Michael Crossley reminds us, 'It is now increasingly difficult to understand education in any context without reference to the global forces that influence policy and practice' (Crossley, 2000: 324). It has been argued by some scholars (e.g. Beck, 2000; Scholte, 2000) that globalization means an irresistible trend towards homogenization and the post-sovereign society, and that the harbingers of this are efforts such as those devoted to denationalizing higher education through intercontinental university alliances, like Universitas 21.

However, this globalization does not necessarily mean that there will soon be a homogenous, internationally recognizable educational product with which the global citizenry will enhance themselves. Sassen (2003) notes that the trends in twenty-first-century globalization are not necessarily cosmopolitan in character. While globalizing forces reach across, into, and against centred national modes of social order, these interactions can be highly localized, and do not necessarily create any measure of emancipatory cosmopolitan effect. People in low-wage, less regulated economies will undergo different experiences than those elsewhere. In the knowledge service sector and so-called knowledge economies, this localization is even more conspicuous. Herbert Kliebard has described how educational issues have consistently involved major conflicts and compromises among groups with competing visions of 'legitimate' knowledge, what counts as 'good' teaching and learning, and what is a 'just' society (Kliebard, 1986).

Furthermore, a globalizing ethic in the knowledge sector, combined with the tendencies encouraging reflexive, entrepreneurial selves creates new dilemmas and new possibilities for further regional differentiation. In 'Governing the enterprising self', Rose (1992) cites a newspaper advertisement in the *Guardian* for 'Self-Helpline', a broker for the many counselling services which have sprung up to help the enterprising self cope with the problems of modern life, to help address issues such as 'Am I in the right job' or 'Becoming a supervisor'. These services, Rose argues, presuppose individuals who are uniquely enterprising in their disposition regarding themselves and their capacities. The self is presumed to be capable of acting upon and cultivating itself, of mobilizing its resources and maximizing its outputs. As Rose notes:

Contemporary individuals are incited to live as if making a *project* of themselves: they are to *work* on their emotional world, their domestic and conjugal arrangements, their relations with employment and their techniques of sexual pleasure, to develop a 'style' of living that will maximize the worth of their existence to themselves. (Rose, 1992: 149)

This is even reflected in contemporary initiatives aimed at enhancing personal fulfilment, which often take a managerial approach (Shilling, 2006). Students can be taught how to 'manage relationships, physical and mental health, negative emotions and how to achieve one's ambitions'. Shilling notes that

This model of the psyche as a kind of small business is an interesting one, and clever, too, because it repackages the austere message of self-discipline and self-denial as absolute virtues into a kind of longer-term hedonism. (Shilling, 2006: 11)

This notion of the self as a free autonomous chooser is closely allied to the sense that post-compulsory education's students are its 'customers'. This has, as we have seen, been embedded in scholarship and policy on the issue. This notion has been grasped with remarkable alacrity by many in higher education, although some of us are deeply uncomfortable with the simplicity of such an idea and its possible consequences. The ease with which twenty-first-century students are now accepted as 'customers' was made clear to one of the authors (SB) at a conference in 2004. A careers adviser from a post-1992 university was giving a presentation to an audience of academics from mixed backgrounds and told them very firmly that students were their 'customers'. There were murmurs of dissent from a few members of the audience, whereupon the careers adviser repeated emphatically that students were indeed their customers. Only one member of the audience persisted in contradicting her, an academic who also owned and ran a small hill farm. He explained that his customers were the people to whom he sold his sheep at the local market and that he hoped that he had a very different relationship with his students. It was clear that the careers adviser had never been challenged at length before on this issue and she failed to mount a counter-argument, although sadly she clearly remained unconvinced, students being referred to as 'customers' again minutes later as the pre-rehearsed presentation progressed. There is much anecdotal evidence and many emerging press reports suggesting that the notion of students as consumers or customers is having a profound impact on the relationship between students and universities and students and the individual staff within those institutions.

Consuming passions: students as consumers of education

From its inception with the vogue for Total Quality Management in the 1980s, the idea of students as consumers has come to change the whole landscape of higher education. The debate recently featured in *The Times Higher Education Supplement* (2006), which asked whether higher education was being killed by a commercial culture and consumer mentality. Colin Bundy, the former director of the School of Oriental and African Studies, replied with a critique of the idea of students-as-customers, suggesting that higher education is the 'new e-Bay' and arguing that under such a philosophy, the educational encounter is diminished, learning is reduced to assimilation rather than being personally authored, and that the 'student-as-customer metaphor ... poses the risk that students are no longer seen as active participants in the hard slog of teaching and learning' but as 'consumers, acquisitive but passive browsers in the knowledge bazaar'. Other contributions ranged from suggestions that students-as-customers would demand a better quality of education and that this would indeed result; that window shopping or shopping around will lead to advantages for the student; to concerns that students being called customers suggests that they may simply purchase degrees. Nicholas Barr, professor of public economics at the London School of Economics, observed that the previous system of students relying on parental contributions 'forced students to be responsible to their parents. But the option of a loan treats them like young adults.'

The implications of consumer tendencies in higher education are still being worked through and considered. What is also becoming clear is that the unit of consumption, the student, is not alone. Nowadays they are accompanied by others, often their parents, but occasionally their lawyers. Thus, in contrast to Professor Barr's beliefs, a recent report (Shepherd and Baty, 2006) documented another aspect of university life that the idea of the student-as-customer is believed to have given rise to – that of unhappy or demanding parents of students. Shepherd and Baty. use terms such as 'hostile' or 'aggressive' to describe the behaviour of the parents and the problem was deemed worthy of discussion at the Higher Education Academy's annual conference. Delegates were told that parents were becoming increasingly aggressive towards university staff and demanded information such as exam results and attendance records. It is reported that Huddersfield University even employs a family liaison officer and the Director of Student Services at Huddersfield was reported as saying that universities need to provide a 'listening ear' to frustrated parents. It is however, difficult to ascertain just how accurate the notion of increasingly aggressive parents confronting university staff is. Deborah Lee, a sociologist from Nottingham

Trent University, is quoted by Shepherd and Baty. as claiming that 'aggressive conduct – between staff, between students, between staff and students, and from parents – has been swept under the carpet'. Lee also observes that 'students are not customers who are always right'. Other lecturers were quoted as attributing aggressive behaviour to the UK becoming more consumer-oriented and others believed that parents were demanding value for money as they were paying more for their children's university education. Professor Miriam David believed that market forces and competition had brought a 'sea change in parental involvement'.

The idea of the customer being 'always right' is attributed to retailer H. Gordon Selfridge in the 1930s and has arrived in the post-compulsory education arena rather later than in other spheres of activity. The mantra 'the customer is always right' communicates the unequal power in the customer–employee transaction, which is also a key aspect of being a target of aggression (Grandey *et al.*, 2004). Nevertheless, it is interesting that now, the 'difficult' behaviour of students' parents is even a matter thought worthy of debate. Students are, after all, adults, and previous generations have proverbially cringed at their parents making contact with the university. Parental contact was usually limited to bringing the student and their belongings to university in freshers' week and then three years later attending the graduation ceremony. The only other circumstances in which students' parents had contact with the university were those such as the student experiencing serious illness. Yet as an academic who is also the parent of a prospective student observed after attending some university open days: '... my guess is that with parents having to pay hefty top-up fees, their impressions about where their offspring should go will count more and more' (Birkhead, 2006).

The liberalized climate that is making inroads into the world of post-compulsory education has had an effect on the kinds of demands faced in the academy. We have for some years been aware of a feeling among many colleagues that students have become more demanding and less deferential. Anecdotes circulate suggesting that students are increasingly litigious or even intimidating towards staff and institutions. Yet stories describing such 'awkward customers' are rife among those employed within the public services – one hears the same allegations levelled at school pupils and NHS patients for example. One thus has to be careful exactly what one deduces from such anecdotes – they could be just as much the consequence of a failing public service or a demoralized staff body as the consequence of a change in the nature and attitude of students, pupils or patients. Recently however, what has previously been discontent discussed privately among university staff is now emerging in the press and even the law courts.

Three years ago a recently retired senior academic told the authors of instances in the university in which he had worked with students caught plagiarising who had still been awarded degrees after threatening the institution with legal action. We had naively assumed that such situations were not that common, yet Baty (2006) reported on an online discussion forum that suggested that academics are hampered when investigating plagiarism and that universities are indeed threatened by, and fearful of, litigation from students under suspicion of plagiarism.

This new litigious spirit among an enterprising student body has made its presence far more robustly felt in the twenty-first century. There have also been a number of well-publicized successful legal actions brought against universities by students. In 2001 a law student from Wolverhampton University received an out of court settlement for £30,000 when the university cancelled courses that it maintained would be available (Swain, 2006a). Oxford Brookes lost a case against 28 osteopathy students after the university failed to gain professional accreditation for their degrees (Baty, 2005). In 2004 a report by the Oxford Centre for Higher Education Policy Studies found that universities were spending £15 million a year as a whole on legal actions (*The Times Higher Education Supplement*, 2004). It was concern over figures like this and a belief that the introduction of top-up fees would possibly result in even more litigation that led to the establishment of the Independent Adjudicator for Higher Education in 2004, to investigate complaints relating to the quality of courses. Yet tales of litigation are still appearing in the press. Students at the University of Wales, Newport are suing the university after the teaching on their course in environmental management was slashed halfway through the course (Shipton, 2006). Former animation students from the University of Lincoln have given damning accounts of the teaching and facilities that were available to them – at the time of writing they are making representation to the Adjudicator and claiming compensation for loss of time, money and failure to gain employment, maintaining that they will sue the university if their complaint is not successful (Hodges, 2006).

This is interesting from our point of view, not just because it shows that educational purchases are subject to the same kind of legally enforceable disciplines as other consumer goods, but for what it implies about the nature of education itself. The idea that litigation is a means of compensating people for what they had hoped from educational experience implies that the legislative framework governing these actions has reached into the subjective world of the student and the speculative world of what a graduate from a particular course might be expected to earn. Moreover, there is an implication in here that the incompatibility between what organizations offer and what students want is resolvable in this way. As if educational establishments could so readily be commanded to offer a quality product. The kinds of processes which were once used for ensuring the quality of physical goods have been transferred to the realm of intellectual or cultural goods, as if they could be regulated in the same way. A further implication is that those who invest in themselves by purchasing a degree are making a legally enforceable purchase in the same sort of way as if they bought a computer to aid them in their work, a new suit or a car.

This spirit of consumption is also visible in the growing number of press reports relating to the take-up of higher education by young people and the 'quality' of higher education on offer now, which frequently talk about 'value for money' (*Independent*, 2006a). The value for money element is apparent in the cases to which we have referred above. What is important here is that the climate has changed and the way we think about education has shifted so that value for money concerns of this kind seem so eminently reasonable now that students are constructed as personally paying so much for their education. Press coverage of these cases is often very sympathetic to students bringing such actions. In the dash to expand university provision, students may be reassured to find that they have statutory protection against institutions seeking to skimp on resources or facilities. This of course also reflects the more and more complex demands which are being made of universities and their staff.

As we mentioned in an earlier chapter, there have been suggestions that universities should be sued for failing to provide adequate care for students with particular incapacities or vulnerabilities such as 'mental illness'. A recent press report (Hsiao-Hung, 2006) detailed some shocking racist attacks on international students, yet lambasted the university for not doing more to prevent this. While the university might be able to encourage tolerance on campus, the attacks in question happened some distance away from the premises, in the town in which the university was situated. This sort of racist violence is regrettably commonplace in many parts of the UK. However, the implication in here is that the university itself was somehow responsible. A university would be hard pressed indeed to effectively tackle such a phenomenon alone. A duty of care which might once have extended to dispensing advice to international students on how to avoid such confrontations, or on what action to take if a student is attacked, has now been extended to cover the cultural climate of the UK itself. To suggest that universities should somehow be responsible for 'doing something' about such behaviour in the local area seems to make very large claims on their capabilities indeed. This kind of thing is more usually seen as the domain of the police and criminal justice system and even they often seem to struggle with the remit of preventing racism. The point is not to suggest that universities are practically or materially capable of curbing the violent or racist sentiments of the townsfolk. What is interesting is that they should be thought culpable or capable of doing something about it as part of their implied compact with the students.

This burgeoning contractualism is evident in other ways too. In September 2006 there was a flurry of press coverage regarding the decision of some universities to insist that their students signed contracts, agreeing to 'good behaviour' and appropriate participation in activities such as lectures and tutorials (Meikle, 2006). The *Daily Mail*'s coverage (Roberts, 2006) of this phenomenon suggested that the rationale behind the contracts was to protect the universities from damages claims from students who had done little work, but who then attributed poor results to bad teaching. Yet the NUS perceived the contracts to be a means of preventing students complaining about tuition standards and noted that the contracts did not stipulate the standard of teaching that could be expected by the students. Wes Streeting of the NUS was reported as saying that 'vice-chancellors and principals are very busy protecting themselves from the customers they have created in a system that they have been fighting for. It is absurd' (Meikle, 2006). Mr Streeting's observations were astute, but we believe that forces greater than vice-chancellors and principals have created the absurdity. They form a part of this progress to a more marketized, neoliberal approach to higher education that is becoming more and more apparent throughout the world. If degrees are commodities and students are customers then specification of the relative duties of each party to the agreement will very likely become ever more meticulous. Should an event transpire that is not specified in the documentation then one or other party will have grounds for litigation. It is not the actual court cases *per se* that make the system turn the way it does. It is their implied presence, the threat, if you will, that lurks at the back of lecturers' and administrators' minds.

The reaction in the liberal press to these contracts of learning that were presented to students in the autumn of 2006 was interesting. Both Marcel Berlins in the *Guardian* (Berlins, 2006) and Johann Hari in the *Independent* (Hari, 2006) wrote scathingly about the contracts, remembering their own student days, observing that had they been subject to such contracts they would have been expelled. They painted a picture of student life familiar to many – poor lectures, an over-indulgent lifestyle and then intensive compensatory work some weeks before exams. What was interesting about these articles was that the writers were clearly not au fait with the reality of much of the present higher education system and the practices within it. Generations of students like Berlins or Hari who found academic work comparatively easy and regularly missed lectures but pursued other educational and cultural interests while at university, would no doubt have found their lifestyles unnecessarily cramped by such contracts. Present day students entering universities do not always find academic work easy and may even be attending supplementary courses designed to improve their 'skills' such as basic literacy or numeracy. Moreover, they may well have been 'statemented' by an educational psychologist as having special educational needs. For example, a young man with a reading age of six recently graduated from a post-1992 institution, according to the documentation that he showed us. If a student in these circumstances misses considerable amounts of teaching time, they are likely to encounter even greater problems with academic work.

In considering the redundancy and unsuitability of contracts, Marcel Berlins makes the point that 'if students don't turn up and don't work, they're unlikely to get their degree'. Many academics can testify that the situation is no longer that simple. If a course does not show a good progression rate or completion rate, this can have dire consequences for its future survival. The staff who teach upon the course are made responsible for ensuring that students pass. The consumerism that now flourishes in the higher education system seems to have encouraged some students to believe that if the fees have been paid, a degree should be dispensed – and often a good degree. Some who follow the guidance that accompanies the coursework assignments are distraught to find that their marks are only in the 50s. 'I've done everything you told me to' as one of them said to one of us (BB) plaintively. Or there are some who, on hearing how their coursework could have been made stronger by the incorporation of more critical discussion of the material covered counter with the claim 'but we've not been told how to do a critical discussion'. Students can and do dispute results and do so regularly, often on the premise that the appropriate solution to the conundrum of getting a good mark has not previously been made sufficiently explicit to them. The proportion of students obtaining first-class degrees, of course, is a matter of concern to universities as this can affect their position in the 'league tables' published by the UK's more weighty newspapers, so these are matters to be taken with the utmost seriousness.

Shrinking markets: universities and the pursuit of student customers

A further manifestation of the treatment of students as customers and the introduction of tuition fees is the emergence of more manifestly commercial strategies on the part of educational establishments themselves. Such a market is actively advocated by Alan Johnson who, at the time of writing, is the UK's Minister for Education. Johnson has stated that he would encourage universities to cut fees to attract students away from rivals and also that universities should be allowed to offer discounts on tuition fees (Frean, 2006). Drummond Bone, President of Universities UK, was quoted as saying that he would be dismayed to see an 'American-style dog eat dog' market for degrees, although he was sympathetic to the notion of, for example, students receiving discounts on fees as a way of avoiding the psychological fear of huge debt (Frean, 2006). In the same article, Gemma Tumelty, the President of the NUS, expressed fears that students would choose courses 'based on their bank balance, not on their brains'. Mr Johnson dismissed such fears, but only days later the University of Gloucestershire announced that students paying the entire £9,000 tuition fees for their degrees when they began their courses would be entitled to a 20 per cent discount (Richards, 2006). This offer was not made available to students needing state help. This particular discount offer seemed to confirm Ms Tumelty's fears and offers little comfort to Drummond Bone's hopes that perhaps discounts would assist those students fearful of debt. The Government is planning to review fee levels in 2009 and of course there is discussion underway at present regarding just how much universities will be able to charge for tuition before precipitating a drop in applicants – the Russell Group have stated their desire to see the £3,000 a year cap lifted as soon as possible (Harris, 2006).

Whatever sort of market in higher education one would prefer, or which one believes has evolved, there is evidence that the market will soon be one that favours the students *per se*, if not each individual student. Tysome (2006a) reported that delegates at the European annual conference of the Council for Advancement and Support of Education were told that demographic trends are expected to bring a decline of up to 20 per cent of school leavers seeking places in higher education by 2010, leaving universities increasingly financially pressured, and predictions were made that universities would have to 'raise standards' and overhaul their marketing and customer targeting. The head of public relations at Northumbria University was quoted as saying 'it used to be that universities assumed that they selected students. In future, it will be the other way around.'

While it is hazardous to predict the future of higher education, the tendency for universities to be chasing a declining number of eligible applicants has been remarked upon by many other authors too. Bekhradnia (2006) of the Higher Education Policy Institute has attempted to determine the likely demand for higher education in the UK up until 2020. His work suggests that universities may well be courting a smaller population of potential students in the near future. He maintains that between now and 2010–11 the population of young school leavers will continue to increase and thus there will be a continuing growth in numbers. After 2010–11 however, the number of young people will decline substantially and rapidly until the end of that decade. However, the decline in the young population will be concentrated in social groups that participate least in higher education, thus making the effect on student demand less conspicuous. The main implication of Bekhradnia's report is that universities will have to manage a short-term increase in potential student population, followed by a much longer-term reduction. Despite the ingenuity with which universities are marketing themselves, and the exhortations on the part of the government itself, Bekhradnia believes that there is no prospect of achieving 50 per cent participation by 2010. However, the change in the balance of the population between social groups will eventually appear to yield an increase in participation rates, although there will have to be other improvements to achieve 50 per cent participation within the next decade.

At present in the UK around 90 per cent of students with the requisite A-levels progress to higher education, so in Bekhradnia's view, there is little scope for boosting higher education numbers from among those with A-levels. Gorard (2006), addressing the same issue, has suggested, to much controversy, that a solution may be to forego academic qualifications as entrance requirements and like some other European nations, allow more or less open entry to undergraduate courses. Furthermore, Bekhradnia notes that the proportion of people taking A-levels hasn't increased for the last four years. However, if boys stop 'underperforming', this will provide more students by 2020. The potential for access courses to increase the participation rate is limited because access courses only provide a small number of higher education students so even a big increase in access courses would make little impact. A further source of additional students for the UK's institutions that could be exploited comes from the European Community. The expansion of the European Union in 2007 may provide a boost to recruitment, particularly if Turkey is admitted – there are strong reasons for thinking that universities will struggle to maintain a large number of students from other European Union nations. Many of the countries in question face similar demographic trends to the UK. The number of young people in the relevant age cohort will reduce by over 20 per cent between 2006 and 2020. Thus it is highly unlikely that increased demand from European Union students will help offset any reduced demand from home students.

To summarize, Bekhradnia's (2006) projections to 2010 and 2020 suggest that in the medium to long term, changes in the socio-demographic balance mean that there is likely to be an improvement in participation, which will go some way towards countering the decline in student numbers (paragraph 22). Between 2010–11 and 2020–21, there may be an improvement in the participation rate of young people, bringing it close to 50 per cent, without any improvement in participation of young people from poor backgrounds, because of differential birth rates in different social classes. The share of higher education participation by poor students is predicted to decline. There is little evidence of positive movement of students from 'AimHigher', education maintenance allowances and lifelong learning partnerships into higher education. Bekhradnia predicts that after two decades of strong growth, higher education institutions are now in a new environment with low increases in student numbers and possible declines in prospect. This may cause difficulty for some institutions as they come to terms with this new reality.

This pattern of participation in higher education forseen by Bekhradina does not include any sign of substantially greater participation by students from hitherto under-represented groups in the UK population. Of course, neoliberal education reform does not arise from a previously egalitarian educational landscape. Schools and universities have long been linked to the perpetuation of inequality among social groups (Rist, 1973; Bourdieu and Passeron, 1990 [1977]). Reproduction theorists assert that the capitalist system relies on inequality in education systems to produce a working class (Apple, 1995). Certainly, existing inequalities around race and class have long plagued the education system. As Lipman (2002) argues, contemporary education reform policy has the potential to exaggerate inequalities, effectively marginalizing and regulating the identities of those who are failed out of the system and excluded.

Marketing neoliberalism as the best way forward

The legitimacy of market ideals and neoliberal ideology is not just naturally *there* in the social order: it is carefully crafted into being. Furthermore, it must itself be 'marketed' to those who will exist in it and live with its effects (Menter *et al.*, 1997: 27). As Apple (2001) reminds us, markets themselves are marketed and made legitimate by a depoliticizing strategy. They are presented as natural and neutral, and governed by effort and merit. As a corollary of this, those opposed to them are by definition opposed to effort and merit and by implication, are in favour of poor service and lethargy. Part of the sales pitch attached to markets is that they are somehow efficient, less top heavy with bureaucracy and supposedly less subject to political interference. They are grounded in the rational choices of individual actors. Thus, where markets and competition are promoted in education, they are presented as if the guarantee of rewards for effort and merit will produce positive yet 'neutral' or impartial results (Menter *et al.*, 1997: 27). Thus, appeals to market or competitive criteria often involve mechanisms being put in place that give evidence of entrepreneurial efficiency and effectiveness. The competitive spirit cannot be left to thrive alone. There are evaluations of teaching quality, research quality, league tables of results for student experience and so on. All of these, of course, require considerable investment of resources, time and energy to work effectively, to ensure the competitive, enterprising, entrepreneurial spirit is evaluated and encouraged. Olssen identifies this as one of the key differences between classical liberalism and the new spirit of neoliberalism:

> In the shift from classical liberalism to neoliberalism, then, there is a further element added, for such a shift involves a change in subject position from 'homo economicus', who naturally behaves out of self-interest and is relatively detached from the state, to 'manipulatable man', who is created by the state and who is continually encouraged to be 'perpetually responsive'. It is not that the conception of the self-interested subject is replaced or done away with by the new ideals of 'neoliberalism', but that in an age of universal welfare, the perceived possibilities of slothful indolence create necessities for new forms of vigilance, surveillance, 'performance appraisal' and of forms of control generally. In this model the state has taken it upon itself to keep us all up to the mark. The state will see to it that each one makes a 'continual enterprise of ourselves' ... in what seems to be a process of 'governing without governing'. (Olssen, 1996: 340)

The landscape of deregulated neoliberal educational policy is not, in the terms favoured by policymakers, a 'level playing field'. With heavier parental investments in post-compulsory education for their offspring, what Ball *et al.* said about schools is becoming true of universities:

> Middle-class parents are more likely to have the knowledge, skills and contacts to decode and manipulate what are increasingly complex and deregulated systems of choice and recruitment. The more deregulation, the more possibility of informal procedures being employed. The

middle class also, on the whole, are more able to move their children around the system. (Ball *et al.*,1994: 19)

This canniness in sustaining or increasing status in competitive environments has been a feature of middle-class responses in the UK to the present environment in higher education. The *Independent* (2006b) reports that since the early 1980s the graduation rate of people from the 'poorest' backgrounds has risen from 6 to 9 per cent whereas that of people from wealthier backgrounds has increased from 20 to 47 per cent in the same period.

Equally, a number of commentators have expressed concern that the competition among students and their parents to gain places has reinforced rather than eroded the distinction in the UK between the 'traditional' universities and the post-1992 sector, with the latter being 'second choice' institutions (Hill and Baty, 2004). Some see the distinctions between institutions being accentuated in the future, with Stephen (2006) predicting that some elite institutions will be able to opt out of the state system altogether, a further stalwart tier of research-intensive institutions into which middle-class parents are keen to place their offspring, and a third tier of provision where less advantaged applicants will study at their local institution. The prospect of a system that is even more divided than at present and which uses the money from increased tuition fees to offer bursaries not to disadvantaged but to 'brighter' students, is one possible consequence of the competitive zeal which is developing in the sector, as is the competition between students, in which those with middle-class parents will win. Reports are appearing of a proliferation of private, fee-paying independent further education colleges where the 'door opening' 'A' grades at A-level are more readily assured, for parents with money to spend who are keen to ensure their offspring a chance at the elite universities (McRae, 2006).

Despite the warnings that have been raised about the difficulties attached to the issue of competition, and the potentially divisive effects for the sector as a whole, universities and colleges themselves have been embarked upon this path now for some considerable time. Universities are competing on many levels. Some traditional universities are racing to join the high status Russell Group and are attempting to headhunt 'big name' researchers in order to add prestige and add to their institutions' likely good performance in the Research Assessment Exercise and its successors. Institutions already in the Russell Group are of course keen to maintain their positions. The new universities have little hope of winning this particular game and instead promote themselves on other criteria – vocational courses, employability, creativity, student lifestyle and so on. Many institutions, mindful of the investment that parents are likely to be making in their children's education, are offering parents' programmes and parent liaison officers. This particular aspect of competition among universities is the one with which most laypeople are familiar – it is the playing of this game that leads to the publication of league tables, leading to headlines referring to the 'best' and 'worst' universities. Competing on these terms attracts students who are usually academically able, also often from higher socio-economic groups and who have usually left their home regions to attend the desired university. Contrast this with the students that new universities often target. In line with Stephen's (2006) predictions, they are often those with fewer formal academic qualifications, often from more disadvantaged backgrounds and also often resident in the immediate locality.

The pervasiveness of competition

Competition is not just happening on an academic level; it has pervaded every aspect of university life. Institutions are now competing with each other in terms of other facilities on offer. Some student accommodation is now surprisingly upmarket. Although much of this luxurious accommodation is owned and managed by private sector companies specializing in student accommodation such as the Unite Group or Opal (Swain, 2006b), some institutions themselves are currently planning or building sumptuous accommodation for students. At the time of writing, the University of Wales, Bangor is developing far more luxurious accommodation for students than has previously been available. This university benefits from a stunning geographical location and many students have chosen to study there because of that; it is a traditional university that doesn't suffer the 'ex-poly' tag; yet the authorities at the University of Wales, Bangor are clearly aware that to attract students it is now necessary to offer more than respectable academic tradition and beautiful scenery.

As we have indicated, competition between universities for students is being positively encouraged by some New Labour government ministers. It also has support among the opposition – Boris Johnson, at the time of writing Shadow Higher Education minister, was been quoted as saying at the 2006 Conservative Party Conference: 'If the funding follows the student, this will introduce a greater degree of competition into the system and drive up standards' (Sanders, 2006a). In the UK, whichever party holds sway, contemporary educational policies are fostering competition, division and stratification (Reid, 2002). The neoliberal ideology of 'choice' becomes more important in this analysis than actual educational outcomes themselves. The neoliberal ideology is repeatedly evidenced in a celebration of 'market competition' in education (Hankins and Martin, 2006). Peck and Tickell, (2002) suggest that neoliberalism has coincided with, and to some degree created, the entrepreneurialism typified by competition between institutions for economic investments and for students themselves.

During the 2006 Conservative Party Conference, it was reported that a constant theme of platform speakers was the need to improve the skills of the UK workforce because of the constant threat of competition from China and India (Sanders, 2006a). Whatever perception one has of the global economy or the skills needs of the UK workforce, the higher education sector in the UK is certainly facing strong competition from institutions overseas.

There is concern regarding the ability of UK universities to continue to attract overseas students, but there is now also a rather newer phenomenon – that of UK students going outside the UK for their higher education. The last year has seen a flurry of media stories featuring high-achieving A-level students who had either not been accepted by Oxbridge colleges, or had actively not chosen to apply to them and had instead gained places to study at Ivy League institutions in the US (Clark, 2006; Purgavie, 2006). (The first high profile example of this of course was Laura Spence, who in 2000 famously failed to gain a place to read medicine at Oxford and in a blaze of publicity went to Harvard – but not to study medicine. This particular case gained notoriety because of the popular belief that Ms Spence had been discriminated against for having been educated at a state school.) The media coverage tended to stress the superiority of the Ivy League over Oxbridge at every level, whether it was academic status, sporting facilities, the endowed wealth of the institutions or the future prospects of graduates. Oxbridge looked curiously parochial by comparison. Competition within the UK, accentuated by competition between the institutions of different nations for the most 'able' students, is presented by policymakers as desirable in terms of the potential it has to drive up standards.

Phillips (2006), while writing about the role of international consultants in higher education, was clear about the globalization of the higher education market and the competition that UK institutions face from overseas. He identified competition for both students and staff and quoted an American-based consultant as predicting 'an enormous competitive threat' from Chinese and Indian institutions. There is also competition in the global market from Australian universities. The authors have encountered anecdotal evidence of less well-publicized competition from outside of the UK. Universities in countries which have recently joined the European Union with their lower entry requirements, living costs and equivalent qualifications, are proving an attractive choice for enterprising students and their parents. UK students are attractive to institutions seeking to demonstrate parity. Competition for the most promising students comes increasingly from outside the UK.

There also promises to be another serious challenge to universities, but this is not from other such institutions. It is instead from other bodies which may be granted degree-awarding powers. One such body is the College of Law, which recently became the first organization to be given degree-awarding powers that didn't have to be first accredited by a university (Sanders, 2006b). This was possible following legislative changes in 2004, allowing teaching-only institutions, including commercial companies, to become universities. Sanders reported Michael Shattock, visiting professor at the Institute of Education, University of London, as saying that the private sector will bring healthy competition to higher education.

The foregoing then provides a few vignettes of the way that competition is becoming manifest in the post-compulsory education sector. Students compete for places, universities compete for students, and there are forms of competition between strata in the university system and between the university systems of different nations. These phenomena, as Apple (2001) reminds us, are understandable in terms of Pierre Bourdieu's analysis of the relative weight given to cultural capital in the contemporary struggles for mobility (Bourdieu, 1996). The importance of cultural capital in conditioning our dealings with educational institutions means that in developed nations we no longer entirely rely on wealth so as to reproduce class privilege. Power is no longer transmitted through property. Instead, there is a growing panoply of ways in which privilege can be sustained through knowledge of the game. Educationally mediated access to cultural capital is stratified by means of this process of competition. Here, 'the bequeathal of privilege is simultaneously effectuated and transfigured by the intercession of educational institutions' (Wacquant, 1996: xiii). This is *not* a conspiracy; it is not 'conscious' in the ways we normally use that concept. Rather it is the result of a long chain of relatively autonomous connections between differentially accumulated economic, social and cultural capital operating at the level of mundane events as people make their respective ways in the world, including as we have argued, in the world of competition in post-compulsory education. Apple (2001) goes on to propose that the competitive spirit in education, with competition between institutions and between pupils and parents, acts to further exclude those from 'blue collar and postcolonial backgrounds'.

In the version of social life envisaged in much contemporary educational policy, people seem to relate to each other not primarily as relatives, neighbours, community members or citizens, but as (potential) owners or recipients of employability or skills (Hyland, 2002), striving for survival in the harsh climate of the global market. Hyland further draws our attention to the scramble for security as new technologies and forms of work make traditional occupational knowledge and skills redundant. As Gray (1998: 72) describes it, in a curiously prescient passage authored ten years ago, this leads to the 're-proletarianization of much of the industrial working class and the de-bourgeoisification of the former middle classes'.

The human resources of competition: never enough staff

In the case of people who work in universities the competitive neoliberal climate is certainly making itself felt. A generation gap is opening between a new breed of ambitious young career-minded academics who embrace the notion of the enterprising self and a performance-management culture and their older peers who cling to traditional notions of autonomy, collegiality and scholarship (Tysome, 2006b). The competitive spirit is thus leading to divisions even within the higher education workplace. The workplace itself is set to have further difficulties in recruitment as universities compete with other careers and opportunities in the labour market which are open to the best and the brightest. Kubler and De Luca (2006) report on a survey of commonwealth institutions which suggests that academic staff recruitment will be an increasingly significant challenge for most institutions. This is prompted by the rising competition from within the post-compulsory education sector itself, and from other employment sectors. The disciplines experiencing most difficulty in staff recruitment and retention were business studies, engineering sciences, medical and clinical sciences, mathematics and physical sciences, information and communications technology, and chemical and biological studies.

As well as the difficulties experienced in recruiting staff, there are potential human resources problems in the pipeline for UK higher education because it is a line of work where people do not want to stay. Lipsett and Tysome, (2006) report that academic recruitment and retention will suffer as staff struggle to balance the triple pressures of increased teaching, research and red tape. Scholarly bodies are suffering because the new generation of academics has scant time available for professional contributions outside their workplace. Tysome (2006c) reports that according to a recent survey, nearly half of UK academic staff intend to leave their job within two years. This implies a major struggle for universities in retaining staff in future. The prospect of staff turnover reaching unprecedented levels follows the flurry of appointments in the run-up to the 2008 Research Assessment

Exercise. The competitive, enterprising spirit takes people away from their workplaces and into other avenues of employment. The rapid turnover fits notions of a market that we might find in introductory economics textbooks, but in practice, it contributes to a lack of organizational memory and a curiously fragmented experience for students and colleagues.

Even at the more senior levels, when vice-chancellor posts are falling vacant, there are suggestions that the rising generation of senior managers is somewhat squeamish when it comes to these kinds of responsibilities. Fazackerley (2006) reports that institutions are facing an uphill battle to find 'high-calibre' vice-chancellors. It is believed that the new commercial spirit in universities, the uncertainty presented by global markets and the new fee structure in the UK, present a set of challenges which is unattractive.

Alongside this, as the higher education system has become more concerned with phenomena such as quality assurance, student evaluations and parent power, there has been a deskilling and deprofessionalization process among the staff. The 'tick box culture' which has taken root in universities and which is seen to have eroded autonomy is accompanied by constant demands for academic staff to be 'trained' in areas in which it was previously taken for granted that they would be competent, such as teaching, research supervision, or in areas that were simply never previously considered their domain, such as mental health awareness. This can of course 'raise the floor' which can be very positive – there are undoubtedly first-class researchers who gain lecturing jobs but who are unable to teach well and we believe that all students deserve good pastoral care. Yet the enormous number and range of staff development courses now 'offered' to academics and indeed the whole notion of 'continuous professional development' which has entered the sector, implies that people who work as (or desire to work as) academics aren't very competent anyway. So paradoxically, all this training is taking place alongside a sizeable deskilling exercise.

Conclusion: higher education markets and the 'portfolio person'

In this chapter we have attempted to identify some of the contradictory trends at stake in the post-compulsory education system under the economically liberal climate of the late twentieth and early twenty-first centuries. As we have shown, under this new variant of liberalism the markets are not merely allowed to develop naturally, as in classical liberalism, but are carefully crafted into being. The design of markets is also in an important sense about the design of individuals, complete with their portfolios of skills, around which a whole industry has grown up to assist their development.

Under the kind of regimes that we have been discussing, the subject of post-compulsory education and the actual and potential students, could be said to be defined through two related themes. One of these is concerned with 'lack' and the other with 'potential'. These themes are intimately connected with governmental priorities for economic life to be successful in neoliberal economies, to ensure an educated and flexible labour force. In the field of education, young people and other potential students of the higher education system are often described as if they were missing something. Skills, literacy, the enterprising spirit, employability and competitiveness, for example; qualities that can presumably be remedied through post-compulsory education. Meanwhile, in the field of labour restructuring, workers are often described in terms of potential, who must have these qualities and attitudes if they are to be competitive, flexible or to have acquired the right experience to fulfil the roles open to them in the labour market. Moreover, they must have these qualities of flexibility and skills if we are as a nation to compete with other nations.

These discourses are intended to construct neoliberal subjects who are as yet unfinished, as if something is missing from them which must be replenished in order for them to fulfil their potential. Lucey *et al.* (2003) have noted something similar in thinking about explanations as to why working-class children do not succeed in the education system with the same alacrity as middle-class youngsters. There is something missing – the social support, family culture or community, as well as the desire to succeed, are somehow deficient. This sense that the person or subject under neoliberalism is somehow always destined to fall short of expectations is a pervasive one. The worker is always a few skills short of a picnic. The school leaver is insufficiently literate; the academic member of staff is not quite as enthusiastic about change or insufficiently entrepreneurial; the senior manager falls somewhat short of meeting the challenges of being a vice-chancellor. In the face of the moral exhortations of neoliberalism we are all sinners.

What is more, the way in which participants in this process are encouraged to interpret this in themselves is increasingly likely to be as if it were an interior, psychological matter, rather than one which is to do with the demands made by political systems. If one is a student, the additional work involved in keeping abreast of the demands of fees and part-time work is seen not in terms of a failure of the system to provide an entitlement to higher education, but in terms of what it is enabling you to accomplish in terms of your future employment prospects or desired lifestyle. For staff in post-compulsory education, there is the manifest intensification of work involved in assisting students with personal problems, literacy and numeracy difficulties, as well as maintaining a record of research and publication, topped off with a required vigilance for opportunities for enterprise and external funding. These competing and at times contradictory demands are not seen as exploitation, but as hurdles or 'challenges' to be overcome if one wishes to make progress in one's career.

This is all ground that has been well trodden. We mention it here because we see it not as a capricious worsening of the situation but as being consistent with other changes in higher education that have not been written about so extensively. We have explained in earlier chapters how as other human service organizations are becoming less tolerant, less consumer orientated and less user friendly, the higher education system is taking on more of that sort of role. The idea of opening up of choice for students and academic staff in the post-compulsory education system as if they were Gee's (2004) 'shape-shifting portfolio persons' assumes a voluntarist subject, who can simply 'make choices' rather than a subject who is positioned at the intersection of a difficult set of social practices and forces and has to find a pathway through them. The neoliberal demand then is that we all become portfolio persons, as if life were a long drawn out selection process undertaken to impress a notional minatory employer who will never quite be satisfied with what we present. The sense of falling short, like sin, guilt and penitence for one's deficiencies through ever more training, interior reconfiguration and increasingly desperate aspiration, is clearly not there by accident.

References

Apple, M. W. (1995), *Education and Power*. Routledge: New York.

Apple, M. W. (2001), 'Comparing neo-liberal projects and inequality in education', *Comparative Education*, 37(4), 409–23.

Ball, S., Bowe, R. and Gewirtz, S. (1994), 'Market forces and parental choice', in S. Tomlinson (ed.), *Educational Reform and its Consequences*. London: IPPR/Rivers Oram Press, pp. 13–25.

Baty, P. (2005), 'Students win £250K payout', *The Times Higher Educational Supplement*, June 3 2005.

Baty, P. (2006), 'Litigation fear lets cheats of hook', *The Times Higher Education Supplement*, October 13 2006.

Bauman, Z. (1994), *The Individualized Society*. Cambridge: Polity.

Beck, U. (2000), *What is Globalization?* Cambridge: Polity Press in association with Blackwell.

Beck, U., Giddens, A. and Lash, S. (1994), *Reflexive Modernization: Politics, Tradition, and Aesthetics in the Modern Social Order*. Stanford, CA: Stanford University Press.

Bekhradnia, B. (2006), *Demand for HE to 2020*. Oxford: Higher Education Policy Institute.

Bennett, T. (1998), *Culture: A Reformer's Science*. Sydney: Allen and Unwin.

Berlins, M. (2006), 'Universities should give students the freedom to think – not threaten them with petty rules and regulations', *Guardian*, September 13 2006.

Birkhead, T. (2006), 'Dog eat dog', *The Times Higher Education Supplement*, October 3 2006.

Bourdieu, P. (1996), *The State Nobility*. Stanford, CA: Stanford University Press.

Bourdieu, P. and Passeron, J.-C. (1990) [1977], *Reproduction in Education, Society, and Culture* (Second edn) (trans. R. Nice). London: Sage.

Bratich, J. Z., Packer, J. and McCarthy, C. (2003), *Foucault, Cultural Studies, and Governmentality*. Albany, NY: State University of New York Press.

Clark, L. (2006), 'Private pupils look to the US for a university', *Daily Mail*, May 23 2006.

Crossley, M. (2000), 'Bridging cultures and traditions in the reconceptualisation of comparative and international education', *Comparative Education*, 36(3), 319–32.

Cruickshank, B. (1999), *The Will to Empower: Democratic Citizens and Other Subjects*. Ithaca, NY: Cornell University Press.

Dean, M. (1999), *Governmentality: Power and Rule in Modern Society*. London: Sage.

Fazackerley, A. (2006), 'Struggle to fill v-c job vacancies', *The Times Higher Education Supplement*, July 21 2006.

Foucault, M. (1991), 'Governmentality', in C. Gordon and P. Miller (eds), *The Foucault Effect: Studies in Governmentality*. Chicago, IL: University of Chicago Press, pp. 87–104.

Frean, A. (2006), 'Universities urged to join price war', *The Times*, September 2 2006.

Giddens, A. (1991), *Modernity and Self-Identity: Self and Society in the Late Modern Age*. Stanford, CA: Stanford University Press.

Gorard, S. (2006), 'Face it, equity initiatives are too little, too late', *The Times Higher Education Supplement*, September 15 2006.

Gordon, C. (1991), 'Governmental rationality: an introduction', in C. Gordon and P. Miller (eds), *The Foucault Effect: Studies in Governmentality*. Chicago, IL: University of Chicago Press, pp. 1–52.

Grandey, A. A., Dickter, D. N. and Sin, H. P. (2004), 'The customer is not always right: customer aggression and emotion regulation of service employees', *Journal of Organizational Behaviour*, 25(3), 397–418.

Gray, J. (1998), *False Dawn: The Delusions of Global Capitalism*. New York: The New Press.

Gee, J. P. (2004), *Situated Language: A Critique of Traditional Schooling*. London: Routledge.

Hall, S. and Du Gay, P. (1996), *Questions of Cultural Identity*. London and Thousand Oaks, CA: Sage.

Hankins, K. B. and Martin, D. G. (2006), 'Charter schools and urban regimes in neoliberal context: making workers and new spaces in metropolitan Atlanta', *International Journal of Urban and Regional Research*, 30(3), 528–47.

Hari, J. (2006), 'No wonder students shun their lectures', *The Independent*, September 14 2006.

Harris, S. (2006), 'Tuition fees may rise to £5000 a year', *Daily Mail*, August 30 2006.

Heelas, P. and Morris, P. (eds) (1992), *The Values of the Enterprise Culture: The Moral Debate*. London: Routledge.

Heelas, P., Lash, S. and Morris, P. (1996), *Detraditionalization: Critical Reflections on Authority and Identity at a Time of Uncertainty.* Cambridge, MA: Blackwell Publishers.

Hill, P. and Baty, P. (2004), 'Cash for grades trend risks Offa anger', *The Times Higher Educational Supplement,* October 8 2004.

Hodges, L. (2006), 'I have wasted three years', *Independent,* July 20 2006.

Hsiao-Hung, P. (2006), 'Overseas aid: international students are big business for UK universities. But when they encounter racism and violence, are institutions failing to help?' *Guardian,* August 29 2006.

Hyland, T. (2002), 'Third way values and post-school education policy', *Journal of Educational Policy,* 17(2), 245–58.

Independent (2006a), 'The universities could do better', *Independent,* July 20 2006.

Independent (2006b), 'We must explore ways to bridge the social divide', *Independent,* June 15 2006.

Kliebard, H. (1986), *The Struggle for the American Curriculum.* New York: Routledge.

Kubler, J. and De Luca, C. (2006), *Trends in Academic Recruitment and Retention: A Commonwealth Perspective.* London: The Association of Commonwealth Universities.

Lash, S. and Friedman, J. (1992), *Modernity and Identity.* Oxford, UK; Cambridge, USA: Blackwell.

Lipman, P. (2002), 'Making the global city, making inequality: the political economy and cultural politics of Chicago school policy', *American Educational Research Journal,* 39(2), 379–419.

Lipsett, A. and Tysome, T. (2006), 'Spiralling workloads stifle staff retention', *The Times Higher Education Supplement,* November 2 2006.

Lucey, H., Melody, J. and Walkerdine, V. (2003), 'Uneasy hybrids: psychosocial aspects of becoming educationally successful for working-class young women', *Gender and Education,* 15(3), 285–99.

McRae, A. (2006), ' "The teachers treat you with respect"; tutorial colleges are just crammers, right? No, they are chosen by the brightest students', *Independent,* June 1 2006.

Menter, I., Muschamp, P., Nichols, P., Ozga, J., and Pollard, A. (1997), *Work and Identity in the Primary School.* Philadelphia: Open University Press.

Meikle, J. (2006), Students told turn up or face expulsion: union condemns university contracts', *Guardian,* September 11 2006.

Olssen, M. (1996), 'In defence of the welfare state and publicly provided education', *Journal of Education Policy,* 11(3), 337–62.

Peck, J. and Tickell, A. (2002), 'Neoliberalizing space', *Antipode,* 34(3), 380–404.

Phillips, S. (2006), 'Hired guns offer aid in today's cut-throat market', *The Times Higher Education Supplement,* May 5 2006.

Purgavie, D. (2006), 'American by degrees', *Mail on Sunday,* August 6 2006.

Reid, A. (2002), 'Public education and democracy: a changing relationship in a globalizing world', *Journal of Education Policy,* 17(5), 571–85.

Richards, J. (2006), 'Top up fee incentive', *The Times,* September 8 2006.

Rist, R. (1973), *The Urban School: A Factory for Failure.* Cambridge, MA and London, UK: MIT Press.

Roberts, L. (2006), 'Contracts that mean lazy students will be expelled', *Daily Mail*, September 11 2006.

Rose, N. (1992), 'Governing the enterprising self', in P. Heelas and P. Morris (eds), *The Values of the Enterprise Culture: The Moral Debate*. London; New York: Routledge, pp. 141–64.

Rose, N. (1998), *Inventing Ourselves: Psychology, Power and Personhood*. Cambridge: Cambridge University Press.

Rose, N. (1999), *Powers of Freedom: Reframing Political Thought*. Cambridge: Cambridge University Press.

Sanders, C. (2006a), 'Johnson promises sector a freer rein', *The Times Higher Education Supplement*, October 6 2006.

Sanders, C. (2006b), 'College of law to offer degrees', *The Times Higher Education Supplement*, May 12 2006.

Sassen, S. (2003), 'Globalization or denationalization', *Review of International Political Economy*, 10(1), 1–22.

Scholte, G. (2000), *Globalization: A Critical Introduction*. Houndmills, Basingstoke: Palgrave.

Shepherd, J. and Baty, P. (2006), 'Staff exposed to parent rage', *The Times Higher Education Supplement*, July 7 2006.

Shilling, J. (2006), 'Is a happy human a good human?' *The Times*, April 21 2006.

Shipton, M. (2006), 'University to be sued by students for "poor" course', *Western Mail*, June 21 2006.

Stephen, M. (2006), 'Quick decision needed: a place of learning or a finishing school?' *Independent on Sunday*, August 20 2006.

Swain, H. (2006a), 'If you treat people like customers, don't be surprised if they behave like customers', *The Times Higher Education Supplement*, March 31 2006.

Swain, H. (2006b), 'Des res for the far from skint student', *The Times Higher Education Supplement*, July 28 2006.

Times Higher Education Supplement (2004), 'Litigation fees top £15m as academic disputes grow', *The Times Higher Education Supplement*, March 12 2004.

Times Higher Education Supplement (2006), 'You pays yer money', *The Times Higher Education Supplement*, September 29 2006.

Tysome, T. (2006a), 'It's students who will do the selecting now heads are warned', *The Times Higher Education Supplement*. September 8 2006.

Tysome, T. (2006b), 'Young guns ditch old values', *The Times Higher Education Supplement*, December 15 2006.

Tysome, T. (2006c), 'Dissatisfied staff plan mass exodus', *The Times Higher Education Supplement*, September 8 2006.

Wacquant, L. (1996), 'Foreword' in P. Bourdieu, *The State Nobility*. Stanford, CA: Stanford University Press, pp. ix–xxii.

Chapter 7

The Picture of Learning: Thinking About the Educational Experience in Neoliberal Times

After having stayed with us through the preceding six chapters, the reader may be in want of some conclusion. In the face of the sometimes painful changes which have been urged on the post-compulsory education sector in the UK, we might at least suggest an alternative. Perhaps there is a way in which students and staff can transcend the various bugbears we have identified and pursue knowledge together, unimpeded by market logics, key skills or employability concerns.

Transcending these difficulties is not easy however. The emphasis on change at an individual and institutional level which is being thrust upon the universities and their students is nested within a broader sphere of political changes that are transforming the relationship between the state and the individual in many developed nations. As we have tried to show, these new incarnations of economic liberalism have bitten deep and their logic has become sufficiently naturalized and ineluctable that they cannot be broken free from readily.

As we, and many other commentators, have noted, social policies on both sides of the Atlantic have increasingly emphasized the desirability of flexibility in labour markets, and the importance of individuals adding symbolic capital to themselves through attending to their education and skills. These new model citizens are infused with an enterprising entrepreneurial desire to improve themselves and continually reflect upon their skills and their attractiveness to potential employers. That, at least, seems to be the theory. In practice we see desperate staff adapting their teaching methods and curricular content to new demands from an increasingly consumerized student body, and where many universities are seen staggering under the load of responsibility in achieving government policy objectives.

What we have tried to show in this volume is how universities, their staff and those responsible for researching this picture, urgently need to be able to think clearly and systematically about what is happening. If the policy seems not to be working, in the present climate people seem just as likely to blame themselves as the policy or the institution. These are not merely personal deficiencies but reflect a deeper malaise and this volume provides some important first steps in finding the tools to unpick it.

Many of the trends that we have identified look set to continue. Presently, rumours include the possibility that the new centrally imposed limit of £3,000 per annum for the fees paid by students at UK institutions will be raised so that some universities will charge considerably more. This will occur especially among those whose symbolic value in the marketplace can command a premium from students or their parents. Widening-access policies have sought with increasing desperation to tempt more students in, yet as we have seen, with the potential for decline in the catchment age group, we may yet see a number of institutions chasing a smaller body of potential applicants.

The topicality and currency of many of the concerns that we have identified in this volume were underlined at the end of 2006 in an article by the Minister for Higher Education, Bill Rammell. He claimed that: 'to succeed, the sector has to be as flexible, innovative and responsive to business as possible' (Rammell, 2006), condensing the dreams of the neoliberal project in every particular. The flexibility of the sector, which presumably will depend on the flexibility of the staff involved too, in meeting the skill agendas imposed by employers is seen to be crucial in ensuring its prosperity in the future. Moreover, according to Rammell, the government's policy will remain focused on skills and improving the skills of the workforce, including both young people entering higher education for the first time and older workers who must continually seek to upgrade themselves.

Despite its continued popularity with policymakers, the notion of skills, as we have highlighted, is problematic. Whereas politicians assure us that higher skills and higher rates of participation in education are important, the literature on skills tells a different story. As we have seen in this book there is some doubt as to the extent and kind of skilled labour force needed given the economic profile of the UK. Some have suggested that the current situation demands workers who are occupationally docile and prepared to accept casualized minimum-wage jobs in the service sector. Here, the skills involve answering the phone in a company-approved way, looking happy for the customers and presenting an image that is consistent with the way the company wants to be represented. The knowledge economy is for the time being at least, still a dream, and that in some cases we have a skills glut rather than a skills shortage, as witnessed by the fact that so many graduates do not work in graduate jobs.

The point is not that we can band together to replace the discourse of skills with something more to our kidney. After all, the present situation seems very far removed from John Henry Newman's idea of a university focused on the cultivation of intellect or the pursuit of knowledge for its own sake. That idea seems very quaint indeed compared to the present situation of universities with multiple activities straddling general education, vocational training, highly-specialized applied and basic research, beset by the painful realities of more aggressive competition for funding. The point is to be able to recognize the nature and limitations of the pieces in this particular game of chess. Talk of widening access and skills will only ever accomplish so much. The key factor is to have the tools to perform the necessary deconstructive work.

In one sense, this vision of docile workers in a service economy is not unlike universities, where the staff are a kind of aesthetic labour to attract students and funding and to project the pre-formulated corporate image desired by the institution. Like the hospitality sector, universities are in pole position when it comes to employing casual staff. They are estimated to number nearly 70,000, if those on hourly pay and short-term contracts are taken into account – which is more than four in ten, according to the University and College Union (Sanders, 2006). So what of this trend? Universities whose prestige and income derives largely from research will surely want to keep their grant-earning staff in a position where they can continue to do so, away from the wiles of an increasingly needy student body. It is here that part-time, fixed-contract or hourly-paid staff are most useful. Equally, universities whose major source of income lies in teaching will have large classes whose coverage often has to be arranged at short notice, whereupon most course leaders have a network of colleagues who might be interested in a little hourly-paid supplement to their usual wage. They may, in some institutions, make use of an agency to supply hourly-paid teaching staff. This is a trend that universities might find difficult to counter as it would mean renegotiating their relationship to a number of fiscal pressures.

The new self in neoliberalism gains what Nikolas Rose (1999) calls 'a serious burden of liberty', in which freedom is an 'obligation'. Choices are opened up to people but they are also accompanied by a burden of risk, inasmuch as one might make the wrong choice and fail to maximize one's potential. From the point of view of policymakers, the issue becomes one of how to manage and govern a population when traditional ties have been taken away by globalization and neoliberalism, rather than being about a simple and positive opening up of choice. Hence the necessity for the new citizen to be an entrepreneur of the self, who immerses him or herself in the project of acquiring status, capital or prestige. As part of this process, as theorists such as Giddens and Beck have noted, the gaze of the citizen is turned inwards. This reflexive scrutiny is sometimes thought of as 'learning how to learn' or 'evaluating strengths and weaknesses' but we would argue that it has a more subtle governmental function. It means that the challenges we face will come to be seen in psychological terms. As Walkerdine has put it:

> While self-realisation is what is expected of the life project and one in which success is judged by the psychological capacities to succeed, the ability to handle uncertainty, the never knowing where work will come from etc., in fact produces an almost inevitable failure that will be lived as a personal failing, hence the necessity for forms of counselling and therapy intended to prop up the fragile subject, to keep the illusion of a unitary subject intact. (Walkerdine, 2003: 241)

There are implications here for the distress, unhappiness and unease that people in the higher education system feel. To describe it as 'stress' is to reduce it to something psychological in pretty much the way Walkerdine describes. It seems to us, looking at the unhappiness of our colleagues and students in the academy, that there is something larger at stake as each of them appears to be yearning for something better.

Of course, where university employees are confronted with students who need extra help, the response of many is to try to assist the student. This is entirely commendable. There are many warnings, as we have seen, concerning the importance of attending to student distress and mental health problems. Lest the situation we described earlier in the book has receded from memory, here is another reminder from Kadison (2004):

> If the mental health crisis is to be turned around, colleges, from the top down and bottom up, must recognise that emotional and physical well-being is part of the educational mission and can affect academic success dramatically. Universities must provide resources for education and assessment. Students can play a key role – young people are most receptive to their peers who can help with education and reduce stigma. In fact, the entire community, including parents, needs to be educated about the symptoms of serious problems and how to make referrals.

By describing the process in this way it makes it look like the sort of thing any self-respecting human being would do. Anyone that is, who is kind and helpful. The relationship between staff and students is refigured in terms which are both psychological and which avoid any mention of exploitation. Moreover, it is clear that certain aspects of characteristics ascribed to the docile worker under neoliberalism are central to this refiguring of the work relation. Workers who work over and above expectations are nice, kind and helpful – rather than militant, difficult, aggressive – are workers with a psychological interiority. That is, they have come to understand their place in the world and their responses to it, in terms of attitudes, thoughts and emotions. Under these circumstances the increasing demands to deal with paperwork, 'challenging new targets' and distressed students are reflected back upon the self, as challenges for the worker to overcome.

Similarly, this language of psychological interiority pervades the student experience too. To those who study in the higher education system the idea that as students their employability is being enhanced allows them to stay in an economically vulnerable and often burdensome position, with part-time jobs, insecure housing and a bottomless pit of debt. In this sense, employ-ability and the lifestyle that goes with a 'good job' become potent fantasies and, in our experience, were discourses used frequently by younger students with whom we have discussed the issue (Baker, 2005). In addition, a fantasy of something better coming along in the future which will take the indivi-dual out of the unfavourable conditions serves a similarly powerful role in assuaging the discomforts of the present. The purpose of work within this discourse becomes the possibility of consumption and thus the achievement of an identity produced through consumption, or even a 'lifestyle'.

We can see that the interior domain of private thoughts, inclinations, dispositions and emotions, then, is a vitally important component of the neoliberal project – once we see how it makes sense in the organizational and political climate within which we are embedded.

Looking to the future, the indications concerning how 'research quality' will be evaluated are worth a moment's speculation. Perhaps it is likely to be based upon combined data on research income, with information on post-graduate students and information on research volume and quality. Thus once again, the research-intensive universities will be recapitalized, and the possibility of movement between the strata will be progressively less likely. Equally, here too we can see how notions of interiority are conflated with the reward structure. Research quality, excellence, originality, brilli-ance and international significance – the very terms in which the quality of research is described connote features interior to the research and, by impli-cation, interior to the researcher. Most of us can easily appreciate that over-worked staff in under-capitalized establishments may have difficulty turning out earth-shattering material. Even if they do, in all likelihood, no one will notice. It requires a budget that will facilitate a certain amount of flesh pressing at the right conferences.

The task we are urging upon the reader is to notice. Notice how those of us involved in the post-compulsory education system are changing. Notice how this aligns with what has happened to other organizations, other spheres of activity and other countries. The markets to whose discipline we are now subject did not just happen naturally, but were carefully nurtured into being and with them come the kinds of concerns and consciousness we have been writing about. This consciousness elides the operations of power just as much as it is an effect of them. So far, education studies has drawn upon theory in a stolid, pragmatic manner – notions of culture from Bourdieu, ideas about measurable psychological characteristics from psychometrics, philosophies from Dewey or Freire. Yet this has left us curiously ill equipped to understand what is happening to ourselves. This is why we have pointed the reader regularly in the direction of Foucault, Rose and those who have drawn upon their work in the educational field. It is this way of thinking which will help link the subjective sense of eternal obligation to be or do something better, the cult of long hours, or the nagging fear that one is falling behind, to the powers, structures and forces that make this yawning sense of personal deficiency possible. Once we can understand, we can act.

References

Baker, S. (2005), *Like a Fish in Water: Aspects of the Contemporary United Kingdom Higher Education System as Intended and as Constructed*. PhD thesis, University of Wales.

Kadison, R. (2004), 'Test minds, but tend them too', *The Times Higher Education Supplement*, October 15 2004.

Rammell, W. (2006), 'Our reforms will make for a prosperous sector', *The Times Higher Education Supplement*, December 22 2006.

Rose, N. (1999), *Governing the Soul* '2nd edition', London: Free Association Books, 123.

Sanders, C. (2006), 'Sort out casuals problem, says UCU', *The Times Higher Education Supplement*, July 14 2006.

Walkerdine, V. (2003), 'Reclassifying upward mobility: femininity and the neo-liberal subject', *Gender and Education*, 15(3), 237–48.

Index